ZEPPELINS AGAINST LONDON

ZEPPELINS

AGAINST

LONDON

KENNETH POOLMAN

ILLUSTRATED

THE JOHN DAY COMPANY

NEW YORK

First American Edition 1961
© 1960 by Kenneth Poolman

Library of Congress Catalogue Card Number: 61-10316

Manufactured in the United States of America

To the memory of

CAPTAIN WILLIAM LEEFE ROBINSON

CONTENTS

"*I do not foresee any other difficulties that prevail against this invention save one, which seems to me the greatest of them all, and that is that God would never surely allow such a machine to be successful. . . Iron weights could be hurled to wreck ships at sea, or they could be set on fire by fire-balls and bombs; nor ships alone, but houses, fortresses and cities could thus be destroyed with the certainty that the Airship could come to no harm, as the missiles could be hurled from a vast height.*"

Francesco Lana, Society of Jesus, 1670.

FOREWORD

By Marshal of the Royal Air Force Sir John Slessor, the first pilot ever to attack a Zeppelin in the air.

In these days of intercontinental ballistic missiles and supersonic bombers, it is permissible to look back with some nostalgia upon what must now seem to us the relatively negligible menace represented by the Zeppelins of the Kaiser's war. One may also wish that the problems of air defense today were anything like as easily soluble as they were at the time of the first Zeppelin attack which, it is not easy to realize, was nearer fifty than forty years ago.

To us whose minds are conditioned by experience of the devastating air bombardments of World War II and by the looming shadow of the H-bomb, it is perhaps difficult to take the Zeppelins seriously at all. To us—at any rate to me—they seem somehow less real than the galleons of the Spanish Armada or the French three-deckers of Nelson's day. Their direct impact upon history was so slight and their useful life so short before it was, in effect, terminated by the arrival of the incendiary bullet, that I doubt whether today one in a thousand of the younger generation has any idea that, not very long ago, these unwieldy gas-bags did appear as a novel and alarming threat to security and personal safety.

Nevertheless, the Zeppelins have their place in history and it is a good thing that we should be reminded of it in this book. Their primitive and short-lived activities were the first attempt in history to strike directly at the will-to-resist of a civilian population in war. One may smile now at the bombastic fulminations of the German press after Linnarz's raid in the spring of 1915 on the theme that "Britain is no longer an island." But the fact remains that the proud integrity which was owed for so many centuries to sea power was in fact lost forever when Blériot first landed near Dover. And it was the crude low-yield bombs of the Zeppelins which first underlined that truth in blood.

The reader may be tempted to wonder whether the author's description of a London "buzzing with fearful excitement" after the raid of September 8, 1915, is not somewhat exaggerated. But among my own most vivid memories is that of the scene in East London (referred to by the author) the day after the raid of October 13th, that year. It is no exaggeration to describe that scene as one not far removed from panic. It was with the more profound relief and admiration that, a quarter of a century later, I witnessed the patient stoicism and good-humored endurance of the people in that same part of London, under a scale of attack compared to which the efforts of the Zeppelins were almost negligible.

The human being is an adaptable creature. And it was that early experience in London that made me marvel in the second World War at the way in which the people of British—and indeed perhaps even more of German—cities were able to adapt themselves to conditions which before would have been thought to be beyond human endurance.

But that is a thing of the past. No people could adapt themselves to endure attack by long-range missiles with hydrogen warheads. It is no longer only necessary for an aggressor to be certain that free peoples would retaliate in kind; what *is* vital is that he should *not* be certain that we would *not* do so. Miscalculation, misjudgment by a potential enemy of the moral fiber of a people, is the real peril today.

PART I

THE WEAPON

"We invent a vessel to swim beneath the sea and at once it is appropriated to increase the terrors of war. We learn to fly like the birds, and at once flying becomes a new arm of military science, and has little other meaning."

–A. G. Gardiner, the *News*, 1914.

1. THE BATTLEGROUND

It is England on a September evening in the year 1916. There has been rain in London and the eastern counties during the day, but it has stopped now. Wisps of cloud drift across the stars and there is no moon. The people of England are thinking, "It's a Zepp night."

The Admiralty and the War Office have known this fear to be a fact since late afternoon. The telegraphers on duty at the Admiralty radio station at Hunstanton, on the Walsh, have picked up a signal from a German Zeppelin airship to its base—the "thorough" Hun is sometimes amazingly careless—and passed it at once down their private telephone line to the telegraph office in the Admiralty basement. From here the message, in code, has gone through the pneumatic tube up to Room 40 in the Old Building where Nelson watches Whitehall and guards the Empire from his whitewashed niche.

In this room, the existence of which is known only to the heads of Admiralty, and in its adjoining complex of offices and cubby holes, work some of the best brains in the country. Old Maskell, the messenger who carries a locked black box from Room 40 to Naval Intelligence twice a day, has a suspicion of what goes on there. He tells his cronies that the inmates of Room 40 have nothing to do all day "but work out crossword puzzles."

The latest "crossword" which has come thudding out of the tube into the waiting basket is solved with comparative ease. Before it is fully decoded others have dropped into the basket from listening stations all over the eastern counties and France. They are all radio signals from Zeppelins—some even give their identification letters—and they soon reveal the general objective of the armada that is gathering.

Shortly after nine o'clock the order goes out from General Headquarters, Home Forces, "Take air raid action." The warning goes to observer posts dotted about the country, to gun sites in and around London and on the coast, and to the headquarters of the Royal Flying Corps at the War Office. The rough-and-ready air defenses of Britain mobilize and wait for the first sight or sound of Zeppelin motors to give them some indication of the particular target. Will it be London? Is it Tyneside's turn? Or the Midlands again? The outermost ring of human observers is aboard the lightships, which are vital sources of information for the defenders because German Naval Zeppelins flying the long haul over the North Sea like to steer for them as signposts to their targets.

About ten o'clock the watch-keepers aboard the Haisboro Lightship, anchored eight miles off the Norfolk coast near Bacton, hear the deep throb of engines above them. Then the noise dies and they can just pick out a huge shape, hovering silently, engines stopped, above their masthead, waiting for her consorts, the bad navigators and the victims of head-winds and rain squalls, to join her for the thrust across darkened England.

Half an hour later the gunners on the coastal sites can hear airship engines approaching them. Their searchlights flicker on and whisk about the sky but the beams rebound off low cloud and the Zeppelins pass overhead unseen and unchallenged. They fan out across darkened Norfolk.

Below them people have been awake in uneasy expectation for some time. They know the signs by now. The animals are restless. Dogs will not sleep, but lift their heads and howl. It is a spine-chilling sound. In the country districts pheasants start up their *whirr-whirr-whirr* of strident alarm. In farmhouse windows the lights go on as ducks sound off in chorus, rooks caw, and all the animals grow restive and excited. Light, nervous sleepers all over Norfolk, then Essex, are startled into uneasy wakefulness by the racket. Wives whisper, "It's the Zepps again," and hope that the children will not wake. Soon the well-known droning comes out of the night like a bad dream, and swells until it is right overhead. People get up, go to the window and watch the sky, hearts hammering. Then the frightening sound recedes. The anxious watchers relax and go back to bed. "It's London again," they say.

A few minutes after eleven o'clock a colonel in the Military Aeronautics Division at the War Office picks up the telephone and speaks in turn to pilots standing by at three small grass airfields located round the rim of the capital. At each airfield there is a machine standing by. At his order "Take air raid action," the duty pilot gets ready to take off from each place and patrol over London as part of a new, yet unproved system arranged to throw as wide a net as possible across the path of Zeppelins heading for London. At the end of two hours' flying, which is the capacity of his gas tank, the first pilot will grope his way back to the little airdrome, endeavoring to land by the aid of a new system of gasoline flares in tins, hoping that the usual mist has not hidden the field, and the second machine will have taken his place in the freezing cold at 10,000 feet.

The machine is trundled out of its rough hangar, which is nothing but a large canvas tent pegged down in the stubble of a field that was high with corn a few months before. It is a frail-looking machine, a B.E.2c biplane which has been developed from a prototype stolen from a French model

6

copied from a Wright Brothers design at the Royal Aircraft Factory at Farnborough, an establishment which, until the last few years, has built nothing but balloons. The letters B.E. stand for Blériot Experimental, and the aircraft is not so very far removed in development from the puny machine which sputtered across the Channel on July 25, 1909, and proved to those who dared to think ahead that the days were numbered when Britain could rest safe behind the shield of the Royal Navy.

It takes the best part of an hour for a B.E.2c to climb to 10,000 feet, its ceiling, a performance easily surpassed by the Zeppelins themselves. It is therefore vital for them to get off the ground in plenty of time to anticipate the airships and be in position above them if there is to be any chance of an attack The machine is armed with a single Lewis gun which is unreliable in action, and fixed to fire upward over the top plane. It often jams, and sometimes the drum of ammunition will slip off and give the pilot a stunning crack on the head. If neither of these things happens then it is strong odds that something else will, probably engine failure, which is a curse of these primitive machines. The airborne gasoline engine is only ten years old, and the 90-h.p. Raf motor in the B.E. was on the drawing board when war broke out. The B.E.2c has only one trump card, and that is its excellent stability. It is a safety factor which is actually a liability in action against the swift and agile Fokker fighters of the German Air Force which have been decimating the B.E.'s of the Corps squadrons on the Western Front. But it is a potential asset for fighting Zeppelins at night, when what is required above all is a steady gun platform from which to aim at the huge, surprisingly elusive monsters.

Until recent weeks pilots have had no effective missiles to use against the airships. Bombs and explosive darts have been tried and have failed, and the normal machine-gun ammunition will pass right through an airship's envelope and gas-bags and out the other side.

Tonight each pilot of the London air defense is taking up with him three drums of a special incendiary-explosive ammunition, mixed with tracer for aiming in the dark, of which government scientists have high hopes. All previous devices have failed to bring down a Zeppelin raider on British soil, and they have got through again and again, killing and wounding civilians unscathed, seriously interfering with war production in the factories and, above all, spreading a defeatist "Zepp" psychosis throughout the country. Until now, ordering the crude airplanes of the Home Defense Wing of the Royal Flying Corps to shoot down the great aerial cruisers has been like sending sailors barehanded against a school of Moby Dicks.

The machine is ready, out on the oily, exhaust-stained stubble, and the flares are lit. But in the last hour a typical Thames mist has crept up the river and is lying over the field. The pilot, a young lieutenant in the Royal Flying Corps, can barely see the flickering flares through it, and for a few moments ponders whether to telephone Headquarters at the War Office and call it off. Then he decides that the air is probably clear a few feet up. Feeling cold, he wishes that he could have worn his British woolies underneath his long leather flying coat, but its swaddling thickness would seriously restrict his movements in the cockpit. He stamps his feet hard and flaps his arms vigorously across his chest two or three times, then climbs up into the shallow, open cockpit.

Take-off is an informal business.

"Choke out." The mechanic centers the heavy, four-bladed wooden propeller and spins it to draw a mixture into the cylinders.

"Switch on."

"Contact." The mechanic centers the propeller again and

gives it a vigorous heave. There is a cough, then silence, as the cold engine, open to the night air, continues to breathe in fog. A second swing, a second cough. The process of starting can sometimes last as long as five minutes. A third swing and this time the engine catches. There is a loud racketing roar and the pilot is relieved to see the tappets chattering in the engine in front of him. The frail bones of the biplane shudder as a life current surges through inert wood, wire and fabric and pulsates through the pilot's vibrating body. The blue and yellow exhaust flames bloom at the tips of the twin, upward-thrusting exhaust pipes beyond the leading edge of the top wing. He opens the throttle to full revs and repeats this several times to flood the engine with heat. When the machine is warm enough and ticking over steadily at low revs he does a final quick methodical cockpit check. He is ready to go.

"Chocks away." Mechanics jerk the wooden blocks from beneath the heavy wheels of the B.E., the pilot opens the throttle, and the machine is bumping down the ravished grass, her engine roaring hoarsely through the fog. The flares rush past his wing tips, flickering as the slipstream sweeps them. A little more throttle and the tail comes up, then the bumping and lurching suddenly stop and the machine is clear and climbing slowly, elbowing the mist aside.

The mist falls away very soon, as he had hoped, and the B.E. climbs into a black night sprinkled with the early autumn stars, their cold light occulted here and there by patches of cloud. The machine spirals slowly up, taking a long, dogged fifty minutes to reach 10,000 feet, then levels out, turns on to its patrol line over the Thames, and the pilot settles down. Below his starboard wing the huddled, naked mass of London sprawls. He can see the river gleaming below like a winding glacier. Shading his eyes he peers into the cockpit nacelle at the green mineral glow of his primitive instruments, the only touch of friendly warmth in the black immensity of the night. Somewhere in the dark two other lonely machines are patrolling the aerial frontier of the capital. A few crude, clumsy biplanes, old-fashioned even in this, the very first decade of aviation, stand between the uneasy, Zepp-haunted multitude and the airship fleet now frightening Essex with the throbbing of their motors and the first screech and shock of their fire bombs. It is a weird battlefield, the like of which has never been fought over before in the whole bloodstained, striving history of man.

The pilot hears the rumble of bombs away in the darkness toward north London. They grow louder, and the sharp crack of the guns joins in. The searchlights are flitting uncertainly about the sky. He can feel the familiar excitement rise in him, making him forgetful of the bitter cold that has numbed him in his open cockpit. He has managed to coax the B.E. to almost 13,000 feet by now, higher than he has ever flown before, and has been in the air for nearly two hours. It occurs to him for the first time that his fuel must be running low. At that moment he notices a fiery concentration of shrapnel bursts in the sky to the northeast. Thinking that where there is so much fire there must be a Zepp, he banks the machine and heads in the direction of the glow. He has been flying for about fifteen minutes when one of the searchlights flicking to and fro out of the blackness below him halts, retracks and fixes on the huge blunt nose of a Zeppelin as it comes sliding out of a cloud. Engine full on, he puts the nose of the B.E. down and steers straight for the Zepp.

As the bow of the great airship begins to fill the whole sky in front of him, the B.E. bucks and cavorts in the fierce blasts of shrapnel near-misses. To a pilot heading toward the Zeppelin from another dark corner of the sky it looks

as if he means to ram the airship head-on like the French-
man Roland Garros in the first days of the war.

But the pilot is diving to position himself beneath the
giant hull so as to rake the underbelly of the airship with
his new bullets. He levels off eight hundred feet beneath the
nose and begins to fly straight and level down the length of
the Zeppelin, immediately beneath its gondola. He reaches
up above his head and with a quick pull cocks the gun. His
finger squeezes the trigger of the Lewis. It is a moment
tense with possibility, a second of time which could be a
turning point in the war, an epoch-making flicker of action.
No one has yet shot down a Zeppelin over Britain. Will he
be the first?

This is the strange battleground of the Zeppelin war, and
these are the duelists, the huge powered balloon, the lighter-
than-air, against the heavy, clumsy airplane—two primitive
machines barely free yet from the long and painful spring-
ing time of flight, locked in a struggle in the darkness,
10,000 feet above the earth.

2. INFERNAL MACHINE

Throughout the last decade of the nineteenth century, the Gay Nineties, a young retired cavalry general of the Imperial German Army worked stubbornly against great difficulties to build a prototype of the astonishingly ambitious lighter-than-air flying machine which had been his paper dream for a long time. Count Ferdinand von Zeppelin did not invent the dirigible airship, but he was the first to put a really successful version of it into the air. The first Zeppelin flew on a spring morning of the first year of the twentieth century. Designed from the start as a weapon of war by its creator, it was used commercially as well from 1911 to 1914, but in 1914 it was put into action against Britain as an instrument of destruction. The "Zepp" was born, the first of the new terror weapons of the air, an invention with a limited future on its own account, but a progenitor of more infernal machines to come.

We cannot put a date to the earliest longing of man to fly like a bird or float above the earth like a cloud. We cannot exactly identify the real prototype of the Zeppelin, but it is generally accepted to be the aerial ship described by Francesco Lana. He dreamed of a craft which would support the weight of two or three men by the buoyancy of four globes of thin copper from which the air had been pumped. His globes were the direct forerunners of the Zeppelin's

multiple gas-bags; oars and sails were suggested to propel his
vessel because there were no internal combustion motors in
1670, which was a century away from the invention of even
the steam engine.

Zeppelin was a southern German, a Württemberger born
at Constance on the smiling lake in 1838, son of an aristocrat of north German descent with a family tradition of
soldiering and state service, and of an attractive, intelligent
girl of French parentage. When he was a small boy playing
on his father's estates at Girsberg, just over the Swiss border,
the family noticed that he was particularly interested in the
working of any new piece of machinery which his father,
the Count, bought to improve the efficiency of his farm.
When Ferdinand was twenty, a short, stockily athletic, energetic, handsome young man with curly blond hair and
frank blue eyes, he succumbed to the trend of fashion among
young men of his class and joined the army, becoming a
second lieutenant in the 8th Württemberg Infantry Regiment at Stuttgart. After only a month of the little world of
an infantry subaltern he entered his name for a year's study
at Tübingen University. His growing appetite for knowledge more varied than the drill book could give him was
further whetted by courses in mathematics, in organic chem-
istry, political economy and history.

When he was transferred to the more suitable environ-
ment of an engineer unit and sent to garrison duty, he had
plenty of time to study new inventions and new military
techniques, and was already a young man of exceptional
ability.

At the end of the war with France, Major von Zeppelin of
the Imperial German Army seemed well set for advance-
ment. In spite of a rash outspokenness, an inability to allow
stupidity in his superiors to pass without biting comment,
and a very thin skin on the matter of his beloved Württemberg and his former service against Prussia in the Austro-

Prussian War, he had got on well enough with the Prussian Army to attract the attention of the Kaiser himself, as well as von Moltke. In January 1872, he was commanding the 5th Squadron of the 15th Schleswig-Holstein Uhlans at Strasbourg, in 1874 the 2nd Württemberg Dragoons, two years later the 19th Uhlans.

In 1884, the year in which he received his full colonelcy, the Renard and Krebs airship appeared. Zeppelin absorbed all that he could read of *La France,* chagrined that it should have been France, Germany's "natural" enemy, and not his own Fatherland, that launched the invention. Three years later he actually wrote to the German Chancellor deploring the backward state of German aeronautical progress in comparison with France. When the "crazy" German, Ganswindt, published his scheme for a monster dirigible of 500 feet, Zeppelin was immensely interested. Trained engineers laughed at such a fantasy, void as it was of any calculations based on sound, scientific experiment, but Colonel von Zeppelin, who had only a little knowledge, did not laugh. He thought Ganswindt's great ship of the air made glorious sense. Its very hugeness appealed to him. Anything worth creating was big. The new Germany was big; a German should think big.

Zeppelin, in spite of his zeal in the cause of the Fatherland and his good professional standing, suffered from being a violently outspoken champion of his native state at a time when Württemberg officers in the German Army were still mistrusted by the Prussians, who held the highest offices in the establishment. At last the pushing, prickly Colonel from Constance went too far for his own good. He had always been especially hot against the practice of appointing a Prussian officer to command the Württemberg regiments in the German Army, and when he actually wrote a memorandum, which the Kaiser read, complaining of the continuance of this insult, the ruling clique of Potsdam had found a perfect excuse to get rid of him. The Prussian Inspector General of Cavalry contrived to find fault with Zeppelin's performance on the drill parade and he was marked unfit for higher command. He was left high and dry, a colonel without a regiment, passed over for a division. In November 1891, he was formally promoted lieutenant general, and on December 29th retired from the German Army with the ironic promotion to general in the suite of the King of Württemberg. His chosen career had come to a jarring halt; his service to the Fatherland seemed over. The Prussian Junkers did not deserve the rich dividends they were to reap from their blunder, and the world would have been a slightly better place without it.

Zeppelin was fifty-two when the army rejected him. For many men this would have been the end, but for Zeppelin, as energetic in mind and body as a young man, it was a long way from the point of no return. He returned to his native state, where a devoted wife and daughter and the soothing atmosphere of a beautiful home on the shores of sunny Lake Constance helped to soften the inevitable hurt. The effect upon him of the disappointment was abnormal, because he was such an unusually self-confident and energetic spirit. With him, whatever bitterness remained was driven deep, strengthening the already tough roots of his independent, stubborn nature, feeding the growth of a new obsession to succeed. From a mere saber-rattling Uhlan convert he underwent a Faustian metamorphosis into the inventor of an infernal machine, multiplying many times his danger to normal human society.

For a time he cultivated his own garden while he cast around in his mind among his many interests for something solid upon which he could build a new future.

It did not take him long. His attentive wife, probably glad in the obvious way to get an unemployed husband out from under her feet and genuinely anxious not to see his undoubted brilliance go to waste, supported him in the strange madness which now struck this middle-age aristocrat. Among the copious notes and references in his diaries a close interest in the future of the dirigible airship had grown up and reached the point where Zeppelin, drawing mainly upon Ganswindt's, and possibly the Alsatian Spiess's, ideas, had formulated a general plan for a large airship with a rigid framework which might have important military use. In his idleness, restless with frustrated ambition and patriotism, it struck him with the force of a brainstorm that he would build this Frankenstein's monster and dedicate it on the altar of the Fatherland as an alternative to the career of a cavalry general. In that cause nothing was impossible. What could no longer run would fly. The spirit imprisoned in idleness would escape into the sky and by conquering it impose its will yet more strongly upon the little earth.

His basic design for the ideal air vessel had matured through years of careful study, and he never departed from it. To realize properly the enormous potentialities which hydrogen gave to the free-floating balloon, it was necessary to design an airship which could fly long distances fast, without interference from the weather and the atmosphere, and carry a paying cargo in the form of soldiers or bombs. Zeppelin decided that all these condtions could only be met by a really large ship of a long, slender shape, pointed at both ends, which could contain a huge quantity of hydrogen. To prevent such a shape from breaking up in the buffeting winds a basic structure of great strength was necessary. If the hull were designed round a rigid outer framework covered with a strong skin, protection could also be given to the gas inside from the temperature changes in the surrounding air and from the sudden shifting of pressure normally brought on by attempting to force the clumsy gas-bag at any useful speed through the air or maneuver against a strong wind. Given powerful enough engines such a Leviathan could succeed. It was Ganswindt's giant given a practical twist.

For real strength Zeppelin wanted a metal frame from which all other parts could be hung in safety. The special engines then in process of development for flying machines were of feeble power, so the girders must be of aluminum, as light and as delicate as the demands of strength would allow. For safety and ease of handling, the hydrogen would be contained in a number of separate cells inside the rigid frame, so that the ship could remain afloat even if several of these collapsed.

On a July day in 1900, this carefully matured image in the mind of Zeppelin, after surviving storms of ridicule and buffeting headwinds of expert opposition as great as the elements could offer to the frail vessel itself, left its floating shed on the lake at Friedrichshaven and soared over the smiling mirror of the water, a clumsy, unfledged but basically healthy flying creature 420 feet in length and 40 in diameter.

Technical difficulties had almost brought down the amateur's dream at the very start. The weakest point in his plan was the lack of powerful engines, a lack which was even more of a serious handicap to the heavier-than-air inventors with whom the currently more successful balloonists were vying. He managed to interest Daimler's in the design, but German light engines were well behind French models and none possessed enough power. Major von Parseval, the Bavarian inventor of the kite balloon, had at that time no faith in the dirigible and could offer Zeppelin neither help nor encouragement. Only news of a new light gasoline engine prevented him from abandoning the project in its first year of growth. The necessity for a new standard of mechanical perfection in the other moving parts of the machinery also held up progress seriously.

Encouragement came only in isolated spurts. Zeppelin per-

suaded a brilliant young aeronautics engineer named Kober to leave the aircraft firm of Reidinger's at Augsburg
and join him. Kober went enthusiastically ahead with the
testing of the special aluminum tension rings, long frame
members and the like for the airship's hull. After five years
of effort, Zeppelin, who had spent a large part of his own
capital on the project, had still failed to interest either the
government or the thriving industrial firms of Germany in
his airship. But he did at last convince the conservative engineering fraternity that there might be a future in his
amateur experiments.

Zeppelin now appealed to German industry with more success than before. Cautiously, a number of manufacturers
agreed to set up a "joint stock company for the promotion
of air navigation" under their management, with Zeppelin
himself putting up half the capital of 800,000 marks. The
company was formed in May 1898, and in the following year
work was begun on the first Zeppelin airship at Manzell,
near Friedrichshaven. There was a serious setback when the
floating shed, which had been built to house the airship and
enable it to take off into whatever wind prevailed, was badly
damaged in a storm. Repairs used up 100,000 marks of pre-
cious capital and Zeppelin had to make it up with another
portion of his now dwindling fortune. But in July 1900,
conveniently ushering in the new century with a German
miracle, the Zeppelin airship flew.

It was a pencil-shaped ship, abruptly tapered to a point
at each end of its 420 feet. Running along the underbelly
was a triangular-shaped lattice aluminum keel giving
strength to the whole delicate structure and serving as a
gangway. In two places this gangway was broken, and ladders gave access downward to a control car forward and an
engine car aft. In each car was a 16-h.p. Daimler motor
driving two propellers mounted one on each side of the
envelope above. A wheel in the control car connected with

a vertical rudder right aft on the hull for lateral steering, and the ship was tilted up or down by moving a sliding weight attached to the keel. The rather primitive steering gear gave trouble, but the huge air vessel was stable enough for a preliminary test, and flew for three and a half miles, part of it against a headwind of 16 m.p.h.

This was an outstanding performance for 1900 and for such a large airship, and Zeppelin counted it a great success. A German had thought big—bigger than any other aeronaut anywhere in the world—in the interests of his Fatherland. And here, actually dominating the new realm of the sky in the shape of the great silver gas-bag, was the working, moving, soaring symbol of his country's promise. Fervently Zeppelin set to work to turn promise into achievement, into an image of German domination.

In six months his company was ruined, his hopes dashed again. His backers had not seen, in three short, cautious trials, enough evidence to continue their investment. After some persuasion, the Union of Engineers came to his support and publicly saluted Zeppelin's achievements. The blessing of experts gave interested parties the confidence which one lone ex-army crackpot could not impart. The Prussian state government made him a grant of 50,000 marks to start again, a Württemberg state lottery raised 124,000 marks, and manufacturers promised materials, engines and gas-fillers free of charge. Zeppelin was sufficiently encouraged to put up 400,000 marks, practically all he had left, and build another ship.

It was 1905. The new ship was wrecked in January of the following year. One day Zeppelin was saying, "I shall build no more airships," the next he had scraped together some more of his own funds, and, helped by the proceeds from another state lottery, built another. By now the army had become interested in the possibility of Zeppelin's airship for reconnaissance, and in October 1907, their observers watched its early trial flights.

In Great Britain, where aviation was almost entirely non-existent, a solitary voice told the British public what was going on at Friedrichshaven. Harry Harper, the first British air correspondent and spokesman for the air-minded *Daily Mail,* wrote on October 5th:

> In anticipation of an early official ascent which will in all probability be followed by its transfer to the German Imperial Government, Count Zeppelin's airship is being rigidly guarded from intruders and investigators.
>
> Out upon the glassy surface of Lake Constance the giant craft lies hidden in the floating corrugated iron shed. Count Zeppelin's crew are at work inside making various changes suggested by the successful trials. When they have finished, Count Zeppelin is confident that he will be able to sail for an unbroken period of twenty-four hours.
>
> German military experts were jubilant over the Count's latest achievements, and are bringing their utmost influence to bear to induce the Government to purchase the ship without waiting for further experiments.
>
> Count Zeppelin's manœuvres with his airship during the past week have been most remarkable, and have convinced everyone that the ship is the most efficient at present in existence.

It was about this time that the world ambitions of militarist Germany became seriously suspect, and small clouds of doubt and fear rose into the clear blue sky of Edwardian England. The only possible purpose of the great fleet of battleships which the Kaiser was building was to challenge the real supremacy of the British Navy, which was the only true obstacle in the way of German world expansion. The Emperor of the greatest military power in the world had said, "I will never rest until I have raised my Navy to the same level as my Army" and "Our future lies upon the water." He liked to play with the title "Admiral of the Atlantic." In October 1907, when his visit to England to stay with King Edward was front-page news, it looked to some experts as if this domination of land and sea was to extend to the air as well.

The German army bought Count Zeppelin's new airship, the Z1, and ordered a second. The latter, the LZ4, was destroyed by fire in August 1908, but Zeppelin's stock with the German people, stirred to admiration by his stubborn persistence, had by this time risen so high that a national fund raised six and a quarter million marks for him and financed the building of a large new works at Friedrichshaven. The government, too, made him a further grant to continue his experiments. He continued to suffer disasters. The Z11, taken over by the army, was wrecked in April 1910, and the next ship, the LZVI, burned in September of the same year. With these continual mishaps, mainly due to ignorance on the part of the crews, the army was cautious in its orders for new Zeppelins, as they now came to be called. To create a wide market for his products, since he was not allowed to sell his ships abroad, and would have considered this unpatriotic in any case, Zeppelin formed a subsidiary company, Delag, (*Deutsche Luftschiffahrt Aktien-Gesellschaft*) and began to operate commercially in their name, although seeing his invention play a major part in the German war machine remained Zeppelin's dominating personal concern.

By the year 1914 a fleet of these commercial Zeppelins was operating all over Germany, flying from sheds erected at Baden-Baden, Potsdam, Frankfurt-am-Main, Düsseldorf, Johannisthal, Gotha, Hamburg, Leipzig and Dresden. There was scarcely a single German who had not seen the *Sachsen,* or the *Hansa,* or the *Viktoria Luise,* or, before them, the *Deutschland* or the *Schwaben,* gliding high up through the boundless sky like a silver chariot of the Teutonic gods. Thirty-seven thousand, two hundred and fifty Germans had bought tickets at the various branches of the Hamburg-Amerika Shipping Line and actually gone up in Zeppelins. Among them these Zeppelins with peaceful names instead of numbers had flown 100,000 miles with passengers—1,600 flights, 3,200 hours—all without a single accident. The old Count was actually planning a Zeppelin flight to the North Pole. But on Sunday, June 28, 1914, a Serbian student shot dead the heir to the Austrian empire, the Archduke Francis Ferdinand, and the troubled surface of the European peace was shattered. On July 28th Austria declared war on Serbia and her ally Germany made accelerated preparations for war at her side.

The captains of the *Sachsen,* the *Hansa* and the *Viktoria Luise* received urgent telegrams forbidding them to operate their airships more than thirty miles from their home bases. Within hours army engineers were fitting tiny wireless cockpits and bomb racks and installing machine guns. The hulls of the ships were hastily lengthened by twenty-five feet to give them greater lifting capacity for bombs. War with Russia came on August 1st. France mobilized in support of Russia in accordance with their mutual treaty and Germany demanded unrestricted passage through Belgium to operate their Schlieffen Plan of attack against France. Great Britain stood by a moral obligation to defend Belgium, and on August 5th was at war with Germany.

A few hours after he had heard the news Dr. Hugo Eckener, economist, writer and in latter years airship captain and colleague of Count Zeppelin, shut up the Delag office in Hamburg and went to see Admiral Dick, Chief of the Dockyard Section of the new Naval Airship Division at Kiel, to volunteer his services as an airship commander with the navy.

Dick said, "There *is* a way we can use you—but you must put out of your head any idea that you are going into battle. Your life is much too valuable to us for training airship crews. We have too few airship commanders as it is."

3. OPENING MOVES

Eckener went to Hamburg-Fühlsbüttel, the headquarters of the Naval Airship Division, as chief instructor, and was received there warmly by his former pupil, now *Fuehrer der Luftschiffe* Strasser. The first naval Zeppelin had been wrecked and the second destroyed by fire, and Strasser, a former gunnery officer, had only one Zeppelin under his command, the L3. But he had ambitious plans. New Zeppelins were being laid down for the navy, and work was well under way on a new operational headquarters at Nordholz on the coast near Cuxhaven. Strasser went further in his ideas than most of the naval staff, who thought of the Zeppelins only as scouts for surface ships.

He saw his paper fleet as an armada of aerial cruisers with which to blast the dockyards and arsenals of England much as German U-Boats and surface raiders would decimate British shipping at sea. There were other naval airship enthusiasts who went much further, officers like Captain von Pustau, who said in a lecture at Kiel, "With airships we have in certain circumstances the means of carrying the war into the British country, and in England one imagines with terror that one can already hear the beating of the propellers of the Zeppelin cruisers."

But the German naval staff had no such bold plans on the table, as the armies of von Kluck and von Bülow smashed

through Belgium in their move to outflank and take Paris
in accordance with the Schlieffen Plan, and the view that the
airships should be lackeys of the traditional weapons was
even more strongly entrenched in the army. Few senior
army officers had imagined a wider use of Zeppelins than as
scouts for Uhlan cavalry, though some of the Junker mili-
tarists savored its tempting potentialities as a weapon of
terror. The army, with nine operational Zeppelins, including the three commercial ships, was in advance of the Naval
Airship Division numerically, but in its thinking marched
a step behind. It was natural that sailors should be quicker
to understand the new weapon, once they had taken it up.
The seaman had a greater instinctive aptitude for the kind
of flying involved in operating Zeppelins; the vast blue distances of the oceans were a better training ground for the
boundless altitudes than the mud of infantry maneuvers.
The navy treated their Zeppelins much as they did their
surface raiders, as "aerial cruisers," and this gave them a lead
as airship aviators.

If the German public had known that the loud voices of
enthusiasts in no way spoke for the High Command, that
the army and navy staffs had no really positive plans for the
use of their Zeppelins—the aerial marvels that owed their
existence to the financial support of the people, no thought
of combining them for a decisive blow, no idea more excit-
ing than their use as mobile kite balloons, they would have
been disillusioned and disgusted and other nations surprised.
The people followed the popular press and the Kaiser in
naming Count Zeppelin "the greatest German of the century," and they expected miracles of the invention which was
to them the eighth wonder of the world. Every day, people,
not only in the Fatherland, expected to read that the great
airships which had flown the length and breadth of Germany and back had spanned the comparatively easy distance
from Belgium to England and bombed and terrorized the

British people. The wine of Germanic propaganda, blended of known German genius, generally accepted Teutonic "thoroughness" and Prussian military supremacy, was a forced, home-grown product, drunk at every German table and exported in quantity to the rest of the world, Great Britain included.

The British too had read all about the Zeppelins. In the press the German airships looked huge and menacing in blurred photographs and artists' "interpretations." They appeared alongside horrific sketches of Signor Ulivi's famous F-ray, said to have the power to ignite any explosive known to man at almost unlimited distances. People who had cheered and shouted hysterically in a packed Whitehall on August 5th, when the news of war came through, awoke next morning with less positive feelings, and some skimmed their papers in that early morning hangover from troubled dreams in which monster shapes had roared overhead and London had been consumed in a second great fire.

The Zeppelins did not come that first night of the war, nor the second nor the third nor the fourth. But when stories of German brutality in Belgium began to appear in the papers, the name Zeppelin, or "Zepp" as it soon became, took on a sinister sound which never left it. It became associated with the U-boat, the other German bogy weapon; only the Zepp was more frightening to a civilian population because it could do to women and children in England what the Uhlan "baby killers" and Prussian "rapists" were doing on the Continent.

Londoners watched the sky uneasily, lay awake at night waiting for the new terror of twentieth-century war to come, snarling and roaring overhead. "Zepp" was an altogether new shape of fear in British hearts. There had been no threat like it since Napoleon's invasion barges, and then there had been the Navy for protection, and the Militia if "Boney" landed. Now. . . . What was there to prevent these monsters from scorching London with their breath of fire?

But the first days of war passed and the Zepps did not come. Not the real ones, that is, though fear created their image in many places. Zepps had been *definitely* seen off the coast, over the Channel, shadowing ships at sea. . . . Most of the reports were of the same order as the stories of train-loads of Russians with snow on their boots who had been positively seen—by someone else—on their way down from Scottish ports. Apprehensive citizens stirred uneasily if they heard a drone in the night sky or saw a dark shape among scudding wrack. When three weeks had gone by without sight or sound of the real thing, the Zepp scare began to fade a little, only to be brought suddenly alive again by the head-lines on the morning of Wednesday, August 26th. The *Daily Sketch* said:

ZEPPELIN'S ATTACK ON ANTWERP

SIX SHRAPNEL BOMBS FROM AN AIRSHIP AT NIGHT

THE KING'S PERIL

TWELVE PEOPLE KILLED AND HOSPITAL DAMAGED

"Antwerp," reported Reuter, "protests against this bar-barous attack on the hospital, which was flying the flag of the Geneva Convention. Great excitement reigns through-out the town. The bombs exploded with terrific force."

There was a picture of the old Count, white-mustach-ioed, in his Prussian *pickelhaube* helmet, smiling. Here was the nightmare pursuer himself, the authentic bogyman of the Zepp scare. Would he be over London tonight? Or-dinary people took it for granted that there was no way of attacking the aerial monsters or driving them off when they came. The few who knew the state of the British defenses were pessimistic about the effectiveness of a few untried guns and virtually unarmed, rickety airplanes.

But the early weeks went by free of attack. The news from the front was not good, but at least civilians at home still slept safe in their beds. Once more the mood of the people became optimistic. Theories circulated to explain the inactivity of the German airships. Perhaps, after all, weather or distance had beaten them. Some technical "experts" even predicted that the eddies and updrafts of air from cliffs or hills or even tall buildings would prevent the Zeppelins from ever being able to operate over Britain. This was very comforting to the public. Another view—which gained ground as the German army slowed down in its great drive on Paris—was that the Germans were using all their available dirigibles to act as the eyes of the army in France and of the Imperial navy in the North Sea—very much on the defensive against aggressive opening moves by the Royal Navy under Winston Churchill's direction.

August passed without the Zepps. September came on. There were rumors that a Zeppelin was hiding in the hills of Cumberland and Westmorland and coming out to reconnoiter at night. The Royal Flying Corps sent Second Lieutenant Hucks up in his Blériot to chase the shadow. Hucks made a thorough search and enjoyed the scenery, but there was no Zeppelin. The threat was still very real, however, and the government took some steps to protect likely targets.

On September 11th the Commissioner of Metropolitan Police issued the first ordinance for the restriction of lighting to safeguard London against airship raids. The threat of living in semidarkness was enough to lower the spirits of Londoners even further. Although the actual dim-out was not to come into force yet, the thought had disturbing undertones of a breakdown in civilization, a plunge into jungle chaos. Uneasy apprehensions took root which the savagery of the Uhlans had already aroused in the minds of the civilian population of England, who had not looked on the awful face of war for three centuries. For the first time people at home in England, and especially in London, began to see that this war with Germany was to be no Crimea, no Boer Rebellion.

Still the Zeppelins did not come, but the signs and portents of their presence were not all shapes of fancy. A few days after Hucks had laid the ghost ship of Grasmere, a Royal Naval Air Service seaplane on patrol from Felixstowe sighted a Zeppelin to seaward. The airship was a good sixty miles away when the pilot first saw it and the seaplane itself some distance out to sea on the terminal mark of its patrol. The Zeppelin did not come any closer and soon disappeared over the misty horizon. No Zeppelins came any closer than this in September.

On October 1st the new restrictions on lighting came into force in London. A large number of street lights were put out and the remainder shaded, and streetcars and buses were darkened. Blinds had to be fully drawn in private houses before gas mantles and oil lamps could be lit. London was plunged into the darkness of the cave and atavistic fears began to stir deep in people's minds. But as the days and weeks went slowly by with no warning signals going off and no constables on bicycles blowing their shrill whistles, no searchlight playing in the sky, no dreaded throb of motors overhead and no bombs screaming down, feeling once again became more buoyant.

October, then November, went by without any sign of German aircraft, Zeppelins or otherwise. Then, at ten-past four on the afternoon of December 15th, the S.S. *Ape,* on her way from Hull to Yarmouth, sighted a Zeppelin just south of the Protector Shoal Buoy, heading in the direction of Mablethorpe. It was raining, and there were heavy patches of mist over the water. The barometer had sunk to

29.15 inches. If the Zeppelin had come to raid England she had chosen a very bad day. But the airship came no nearer than the coast and soon vanished in the mist to seaward. She was probably on a reconnaissance of the English coast.

Then, at thirty-five minutes past twelve on the morning of the first Christmas Day of the war, while Commodore Tyrrwhitt's cruisers in the Heligoland Bight were awaiting the return of the naval seaplanes which had gone to attack Nordholz, an Albatross seaplane appeared over Sheerness, flew as far west as Gravesend, went inland to Dartford, northwest to Erith, passed over Purfleet and Tilbury, crossed the river again at Shornmead Fort, and dropped two high-explosive bombs just south of Cliffe Station. Eventually the plane went out to sea again over Thanet and Minster, having survived attacks by R.N.A.S. machines from Eastchurch and the Isle of Grain and made a good reconnaissance of military targets and defense installations all around the Thames Estuary. But when the New Year came in no Zeppelin had taken advantage of his efforts. Britain remained relieved—and surprised. Why were the Germans holding back?

Had she known the reason she would have been even more surprised. The German High Command had not used their world-renowned Zeppelins simply because they had not for a moment thought that they would need them. The army, "the greatest on the planet," was supposed to win the war in a few weeks.

Immediately after the German defeat at the Marne the army and navy staffs met urgently, and Zeppelin raids upon England, for a long time the demand of a few army and navy fanatics and of the general public, were discussed and recommended. But the High Command had not planned for the emergency, and there were simply not enough airships for the double task of bombing England and maintaining the important work of reconnaissance with the fleet and the army in the field.

On August 4, 1914, the German army, with the addition of the *Sachsen, Hansa* and *Viktoria Luise,* had owned ten of the eleven operational rigid airships in Germany. Only one was in the hands of the navy, with another building. Of the army airships, four were new military Zeppelins. These were stationed on the western frontier. There were two older, smaller ones, and one of the wooden-framed Schütte-Lanz ships, the SL2, on the eastern frontier. It was, to start with, too small a force to do any great material damage to targets in England. The High Command had not expected Britain to come in against her when she did, but had looked forward to dealing with her in leisure at a later date, with a vastly expanded fleet and air force, and thus had neglected building the one weapon which could attack Britain unscathed.

Even this meager force became rapidly depleted in the first months of war. Early in August the Z6 at Cologne was ordered to take off in bad, cloudy weather, to bomb the fortress of Lutetia in support of the army. It dropped its bombs on target, but cloud forced it to come down so low that it was hit again and again by shrapnel and rifle bullets and was completely wrecked trying to return to base. A similar disaster destroyed the Z7 in Alsace and the Z8 at Badonvillers. In this way, through ignorance of its use, the generals wasted three of their four new Zeppelins. Like bad players they blamed their cards, and the surviving ships were left to swing on their moorings.

Commanders grew restless and frustrated, and crews became bloody-minded. Captain Ernst Lehmann of the *Sachsen* and the airship's General Staff officer, Lieutenant Colonel Max von Gemmingen, nephew and colleague of Count Zeppelin himself, complained with effect of the uninformed use of the army airships, and Zeppelin commanders were al-

lowed more control over the operations of their ships. Lehmann raided Antwerp in the *Sachsen* late in September
and shortly afterward nursed a new Zeppelin, the Z9, under
Captain Horn, through several attacks on Antwerp and Ostend. On October 8th, Flight Lieutenant Marix of the
R.N.A.S. flew from Antwerp in a Sopwith Tabloid and
bombed the Z9 in its hangar at Düsseldorf, reducing it to
ashes.[1] A month later three more R.N.A.S. pilots, operating
temporarily from Belfort, made a very daring and dangerous
raid upon the almost sacred heart of the whole Zeppelin invention at Friedrichshaven and destroyed another new airship which had been almost ready for service with the navy.[2]

If raids on Britain were not begun soon, it looked as if
there would be no Zeppelins left. Strasser, head of the naval
airships, proposed a naval raid on Britain; it was turned
down, but building plans were accelerated still more, and
by the end of the year the staffs felt that strength was sufficient to begin tentative raids on England. The blockade of
Germany by the British Navy had incensed the German
people and they were demanding a spectacular revenge upon
the comfortable English civilian population, whose navy
brought them all the luxuries and necessities of life.

The new airship plant at Potsdam delivered its first Zeppelin on November 11th, and by mid-December the navy
had taken delivery of five new Zeppelins and the army two.
Admiral von Pohl, the naval Chief of Staff, suggested a joint
attack upon targets in England, but the idea was dropped
because the army staff wanted to use its Zeppelins to attack
the fortresses of Nancy, Dunkirk and Verdun.

And there were other objections. The German Chancellor, Bethmann-Hollweg, did not want London bombed,
for he thought there was still a chance of a patched-up peace
with Britain; and the Kaiser remained absolutely opposed
to attacks of this sort upon a country with whom he had so

[1] Appendix A.   [2] Appendix B.

many ties. But on January 7, 1915, von Pohl presented another memorandum vigorously urging Zeppelin attacks on
England. London, he argued, was a defended city in the
sense of The Hague Convention definition and contained
targets of great military value. His airships would take all
possible care to avoid damaging historical buildings or private property. The effects of such a raid on the enemy's
capital would be far-reaching upon morale and matériel.
On January 9th the Kaiser gave way to the pressure of his
war lords and gave official permission for his Zeppelins to
bomb England, with the exception of London.

In the High Command, the advocates of terror raids on
England, of whom Ludendorff was one, recognized the thin
end of the wedge and were temporarily satisfied. A beginning could now be made and swiftly accelerated until the
scheme which they had in mind for burning London to the
ground, using a fleet of Zeppelins armed with three hundred incendiary bombs each, a plan which Army airship
commanders had confirmed reluctantly was technically possible, could be realized.

At the Fühlsbüttel Naval base *Kapitan-Leutnant* Magnus
Freiherr von Platen, commanding Zeppelin L4, *Kapitan-
Leutnant* Johann Fritze, in L3, and *Oberleutnant* Horst
Freiherr Trensch von Buttlar-Brandenfels, with L6, at the
new Naval Zeppelin Headquarters at Nordholz, awaited the
order to take off for England. Bad weather held them up for
some days, but on the morning of January 19th they left
their sheds and headed for the southeast coast of Britain into
a belt of uncertain weather. Von Buttlar turned back halfway with engine trouble, but at twenty minutes to seven
that evening a young man at Ingham in Norfolk, a mile and
a half from the sea, saw, as he said, "two bright stars moving,
apparently thirty yards apart." They were the navigation
lights of von Platen and Fritze. Before coming over the
land at five minutes to eight they separated, L3 coming in-

land via the Haisboro Lightship, L4 making along the coast in the direction of Bacton. The first Zeppelin raid on Britain had begun.

Meandering about mist-veiled Norfolk, uncertain of their navigation and freezing cold in their open cars, they dropped their bombs indiscriminately wherever they saw a large cluster of lights. Fritze dropped nine high-explosive bombs on Yarmouth, killed one man, wrecked a few houses and damaged a steam drifter in the river. Von Platen did more harm. Following a course Bacton-Cromer-Sheringham-Beeston-Thornham-Brancaster-Hunstanton-Snettisham-King's Lynn, he scattered his bombs as he went. A high-explosive aimed at the radio listening station at Hunstanton—specially tuned to Zeppelin wavelengths—missed by three hundred yards, but at King's Lynn he demolished houses, hit the engine house of the Docks and Railway Company's power station, and killed and injured several people. In all, two men and two women were killed in the raid; ten men, four women and three children injured.

Von Platen reported that his ship had been heavily shelled and held in searchlights over King's Lynn, and thought he had bombed the mouth of the Humber. The "searchlights" were the glare of the lights of Lynn reflected in the mist, and the guns were pure invention. The crews of both ships were specially decorated with Iron Crosses, which they did not have long to enjoy, because both the L3 and L4 were lost in a storm off the Jutland coast on February 8th.

The morning after the raid, Mr. Halcombe Ingleby, Member of Parliament for King's Lynn, motored from his house near Sedgeford to King's Lynn, stopping on the way at Snettisham Church, where an excited and bewildered group was assembled, talking about the raid. The vicar appealed to Ingleby to confirm whether the raider had been a Zeppelin or an airplane. Only two of the others claimed to have actually seen the aircraft. One of these affirmed very strongly that it was a biplane, and that he had seen it very plainly dropping a bomb—"Does a Zeppelin travel sideways?" The other, a woman, exclaimed, "All I can say is it was the biggest sausage I ever saw in my life!" A villager described the aircraft as looking "like a church steeple sideways."

A spate of spy stories circulated immediately afterward. Breathless witnesses reported an impossible number of suspicious vehicles signaling to the raiders—a "dark, closed car with a green light on top," a "car with a fiery light," "a brilliantly lighted motorcar with two powerful headlights," a darkened silent car with four occupants in "strangely muffled head gear." There was an atmosphere of unreality about the Zeppelin raid on Norfolk. People could not believe their eyes when they saw quite plainly the heads of the German crew as the control car of L4 almost fouled the spire on the school building at Thornham. In the United States on January 20th the Milwaukee *Free Press* ran the headlines: "Zeppelins Bombard Sandringham As King George and the Queen Flee. Panic Grips Capital As Foe Steers Course for London."

The raid was an experiment, a first try. Bit by bit from then on through the spring and summer the airship services worked up toward the major effort—the all-out attack on London. In February the Kaiser, under considerable pressure, permitted the bombing of military targets east of the Tower. On February 26th the L8 took off for England from Düsseldorf, but strong headwinds forced her to turn back and land at an army field in Belgium. From here she made a second attempt on the night of March 4th, but got into difficulties when a gale struck her out of the unchartable west, and she was shot down in France.

The L8 was replaced by a new ship, the L9, commanded by a Lieutenant Commander Mathy, a new Zeppelin commander. Mathy began to get his hand in on April 14th by an impromptu raid on Tyneside while on reconnaissance in which he did some damage and killed a woman and a child. The following night his colleagues Böcker in the L5, von Buttlar in the L6, and Peterson in the L7, with the director himself, Peter Strasser, on board Peterson's ship, made an attempt to raid the Humber. The heaviest attack was made by the L5 which dropped its bombs on Henham Hall, Southwold and Lowestoft, well to the south of the target. Von Buttlar's L6 returned with its gas cells punctured by rifle bullets.

These early naval Zeppelin models did not have the range of London, but in the spring of the year the army had made good their earlier losses by the addition of a batch of new ships. Based upon their newly built sheds in Belgium, which allowed them a short haul to London, they began concentrated action against the eastern sector of the British capital, led by Hauptmann Linnarz, the best of the army pilots, in his LZ38. On May 10th he made an attack upon Southend. He was driven back over Canvey Island by an unexpected burst of gunfire but left behind a card threatening, "You English. We have come and will come again. Kill or cure. German."

Two further raids upon the Thames Estuary gave Linnarz the experience he needed, and on the night of May 31st he extended his activities. Steering over Ramsgate and Margate he crossed the Estuary to the north shore at Shoeburyness, went west over Brentwood, then turned south and bombed the northeastern sector of London. On districts from Leytonstone to Shoreditch he dropped his cargo of incendiary bombs and murderous grenades, and got clean away. The following night Lieutenant Commander Hirsch in the L10 from Nordholz tried to outdo Linnarz but only succeeded in bombing Sittingbourne and Gravesend, which he thought was Harwich, with poor results.

Linnarz's attack was the first serious raid on London, none

of the previous attempts having been more than uncertain lunges. Neither the forty-two casualties—seven killed, thirty-five injured—nor the estimated $100,000 worth of damage were serious in themselves, but the threat of large-scale attacks had been brought home. Linnarz became a popular hero in Germany: the bombing of London satisfied the growing demand for retaliation against the British public on account of the "hunger blockade," and the German press reveled in extravagant versions of the exploit. The *Neueste Nachrichten* of Leipzig said:

"England no longer an island! The City of London, the heart which pumps the life-blood into the arteries of the brutal huckster nation, has been sown with bombs by German airships, whose brave pilots had the satisfaction of seeing the dislocated fragments of docks, banks and many other buildings rise up to the dark skies in lurid tongues of flame. At last the long yearned for punishment has fallen on England, this people of liars and hypocrites—the punishment for the overflowing measure of sins of ages past. It is neither blind hatred nor raging anger that inspires our airship heroes, but a solemn and religious awe at being the chosen instruments of the Divine wrath. In that moment when they saw London breaking up in smoke and fire they lived through a thousand lives of an immeasurable joy which all who remain at home must envy them."

After the first raid on Norfolk in January, the few guns dotted around London and the R.N.A.S. aircraft which, the R.F.C. being too short of aircraft, had been allotted to the air defense, flying from coastal stations around East Anglia and airdromes around the perimeter of the capital, did what they could to interfere with the ever more enterprising Zeppelins. But the guns were of very limited performance, and the slow, unstable and almost unarmed machines of the R.N.A.S. found the hitherto untried business of flying at night difficult and very dangerous. Pilots were killed frequently in crash landings and only rarely did they even sight a Zeppelin. Only at low heights were the airships in any danger from the R.N.A.S. machines.

On his second raid upon the Thames Estuary Linnarz was hovering casually at 2,000 feet when he was fired on by Flight Lieutenant Mulock from Westgate air station. The gun on Mulock's Avro jammed at the critical moment and nothing came of the attack except a warning to Zeppelin commanders to make proper use of their great superiority in rate of climb and ceiling. On the whole, the very courageous sorties by the R.N.A.S. pilots of the air defenses were ineffective.

At their home bases, however, the R.N.A.S. gave the new army Zeppelins serious trouble. Continental-based Royal Navy machines lost no opportunity in attacking the raiders in and about their sheds there. On the night of June 6th three Zeppelins took off to attack London from their sheds in Belgium. Fog confused them and forced them to break off the flight, and at one o'clock on the following morning Flight Sublieutenant Warneford, who had left Furnes in a Morane monoplane to bomb the Zeppelin sheds at Berchem, sighted one over Ostend, chased her, and near Ghent got above her and bombed her into a flaming, falling wreck, almost losing his own life in the tremendous explosion when the airship's gas tanks blew up. Meanwhile Linnarz had taken his Zepp back and seen her safely housed in her shed at Guère near Brussels.

While Warneford was grappling with the LZ37, Flight Lieutenants Wilson and Mills flew in the dark to Guère, bombed the sheds and completely destroyed Linnarz's ship. Particularly after these disasters, the new Belgian airship bases, of which so many high hopes had been entertained, became too vulnerable to be used except as emergency landing fields. The German army airship campaign against London had been defeated.

On June 18th, twelve days after the German army Zeppelins had met with such disaster, Admiral Bachmann, Imperial navy Chief of Staff, wrote to von Falkenhayn, the Minister for War, asking for his approval on the removing of all restrictions upon bombing London. In his reply on the 22nd Falkenhayn agreed that London should be unequivocally cleared for raids, but warned the Naval Chief of Staff against acting precipitously. Present Zeppelin strength, he said, was inadequate for the job of inflicting "the maximum damage on the enemy," which was the sole object of raids, "not to raise the spirit of the German people," particularly during the period of short nights which then prevailed. Nothing, in fact, short of a very large squadron of Zeppelins accompanied by giant bombers and fighters would do. He proposed that the chief of the army air force should take charge of a combined mass attack on London.

The Imperial navy had meanwhile begun to take delivery of a new, more powerful type of Zeppelin, designed to be able to reach London comfortably, which previous models had been unable to do, and two Schütte-Lanz-type airships. Bachmann thought that Zeppelin attacks should continue right away so as to strike while the English people were still seriously alarmed and to forestall the bad weather which was forecast. Now that he had persuaded von Falkenhayn to support the removal of the Imperial veto upon the bombing of London, he was able to press his point with success, and on July 9th the Imperial Chancellor agreed to allow attacks upon the City of London, though only between Saturday afternoons and Monday mornings.

When the order was submitted for his approval, however, the Kaiser refused to allow it, and on July 11th permission was withdrawn. But Bachmann was able to point to the bombing of open German towns by French aircraft, and after Karlsruhe had been raided, with heavy civilian casualties, the Kaiser was forced to consent at last. He absolutely banned the bombing of St. Paul's and Westminster Abbey, and at first insisted upon the original restriction to week-ends. But reluctantly he was compelled to admit that such a condition, coupled with the unsuitable weather and short nights, could limit the chances of raids to a ridiculous extent, and he withdrew it.

Strasser was now free to put into action his new Zeppelins of the L10 class, bigger, more powerful, better designed craft able to make London easily from Nordholz, Hage or Fühlsbüttel, given good navigators and determined handling. The short distance of the army LZ's from British continental airfields had been turned against them by the vigorous cutting-out tactics of the British naval airplanes, but the much more remote German naval airship stations in north Germany could not be so attacked, nor could the naval dirigibles be so easily intercepted in the wide misty hunting grounds of the North Sea. By August 1st, Strasser had received four of the new Zeppelins as well as two Schütte-Lanz airships.

It had taken a long time for man to find the means of turning Lana's copper globes propelled by oars and sails into the L13, the latest, most potent product of the old Count Zeppelin's stubborn will to success. Commander Mathy's new ship, the L13, was a refinement, but only a refinement, upon the original Zeppelin which had floated lightly in the summer breezes over a shining lake at the opening of this century of violence. She was bigger—536 feet long as against 420; her engines developed more power—210 h.p. to the old ship's 32, giving a speed of 60 miles per hour compared with about 20; the old sliding weight had long since given place to a system of horizontal rudders, fore and aft; gondolas, though still angular and unstreamlined, were no longer open as they had been in all the early ships including Fritze's, and von Platen's L3 and L4, and the triangular keel-plus-gangway had been removed up into the hull for greater strength and accessibility. But in her main essentials Mathy's ship was the same as the original gleam in the inventor's eye.

The main problem set by the rigid airship was the combination of strength and lightness in her frame. The lifting power of her hydrogen had to be balanced against the dead weight of the aluminum skeleton and all the other weights, like gondolas, engines, bombs, guns, fuel, and water ballast, which it supported. These two forces pulled in opposite directions and had to be distributed as evenly as possible along the entire length of the ship to give her equilibrium, not only with regard to normal flight but to the sudden loss of weight at different points caused by the dropping of bombs or the deflation of a gas cell.

To meet these requirements a delicately balanced structure had been evolved. When she was in her early stages of building in the construction shed, a Zeppelin looked like nothing so much as a huge, frail bird cage, but the structure was stronger that it looked. The first step was the building of a nineteen-sided polygonal ring by riveting aluminum girders together. Steel stays were then fitted between the joints of the girders to make the whole ring rigid. Sixteen of these rings were suspended in their correct relative positions along the construction shed, eleven yards apart and linked at every corner by longitudinal tie girders riveted to them and running from bow to stern of the entire hull. Halfway between each two main girder rings an auxiliary ring was fitted to brace the longitudinal tie girders. That completed the first stage of the building. The bird cage was in existence, a huge one, fifty feet across.

Over this great framework the outer skin was then drawn, well-stretched to give extra strength and rigidity to the hull by counteracting the internal gas pressure and so reducing the strain on the girders. The gas pressure was taken directly by the gas-bags, which transmitted the pressure to the girders by means of a tautly stretched net of rhea fiber cloth, the ends of which were connected to the girders. A slack outer cover could result in girders being bent outward by the gas pressure until they gave way, as well as greatly adding to wind resistance in flight. Several coats of a dark yellow dope compounded of rubber and linseed oil also prevented flabbiness, made the envelope weatherproof and inelastic, and further streamlined it by giving it a smooth outer surface.

With the framework complete and the envelope in place, the control and engine cars were slung underneath the ship and the driving shaft mechanism and propellers fitted. The next step was to hang, in the compartments formed by the spaces between the main girder rings in the hull, the gas cells. In prewar ships these cells, which had to be as light as possible and impermeable to gas, were made either of one or two layers of rubberized cotton or of seven thicknesses of goldbeater's skin. The rubber material, however, was discarded because of its weight and conductivity to electricity, and the war made pure goldbeater's skin, in any case too easily torn by bullets or shrapnel, too scarce and expensive. So an ersatz fabric made of one layer of linen and several layers of goldbeater's skin glued together was adopted. The gas cells were hung from the upper part of the main framework, and pumps automatically compensated for any gain or loss of gas volume caused by changes in the temperature of the outside air.

Inside the hull, running from bow to stern, and broken only by ladders leading down into the control and engine cars, was the gangway, the *Laufgang,* built on triangular trestles. Along this narrow corridor all the extra weights taken on board for the flight were located, the gas cylinders, oil and fuel tanks, bombs and water-ballast containers, as well as the rudder-control cables, bomb releases, telegraph and telephone wires, electric lighting wires and speaking tubes.

With these new ships, guided by lessons learned from pre-

vious raids, especially Linnarz's solitary attack of May 31st
on London, a really ambitious, large-scale offensive directed
against the British capital as the principal target was planned
for the anti-cyclonic period of fair weather predicted by the
weather experts for the late summer and autumn. No longer
were raids to be made on moonlight nights, a precaution
which the army ships had ignored, and a much closer study
of the weather was made.

The first two attempts were failures and were charged to
experience. Bombs were wasted, and Peterson crashed his
new L12 in Belgium after she had been crippled by a lucky
shell from below. Here the disabled airship was bombed by
the ever vigilant R.N.A.S. and completely destroyed. But
Strasser and his captains persevered. On August 17th Wenke
in the L10 came in alone and bombed Leyton, killing ten
persons and injuring forty-eight, spotting the railway station
with a high explosive and damaging a chapel. Böcker in the
L14, and von Buttlar in the L11, dropped their bombs over
open country or in the sea and did no damage, although they
were credited in German official communiqués with successful attacks on east London and the Ipswich area.

On September 7th the army's badly blunted determination
revived, and three of their ships set out for London. Only
one, a Schütte-Lanz airship, got through, but she made herself felt, killing six men, six women and six children in southwest London, injuring thirty-eight more people, and doing
some damage to private property. The score was mounting,
although no raid so far could be described as more than be-
ginners' fumblings.

On the morning of the day following this army effort,
Captain Strasser studied his weather charts keenly to see if
the skies to the westward would give him a chance to outdo
the army.

PART II

THE CAMPAIGN

"As to an airplane corps for the defense of London, it must be remembered that it takes some time for an airplane to get up as high as a Zeppelin, and by the time it gets there the airship would be gone. . . ."

Kapitan-Leutnant Heinrich Mathy,
Imperial German Navy, 1915.

4. MATHY

Nordholz, the headquarters of the Imperial German Naval Airship Service, was sited in a particularly dreary and isolated spot on a long stretch of sandy soil and scrub a few miles from Cuxhaven on the mouth of the River Elbe, on the railway line running between that town and Bremerhaven to the south. It was cold, bleak and desolate there for most of the year, and duty at Zeppelin H.Q. emphasized the description of war as long periods of boredom punctuated by bursts of fear and excitement.

Action, when it came, could take one of two forms. Mostly, the airships were used for reconnaissance work with the High Seas Fleet, the job for which they had originally been ordered by the navy. This was tedious, monotonous, unrewarding work. But when a period of moonless nights and good flying weather coincided, Nordholz transformed itself into a frenzy of preparation for the Zeppelins' bigger, more spectacular role—a raid on England.

The weather chart on the morning of September 8, 1915, showed the right conditions. An anti-cyclone extended from the Irish Sea to Scandinavia, with its center over the North Sea, maintaining very quiet conditions over the British Isles and the adjacent continent. Light westerly winds prevailed below and aloft. Zeppelin aviators liked this sort of weather. A light westerly wind gave an airship the best conditions for an attack on England, because it facilitated her retreat from the target if she were being attacked or if one or more of her motors stopped. It must not be too strong, or the chances of reaching London, Liverpool or the Tyne would be too great to risk.

But this morning Strasser, the Director of Airships, thought the weather about perfect. It promised to be generally fine over the target, with a chance of light ground mist, which was bad for whatever odd airplanes the British naval air service might try to get aloft, but good for a bombing Zeppelin, because you could still see buildings like Tower Bridge, the Bank of England and the forbidden Buckingham Palace and St. Paul's quite clearly, still identify the unique serpentine twists of the Thames. And tonight there would be no moonlight to assist the few fumbling searchlights and the dozen or so short-ranged inaccurate guns which the British had located in and around their capital. It was England tonight.

There had been, for the first five months of the war, so many maddening delays and disasters in the Zeppelin arm, so many sentimental restrictions placed on it by the Kaiser and by the Imperial Chancellor. But since raids on England had begun in January, when von Platen and Fritze bombed Norfolk, the airship attacks had gradually been stepped up in weight as the situation in France remained at stalemate and the High Command turned to their two secret weapons of silent terror, the U-boat and the Zeppelin, now coming in more efficient form from the factories. The provincial cities of Britain had felt the force of the Zeppelin service since then, though for some time the Kaiser had refused permission to go to London, the enemy's capital, the heart of his resistance. Now, when the naval airship service, after a slow start, was getting into its stride and beginning to outstrip the army Zeppelins, London was going to experience the full force of terror and destruction by fire of which the new ships were capable.

The raid was on. Strasser issued his order to prepare for the flight, and the crews of the four airships selected to make the attack—Lieutenant Commander Mathy's L13 and Lieutenant Commander Loewe's old L9 from Hage, Lieutenant Commander (Reserve) Böcker's L14 from Hamburg-Fühlsbüttel, and Lieutenant von Buttlar's L11 from Nordholz—hurried to take the necessary action. They had about two hours from the time of the order to the time for take-off to prepare the ships.

In the moonless period the airships were always kept ready for action, and as far as possible everything had already been done. The huge doors of the double hangars at Nordholz had been rolled aside, the handling party were standing by and the L11 was ready for flight. The men in charge of the filling operations had been up at dawn hustling about their jobs in the cold air, and the hydrogen gas had gone hissing into the great containers inside the envelope, leaving a sickly-sweet stench everywhere. The gas-bags were full, the envelope hauled tight. Mechanics had revved up the motors on test, and clouds of sand had gone whirling high in the blast of air from the propellers. The fuel, the machine guns and ammunition, everything needed during the flight, were in the ship.

Now the bombs had to be hung in position. They were brought out from the munitions depot on small hand carts and placed under the ship. The light-caliber bombs were carried into position in the corridor which ran the whole length of the ship inside the envelope by men of the airship's care and maintenance party. The medium- and heavy-caliber bombs had to be hoisted into position with the help of tackles, and suspended by hooks to the bomb frames. The men worked hard and cheerfully and made coarse jokes as they patted the bombs and wished them good hunting among the English, who were starving German families with their blockade. In this bomb load there was a preponderance of incendiaries. London was going to feel the fire tonight.

One or two of the crew members of L13, Commander Mathy's ship, had prepared specialities of their own, little presents for the smug citizens of London, which would dangle on little parachutes and fall into the back gardens in Finchley or Plumstead or even, with luck, on the doorstep of the warmonger Churchill at the British Admiralty in Whitehall.

They carried one especially spectacular contribution. This was a huge bomb of 300 kilograms (660 lbs.), the heaviest ever put aboard a Zeppelin, and it came especially to Germany's leading airship captain from the factory as a "love gift," a *Liebesgabe*. What little home in Leyton would receive this one? Would it demolish Sir Christopher Wren's immortal monument, or wreck the gateway to the capital at Tower Bridge, or blow up the Houses of Parliament at last or, biggest prize of all, shatter the Bank of England and ruin the bloated system of capitalist finance which was promoting this war against Germany? If it should go astray and land fair and square on Buckingham Palace and kill the King of England, who would be sorry in Germany but the Kaiser? And his word counted for less and less these days. There was an extra excitement about the operations for this sortie, an anticipation of history about to be made, a feeling that tonight Commander Mathy was going to excel himself.

The crews of the four Zeppelins, at Hage, at Fühlsbüttel and at Nordholz, the bombing-up completed, put on their warm clothing, their furs and watchcoats, and looked for thermos flasks and lifebelts, which was about all they were allowed to take in the way of extras. The space in the control and engine gondolas slung beneath the hull, and in the narrow gangway inside the envelope, was so constricted that even the lifebelts were a specially designed, small type, which hung flat on the body and were inflated in the water. The airship captains received final information, orders and instructions and a blessing from Strasser, whom everyone in the naval airship service respected and called "The Kaiser" in affection.

The quick meal over, packets of bread and butter and sausages made up, and thermos flasks filled up with hot coffee—it could never be too hot for the icy altitudes above the North Sea—it was almost time to go. But before the airships could leave their sheds and go aloft they had to be "weighed," and for that every man of the crew and every last article to be taken on the flight had to be on board.

Zeppelins and U-boats were strange, unholy creatures, with much in common. Each was a totally submersible vessel, a Zeppelin in the air, a submarine in the sea. If a U-boat had too much air in her buoyancy tanks she would rise of her own accord, likewise a Zeppelin with her containers full to bursting with the lighter-than-air hydrogen; if either had too much water ballast she would sink out of control. For positive control by her commander's hand each had to be balanced carefully so that she would float motionless in her fluid element, a state known in submarines as "neutral buoyancy."

To achieve this state, to counterbalance the amount of "lift"—equal to the amount by which the airship with its hydrogen was lighter than the amount of air it displaced—which a ship naturally took on as soon as her gas-bags were filled, she was loaded with weights corresponding to the "lift," namely the crew, the fuel, the lubricating oil, the guns and bombs, and the water ballast. These combined weights had to be adjusted accurately so that they exactly equalled the amount of lift, and this was done by altering the amount of water ballast. Enough ballast had to be discharged to ensure that the ship had no tendency either to rise or to sit too heavily on the ground. When the ship was properly ballasted she floated in the air, and the strength of one man was sufficient to push her up or pull her down. When this state of neutral buoyancy had been reached she was ready to be brought out of the shed.

When Commander Mathy made his entrance through the hangar doors at Hage the officer on duty reported that all was ready. At a signal given by a blast on a whistle the handling party, which had been standing by for some time, seized the handrails running along the bottoms of the gondolas. "Airship forward!" A good heave, and L13, 530 feet long, huge as an ocean liner, moved delicately forward out of the hangar.

Gently controlled by the men on the trailing guide ropes, it glided out, its runners squeaking along their steel rails. A blast from a megaphone signaled that the stern had emerged and the airship was free of the hangar.

"Slack off." Mathy gave the order, a signalman passed it to the crew by flag, the ropes at her bows were released and soon the Zeppelin was swinging gently in the light breeze over the landing field, 200 yards from the shed.

"Hands off. Ease up the guys." Most of the remaining rope handlers let go and the landing party stepped back clear of the gondolas. For a moment the great swollen bulk of the L13 hung motionless, then began to rise majestically upward. "Hold on!" Hand rails and guy ropes were grabbed again and she was hauled down. Commander Mathy climbed up into the for'ard control gondola. "Cast off!" To a hoarse chorus of "Good luck!" and exhortations to give the English hell, the gondolas were shoved upward by a cluster of strong arms. The captain signaled "Motors full speed ahead" on the engine telegraphs. The motors coughed and roared into life and Mathy took his ship up and away from the field in a wide curve toward the sea.

When all four ships were in the air they set course to rendezvous over Heligoland.

It was 1 p.m. when Lieutenant von Buttlar had the usual signal of departure coded up and sent back to base from the tiny radio cockpit in the control gondola, then the Zeppelin followed the familiar aerial course which took her out over Steil Sand, now submerged by the gleaming tide. Far away to the west on the other side of the great stretch of mist-clad sea which they had yet to cross, a British listening station had picked the L11's laconic signal out of the crackling static and passed it immediately down the private telephone line to the telegraph office in the basement of the Admiralty in London. From here it was dispatched swiftly up the pneumatic tube to a secret department for decoding. Here the code was quickly broken.

Presently, other signals came in, all of the same nature, and it was not very long before Admiral Hall at Naval Intelligence, the Home Office and General Henderson, Director General of Aeronautics at the War Office, were in possession of all the known facts. Four unidentified Zeppelins had left their bases and in their formal departure signals had included the words, "Only H.V.B. on board." British Admiralty Intelligence was by now well acquainted with this message and its significance.

"H.V.B." or *Handelsschiffsverkehrsbusch,* was the German Mercantile Marine code book used by German outpost vessels and airships. A copy of it had been captured in Australia early in the war and yet another found in the nets of a Lowestoft trawler. The Germans were well aware of the loss but they continued to make use of the signals in the book, obscuring them by constant translations into a different cipher, ignorant of the skill of the British Admiralty code experts. Airships used it when raiding Britain because its value to the enemy, if they were brought down and captured, would be small, whereas it was laid down in orders that they must leave behind the more confidential naval signal book and notify base to this effect when setting out. Hence "Only

H.V.B. on board," hence the certain knowledge at Admiralty Intelligence that tonight the Zepps were coming again. Sometimes, infrequently, airship commanders or their radio operators were careless enough to reveal the identification letters of their ships and occasionally even their targets in Britain. The objective was Britain, but for further information the British anti-airship defenses would have to rely on human ears and eyes in ships at sea or along the East Coast. Meanwhile, the warning went out to such scratch defenses as existed.

The Zeppelin squadron which hovered over Heligoland was already depleted by one. Von Buttlar, as he so frequently did, had had to return to Nordholz with engine trouble. The reduced force split up and proceeded otherwise according to plan, Loewe in his old L9, steering a course which was by now well known to him in the direction of the north Yorkshire coast; Mathy and Bocker in the L13 and L14, making for their own familiar marker, the Haisboro Lightship, anchored twelve miles off the northern Norfolk coast.

The picture of long gray shapes droning westward over light, drifting cloud suggests two marauding longships plowing a course through the cold sea and baffling mist for England. Their commander, stiff and straight behind the helmsman up in the eyes of the control car beneath the lofty nose, completes the image—Commander Heinrich Mathy, young, coldly handsome, bold, competent, fanatical in duty and love of Fatherland and quite ruthless in its cause, the very figure of a Nordic warrior, with the added refinements of a Prussian aristocrat; Mathy the hero-worshiped ace and idol of the airship services of Germany, the born navigator, the quick and resourceful thinker, the precise and unemotional killer, unlikely to mistake Burnham-on-Crouch or Bishop's Stortford for the enemy capital, and once there the least likely to waste his *Liebesgabe,* the present from the workers of Imperial Germany to the people of England.

The voyage to the west was generally quiet, and this one was no exception. The two ships flew low over their own coast for as long as they could, keeping a sharp lookout for enemy cruisers in the Heligoland Bight. But they saw nothing in the danger zone, not so much as a fishing boat, from the time they left the German coast. For most of the crew, this part of the flight was dull, even boring, especially to the lookouts. The commanders had much to occupy their minds. They had to concentrate all the time on navigation, not so simple in an airship, where they had to deal with strong changes of wind. Mathy did not like to steer too close to the Dutch coast to plot a fix. It was stupid to tip off the enemy agents there and give the English a warning so early in the day unless the airship was badly off course. As the two ships swayed on through the hazy evening, their charts marked for London, each one was a beautiful and stirring sight to the men of the other, as twilight settled upon the Dutch islands on their port beam and the setting sun touched their mat flanks with gold.

After nearly five hours' flight across the misty sea, the mechanics, crouched beside their engines, were feeling the first attacks of fatigue, deafness, nausea and fear. In all the long hours of flight there had been little relief for them. At rare intervals a man would be allowed to go for some refreshment. To do that he might have to climb out of his engine car into the cavernous dark hull of a ship swaying through the dusk, walk a hundred yards and more along the little gangway eighteen inches wide all in the dark, at an icy temperature, with the wind whistling through the joints of the envelope and the heavy reek of gas all around, take a quick gulp of coffee from a thermos flask, and return again to be stationed for hours at a stretch at his engine, watching the chattering machinery, inhaling the hot, stifling stink of oil and exhaust fumes, ignorant of what was happening to the ship, his only contact with the others a hoarse order roared at him through a megaphone perhaps once every hour.

It was all right, he grumbled, for the control car crew. They could stick their heads into the fresh air whenever they liked, they could see where they were, they could cadge hot food from the captain's special hot-plate which he had had tapped off an exhaust pipe. The frozen officers and petty officers up in the control car, on the contrary, envied the engineers their warm billets next to the motors, and wondered how on earth those first men to raid Britain in the open cars of von Platen's and Fritze's old ships could possibly have stood it.

Cruising near the Haisboro Lightship, the men of the two trawlers *Conway* and *Manx Queen* were feeling the cold too. Their guns had been alerted as part of the air defense along with the naval aircraft at the coastal stations and the London guns, and they were on the lookout for Zeppelins. About twenty minutes past seven they heard engines droning nearby and the huge shape of a Zeppelin loomed out of the dusk, low and well within range of the *Conway*'s one-pounder gun. Böcker in the L14 saw the ships dimly below him in the poor light and thought he had run into a light cruiser squadron. His shout to the helmsman was almost simultaneous with the sharp crack of the *Conway*'s first round. Seven more followed before the L14, tilted upward at a sharp angle, climbed well out of range and disappeared in the direction of the coast.

Fifteen minutes later a second Zeppelin blundered into the *Manx Queen*'s gun sight. The trawler got off nine rounds at her before she too climbed rapidly out of range and continued on course. This was Mathy in the L13. The two airships pursued their separate paths towards the target in the gathering darkness.

As the L13 neared the coast Mathy ordered the elevating planes to be set for climbing and they went still higher so that the din of their motors should not give away their presence too soon. The men went to their action stations, the bombing officer and his party to the catwalk amidships, the machine-gunners to their stations in the control car. The top gunner climbed the swaying fifty-foot ladder through the gas stench and darkness of the swaying hull to reach his lonely post right on the upper surface of the envelope and begin a cold, nerve-racking watch for planes.

There was some mist over the coast. A quarter of an hour after his brush with the *Manx Queen,* Mathy turned out to sea again, heading east, then at five minutes past eight was sighted over the land again at Brancaster. Mathy, the careful navigator, was coolly feeling his way toward the mouth of the Wash. From that point on, given a reasonably clear sky the course for London was well signposted for him. He did not reach the Wash until twenty-five past eight. Then he turned gradually to the south, following the coast, and passed over Hunstanton at eight-thirty heading inland. Near Sedgeford he discovered that he was going deeper inland all the time and turned southwest again toward the sea.

Off Dersingham the L13 was sighted going slowly over the water by a fishing boat. Keeping the coast well in view she groped her way in to the mouth of the Lynn Cut, where she was seen from the S.S. *Annandale,* steaming slowly up the Ouse. For four minutes the airship hovered, engines stopped, at a height of 1,500–2,000 feet, checking her position. At eight forty-nine she started her engines again and this time made a determined set at her objective, steering between King's Lynn and Torrington St. Clement to the west, leaving the sea behind her. Picking up the Ouse near Wiggenhall St. German, Mathy now laid off his course for London.

Following the river and railway he reached Downham Market at nine o'clock. Here he made a mistake in navigation and followed the Bedford Level, thinking it was still the railway line which would lead him south near Ely. When he

was over Nepal, eight miles to the west of Ely, he realized
that he was off course. A minute later he dropped a flare
over Sutton, startling the villagers, most of whom had been
disturbed by the engines of the prowling Zeppelin and had
come out to see if they could spot her. The light of the flare
showed him his error and he left the line of the Level, heading south again. He crossed the branch line running west
to St. Ives and Huntingdon, passed Haddenham on his port
side, crossed the Old West River, passed over Denny Abbey,
over Cottenham, and at nine-forty was over Histon. Five
minutes later the L13 flew over the northwest sector of
Cambridge, and her crew could see the glow of their target
far away ahead of them in the darkness. At ten o'clock she
passed Royston, at five past ten Buntingford, at ten fifteen
Ware, and Mathy turned south-sou'west, with the idea of attacking London from the northwest. At ten twenty-eight the
L13 was over Potters Bar, at ten thirty-two High Barnet. At
ten thirty-five, steering south now, she was above the Great
Northern Railway viaduct over the Dollis Brook, between
Finchley and Mill Hill. Then Mathy turned gradually and
headed to the south-sou'east, getting his bearings from the
Thames, reducing speed as he carefully pinpointed his way
to London.

The river was an indestructible guidepost, a sure road to
the great city. The English could darken London as much
as they wanted, but they could never remove or cover up
the Thames, and from the shining surface of its easily fixed
twists and turns a Zeppelin commander could always get his
bearings and pick up any point in London.

The great city lay ahead, still and silent below in the night.
There were dark patches which stood out from the blur of
lights in the well-lit parts—the residential sections were not
darkened very much. It was the dark patches which Mathy
particularly sought, for they marked the railway stations,
bridges, industrial targets of the commercial city, "the heart

which pumps the life-blood into the arteries of the brutal huckster nation," and it was this vital sector of British power which he, for the first time, was briefed to attack to-night. He had strict instructions to do everything possible to avoid hitting St. Paul's Cathedral and other churches or museums, the Palace, Westminster Abbey, and the Houses of Parliament, and he was not especially interested in residential districts as targets.

Of the London defenses Mathy knew that the guns were the most to be feared, but his first thought was to hit the airdrome at Hendon and stop any sortie likely to originate from there before it could be mounted. His bombs missed the airfield but hit the residential suburb of Golders Green, nearby.

The L13 flew slowly on over northwest London, as Mathy headed down the dark patches which were his target. A sudden flash, and a narrow band of brilliant light reached out from below and began to feel around the sky. A second, third, fourth and fifth came out, and soon there were more than a score of criss-crossing ribbons. It looked to the Zeppelin aviators as if the city had suddenly come to life, and was waving its arms around the sky, sending out feelers for the danger that threatened.

In the control car crewmen looked at each other. London was keeping a good watch over the sky. The L13's motors and propellers now began to give away her position to the searchlights. First one, then another of those gleaming ribbons of light picked her up. From below came an ominous sound that penetrated the noise of the engines. Little red flashes and short stabs of fire glowed prominently against the shadowy background of buildings, winking to north and south, to port and starboard of them. Following the flashes there rolled up from below the sound of the guns. When the first searchlight picked you up and you saw the first flash of guns from below, your nerves got a shock, then you steadied

down and put your mind on what you were there for. Mathy
picked out St. Paul's and with that point of orientation laid
a course which he thought would take him over the Bank of
England.

Although they had been fired on with great inaccuracy
from all points, they had not yet dropped a bomb on London
proper. Picking up the speaking-tube connecting him with
the lieutenant at the firing position, Mathy ordered, "Fire
slowly!" A mixture of incendiaries and high explosives left
the racks in widely spaced bunches and they soon observed
flames bursting out from several places.

The first bombs fell in the neighborhood of Euston Station. At ten forty-five two incendiaries fell between Woburn
Place and Upper Bedford Place and one in Russell Square
at the junction of Woburn Place and Southampton Row.
Fire broke out in a hotel in Bedford Place. A high-explosive burst in the center of Queen's Square and broke all the
windows in the Square, but luckily did no other damage to
the buildings, which included several hospitals. Five incendiaries fell in Osmond Yard, followed by others in East
Street, Emerald Street, Theobald's Road and Lamb's Con-
duit Passage, where a high explosive also fell. The incendiaries did a great deal of damage before they were put out.

At ten fifty-one, still steering a straight course from Euston
Station toward Tower Bridge, the airship dropped a cluster
of seven incendiaries over the Gray's Inn area. But Mathy's
mind was set upon wrecking Tower Bridge and disrupting
river and road traffic, not to mention striking at a revered
British institution. His navigation had not been perfect, but
he had a reasonable idea where he was. At ten fifty-six the
L13 crossed the main boundary of the City of London. "Over
Holborn Viaduct," he reported, "in the vicinity of Holborn
Station, we dropped several bombs." Passing over Smithfield
Market he dropped three incendiaries, which fell in the road-
way south of Central Avenue. It was then he ordered his

pièce de résistance to be dropped. The 660-pounder, Mathy's "love gift" to London, fell in Bartholomew Close. The monster missed the ancient church, but seriously damaged all the buildings in the Close and some in Little Britain close by. Three incendiaries following the *Liebesgabe* down set fire to the wreckage. Two men were killed and a boy and two women injured. It seems likely that at this point he actually thought he had reached the Bank of England. He would be unlikely to have used the *Liebesgabe* on a lesser target, and his report indicates that he had by now somewhat overestimated his real progress.

Mathy was now in fact drawing closer every second to the Bank of England. He dropped a high explosive and an incendiary between Aldermanbury and the Guildhall. One block of offices was seriously damaged and many of the windows in Aldermanbury broken. The next two bombs were dropped together and fell on the other side of the Guildhall, which was not damaged.

It was at this point, when his last bombs had exploded almost on the doorstep of the Bank, that Mathy altered course, abandoning the path which would have led him to the Tower. "From the Bank of England to the Tower—a short distance—I tried to hit the Bridge and believe I was successful, but to what extent damage was done I could not determine." If this was an honest record of his impression at the time, then he had turned away from the two prime targets of his attack on their very threshold, believing that he had made at least a good attempt at hitting both of them.

He did recognize his whereabouts well enough shortly after this. "Maneuvering and arriving directly over Liverpool Street Station," he reported, "I shouted, 'Rapid fire!' through the tube, and bombs rained down. There was a succession of detonations and bursts of fire, and I could see that I had hit well, and apparently done great damage. This has been confirmed by reliable reports we have since received."

Turning northwest over the Bank end of Moorgate Street he dropped three incendiaries at Salisbury House, between London Wall and Finsbury Circus, where there was a searchlight. The bombs fell on the roof and were put out at once. A high explosive fell on London Wall Building, Blomfield Street, which wrecked the London Territorial Force Record Offices, and another which exploded at the corner of that street and Liverpool Street fell directly on a bus, killing three men and injuring several others. Another high explosive in Sun Street Passage, between Broad Street and Liverpool Street Stations, blew up the pathway, damaged a brick railway arch and severely injured a man. This was the last bomb dropped on the City itself. A high explosive then hit the track of the Great Eastern Railway north of Liverpool Street Station, damaging about twenty feet of track and some arches used as stores. The L13 now had one bomb left in her rack. With it Mathy delivered a grim parting shot. The bomb, a high explosive, fell in Norton Folgate, blowing in the front of a shop but spending its main force on a passing bus. The bus had twenty people on board, including the driver and conductor. Nine were killed and eleven injured, including the driver, who had both his legs blown off.

Mathy had now done with London. At Edmonton a single shell, probably fired from a gun on Parliament Hill, appeared to burst close to the airship. She immediately tilted her nose upward at a violent angle and climbed from about 8,500 feet to over 10,000 and disappeared, shedding water ballast in a cloud of greenish-gray vapor. She passed over Norwich at half-past one, and shortly after two o'clock passed out to sea between Caister and Yarmouth heading for Germany.

A shaken London waited for more Zeppelins to come, fearfully suspecting that this was to be the great fire raid which the German press had been promising for so long. But none appeared. Another airship was known to have crossed the coast but she never reached the capital. Engine trouble over East Anglia caused Böcker to abandon the main attack and saved the city from even worse damage and shock than Mathy had inflicted. He bombed a well-lit yeomanry camp, then dropped the whole of the rest of his load, twenty-four high explosives and sixteen incendiaries, over East Dereham. In all, four men, including two soldiers, were killed, and four men and three women injured, besides some damage to three houses. In a meadow at Scarning on the outskirts of East Dereham was found afterward a German officer's cap and a small parachute to which a bundle of German newspapers was attached. Stuck in the papers was a leave pass dated "Nordholz, 7th September, 1915."

One army airship, the LZ77 under Captain Horn, had made an attempt to collaborate with the naval ships that night. This ship was seen over Dunwich at eight forty, after which she went south and dropped eight high-explosive bombs near the Galloper Lightship about half-past nine. She was seen again only once, off Walmer heading east, at ten forty. Horn, the man who had carried out the first airship raid, the attack on Antwerp on August 14th, was a daring commander and knew his way to London, but some serious obstacle, probably fog at sea, must have got in his way.

While London was gaping and wincing at Mathy's attack, Loewe's L9, Mathy's old ship, was approaching her target in the north. She came in over the Yorkshire coast at about nine fifteen and dropped some incendiaries and high explosives.

Shortly before the war, German contractors and workmen had installed a benzol plant and other machinery at the big iron works at Skinningrove. The Germans had therefore detailed information on the topography of the plant, and Loewe had been very fully briefed to destroy it. He was over the plant, an easy, well-lit target, at nine thirty-five, and dropped his main load of nine high explosives and twelve incendiaries. The bombs exploded in clusters of fire and debris. The water main and electric-light cables were severed. An incendiary hit the roof of the benzol house, but did not penetrate the thick concrete. A high explosive dropped within ten feet of it, causing heavy damage, but left the house untouched. Had this bomb hit the house, with its 45,000 gallons of benzol, most of the factory would have been destroyed. Another high explosive narrowly missed the T.N.T. stores. There were no casualties, as all the workmen had taken shelter in neighboring mines at the first alarm.

Loewe made off in the direction of Hinderwell, heading toward Kettleness again. There he turned south and went out to sea at nine forty-five near Sandsend. Three R.N.A.S. aircraft from Redcar chased him, but were defeated by thick smog over Middlesbrough, though one pilot searched for the raider for an hour and a half.

Meanwhile, a London buzzing with fearful excitement awaited the dawn to inspect its wounds, fully aware that this night's work was the worst attack yet, and certain in the uneasy knowledge that it was only the forerunner of many more and heavier assaults. From Euston to Liverpool Street the crescent scar of fire and ruin where Mathy had thrown his bombs burned and crumbled, as thousands of dollars' worth of goods and property went up in smoke, and dazed and fearful people searched the wreckage for the missing. There was no catastrophe of this kind in the living memory of Londoners. Nothing like this had been heard of since the San Francisco earthquake or experienced in England since the Civil War, including the German naval bombardment of Scarborough, Whitby and Hartlepools the previous December, which had been a rather breathless hit-and-run affair by the German fleet, in general well bottled up by the Royal Navy, and unlikely to be repeated.

It was a neutral observer, William G. Shepherd of the American United Press, who most clearly saw the significance of that grim night of September 8, 1915. Shepherd was sitting in a theater listening to the orchestra playing an entr'acte when a deep booming noise drowned the sawing violins. A young girl in front of him exclaimed, "It's a Zepp!" The Scottish officer with her tried to soothe her. "No, it's a door banging." An excited, nervous whisper ran through the audience.

"The curtain goes down," Shepherd wrote. "You file out of the theater into a crowded street. Traffic is at a standstill. A million quiet cries make a subdued roar. Seven million people of the biggest city in the world stand gazing into the sky from the darkened streets. Here is the climax to the twentieth century. . . .

"Suddenly you realize that the biggest city in the world has become the night battlefield in which seven million harmless men, women and children live. Here is war at the very heart of civilization, threatening all the millions of things that human hearts and human minds have created in past centuries."

Pathetic and poignant scenes, of which Londoners had had a foretaste already, were multiplied all along the L13's swath of destruction. A bomb fell on the roof of a big block of workmen's quarters, right above a little room where four children had been put to sleep. The two older children had got up and stolen out, with giggles and loud whispers, to make some tea in the next room. They were saved, but their empty beds were burned to blackened shreds, and the other two sleeping babies were killed.

Another bomb fell through the roof of a stable yard, set a car alight, and soon had the whole place on fire. The stableman and his wife rescued eleven terrified horses and led them one by one out into the street. They also saved their watchdog, and the woman even managed to rescue a canary from the first floor, right above the fire, although as she was carrying it down the stairs she was blown off her feet by the blast from another bomb exploding in a neighboring courtyard.

The bomb which killed a man on the corner of Red Lion Street blew in the front of the public house behind him, reducing the stock to a mere mass of broken glass, over which floated for hours afterward an indefinable odor of assorted forms of alcohol. The explosion took off the top of the grand piano on the floor above the bar, twisted the iron bedsteads and injured a woman sleeping there, and reduced what had been the carefully kept living quarters of a small family to a mass of soot, dust, plaster and broken glass.

The driver whose legs had been blown off by the bomb which wrecked his bus at Norton Folgate died shortly after he had been admitted to the hospital.

To Londoners, to the sort of ordinary people whose experience of such horrors had been confined for a century and more to newspaper accounts of earthquakes and natural disasters in far-off countries and romanticized poems, pictures and stories of British Redcoats in remote foreign wars, the events, and even more the rumors which succeeded the actual bombing, were a savage shock. It took time for their deepest feelings to break through the stunned silence which shrouded the City of London on that morning of September 8, 1915.

Presently, from private individuals, from the press and from angry men on the floor of the House of Commons, arose an outcry in which rage against the "Murder by Zeppelin," as the papers called Mathy's attack, mingled with loud dissatisfaction at the ineffectual display put on by the air defenses. Londoners had heard the guns go off and seen their shells blossoming in the sky, but only one shell in all that wild barrage had made the Zeppelin commander abandon his leisurely, almost casual, course over the city. A very uneven, mixed collection comprising twenty-six guns had been set off at the L13, if a certain amount of rifle fire and five rounds from a .45 M.H. gun at Waterloo are left out of the reckoning. Mathy himself had no knowledge of the six hits which were claimed, and the envelope of the L13, safely back in its shed at Nordholz, had not a mark on its smooth yellow hide.

Still more disappointing had been the total failure of the airplanes even to sight any of the four Zeppelins to come to her shores that night. It was not the fault of the pilots, who ran risks every time they took off at night, but the public had expected more of them than it had been within their power to achieve at this stage in the development of British aeronautics. An appendix to the official count of the raid by General Headquarters, Home Forces, lists, under the heading, "Action of Airplanes," a total of six sorties made by Royal Naval Air Service machines that night, and adds, formally, "Royal Flying Corps. No action." This was an alarming state of affairs, and was the result of the very late development of flying in Britain, in comparison with France and Germany.

Until a year or two previous to the outbreak of war Britain, confident in the power of the Royal Navy, had done little more than keep in touch with trends in the development of floating or soaring flight. The experiments at Woolwich at the time of the American Civil War by Lieutenant Grover were the first steps in the persistent, and for almost fifty years the solitary, practical interest taken in flying machines by the Royal Engineers, and led to the establishment of a Balloon Equipment Store in 1878. In that year the very first air estimates were published—£150 for the purchase of one balloon, the *Pioneer*. By 1902 both France and Germany were well ahead of Britain in aviation, and an observer went to Paris to observe Santos-Dumont's remarkable little airships in action. Two years later two British balloons were planned. In 1904, too, the first aero-engine developments began at the

Balloon School, and research began upon spherical and elongated balloons, kites, aerial photography and signaling, and
balloon winches. The War Office refused to finance Colonel
Capper in his idea of bringing the Wright brothers to work
at the Balloon School. In 1905 the balloon factory was
moved to Farnborough and a balloon section set up there as
well.

It was in 1906 that aviation in Britain at last began to show
some real promise. Capper came to Farnborough, the flam-
boyant American Samuel Cody was appointed chief instructor in kiting at the School, and Lieutenant J. W. Dunne,
R.E., was attached to the factory for full-scale experiments
with inherently stable airplanes. Cody asked permission to
convert a man-lifting kite into a power-driven airplane. In
May 1908, he made the first flight of such a machine in England. In the following month a struggling young aviator
named A. V. Roe also made his first hop off the ground in a
machine he had designed and built himself. Later that year
Wilbur Wright flew for the first time in Europe and gave
aviation there tremendous inspiration. By 1911, flying in
Britain had reached a sufficiently promising stage for the War
Office to form an air battalion at Farnborough. A year later
this experiment was developed and the government created
a Royal Flying Corps.

The Flying Corps had two divisions, a naval and military
wing, the naval section being set up at Eastchurch on the
Thames Estuary, the military at Farnborough. A Central
Flying School at Upavon on Salisbury Plain was to serve both
wings. From the establishment of this organization the naval
wing went ahead of the military, largely through the enter-
prise and energy of its first director, Captain Murray Sueter,
and of the air-minded young First Lord, Winston Churchill.
Whereas the military wing looked mainly to the Royal Aircraft Factory at Farnborough for its machines, and suffered
thereby from a combination of War Office short-sightedness

and a genuine desire for engineering perfection on the part of the factory, the Navy bought most of its aircraft from the new private establishments, firms like Avros and Sopwith, whose founders were men of great flair and imagination and provided the infant naval aviation with a flow of excellent machines.

In June 1912, the Technical Subcommittee of the Committee of Imperial Defense, which had been set up to provide an answer to the serious threat from German military aviation, especially the Zeppelin fleet, sent two of its members, Captain Sueter and Mervyn O'Gorman, Director of the Royal Aircraft Factory, to France, Austria and Germany to report on the state of aviation there. Commenting on their subsequent findings, the Technical Subcommittee said, "The report also shows that German airships have covered a distance equal to the distance from Germany to the British coast without replenishing fuel." At Eastchurch the naval wing began experimenting with an explosive grapnel, which could be hung from an airplane to make contact with and destroy an airship. This scheme was abandoned in favor of light bombs which could be dropped or thrown upon the airship, though it was found to be impossible to make a bomb which could be guaranteed to explode on contact with the airship's envelope.

More faith was placed in the Hales grenade, which was supposed to blow a six-inch hole in a Zeppelin's gas-bag when fired from a rifle. In October 1912, the Admiralty had also looked ahead by planning a number of airplane bases in Britain chiefly dotted round the coast from Calshot to Scapa Flow. The first of these was already established at Eastchurch, the principal naval flying center. The next to be completed was the seaplane station at the Isle of Grain, commissioned in December 1912, and this was quickly followed in the first half of 1913 by Calshot, Felixstowe, Yarmouth and Cromarty. Kingsnorth at Hoo on the Medway was completed in April 1914, in time to house the half dozen small nonrigid airships in British service, recently handed over entirely to the Navy.

On July 1, 1914, the naval wing of the Royal Flying Corps was transferred from the control of the War Office wholly into Admiralty hands and formed into the Royal Naval Air Service. On July 29th, when war seemed very near, instructions were given to the R.N.A.S. that the duties of scouting and patrol were to be treated as secondary to the protection of the country against hostile aircraft. This meant Zeppelins. Winston Churchill had advocated a strong force of fighting aircraft stationed partly on the Continent to attack the Zeppelins in their sheds, partly at home to attack those which reached our shores. When war came it was at once clear that the R.F.C. could do neither of these jobs, that it would in fact have its work cut out to supply the Corps squadrons working with the Army in France.

It was logically the Army's job to protect the citizens of Britain on land, as it was the Navy's to shield them at sea, but the R.F.C. had no machines to spare for air defense against the Zeppelins. The R.N.A.S., on the other hand, had about forty machines ready for operations. The main part of the air defense of Britain was therefore placed in their hands.

The aircraft were disposed to patrol the coast between the Humber and the Thames, from Immingham to Clacton. The Wash was considered to be the most likely landfall for a Zeppelin raider and a particularly close lookout was kept there. The R.F.C. did scrape together a few obsolete, untrustworthy machines, which patrolled the Scottish coast and the area from the Thames Estuary southward.

How effective the combined strength of the two air services would be if a Zeppelin fleet attacked was doubtful. Only two of the naval airplanes and one of its airships were fitted with machineguns. One of the machines carried an old

Maxim repeating rifle, the other a Lewis gun loaned to the
Admiralty by Colonel Lucas of Habland Hall in Yarmouth.
The only weapon which had been specially designed to damage Zeppelins was the Hales grenade. Two hundred of these
had been made for the naval wing, but many of them had
been used up in experiments. The remainder were hastily
distributed on August 4th amongst the East Coast flying stations in order of importance. Felixstowe, for example, and
Hendon—the airdrome for the defense of London—had
twelve each, and the Isle of Grain four. What happened
when this thin supply ran out was doubtful. Presumably the
airmen threw what ordinary bombs and grenades they had,
like David's stones, at the huge Goliaths, and shot at them
with rifles. They did not even have many of these conven-
tional weapons. Eastchurch, which was the best equipped,
had only a hundred and fifty hand grenades, forty-two rifle
grenades, twenty-six twenty-pound bombs and a Maxim. For
want of anything better, six-inch shells were fitted with vanes
and called bombs.

As it turned out, none of this primitive equipment was
called upon. The year 1915 arrived and the Zeppelins had
not come to Britain. R.N.A.S. airplanes had successfully attacked them in their sheds at Düsseldorf and Friedrichshaven
and had attempted to raid Nordholz on Christmas Day, 1914,
and when the raids on Britain did begin they continued to
destroy them by bombing their Belgian bases. These attacks
caused the German army airship offensive upon England to
be abandoned in the summer of 1915, but of all the sorties
which had been made by them from bases in Britain against
raiding Zeppelins crossing the coast, only one, that of Flight
Lieutenant Mulock against Linnarz's second attack on the
Thames Estuary, had come even near a promising attack.

The Zeppelins attacked by night. Night flying had been
neglected, and many of those who took off without crashing
and survived weary, dangerous hours in the cold and dark

looking for a Zeppelin—which could be astonishingly elusive, especially on cloudy, misty or moonless nights—crashed on landing and killed or seriously injured themselves and wrote off their machines.

But it was against the German naval Zeppelins coming in from northern Germany across the North Sea that the defenders were most powerless. Stationed on the coast as most of them were, they were unable to get warning of these approaching naval airships soon enough to rise into a commanding position first and thus overcome the great advantages in speed of climb and ceiling which the airships possessed. Hence it was that when Mathy and Böcker crossed the Norfolk coast on the night of September 8, 1915, their total of crashes and fatal accidents was high, and their score in Zeppelins fired on, let alone brought down, nil.

These sorties R.N.A.S. pilots made that night were typical of all that had gone before whenever Zeppelins had made for Britain. Seven machines took off altogether. Three went up from Redcar but did not sight the L9 at all. Flight Sublieutenant Nichol in a naval seaplane, one of several attached to trawlers for anti-airship duties, took off from alongside his parent ship, the *Kingfisher,* forty miles out to sea east of Yarmouth, but it was misty and he saw nothing. Three more aircraft took off from Yarmouth in an attempt to attack Mathy and Böcker. At seven forty-five Squadron Commander Ireland took off, but was forced to land again with engine trouble, and Flight Lieutenant Cripps took his place. At ten past eight Flight Sublieutenant Hilliard went up. At five-past nine Cripps's engine cut out and he was forced to come down. Afraid that his bombs would blow him and the aircraft to pieces, when his altimeter registered a hundred feet Cripps very coolly climbed out on to a wing, with his hand still on the stick, and judging the time it would take for the machine to hit the ground, counted off six seconds, then jumped. He fell on his shoulder on soft marshy ground, and was able to walk away unhurt, but Hilliard was not so lucky. At five past ten he finished his two-hour patrol, came down to land on the airfield at Bacton, crashed into a field adjoining the airdrome, and was killed by the explosion of his bombs.

5. KITCHENER DEMANDS . . .

On the morning following Mathy's raid there was found on the grass in Wrotham Park, Barnet, in north London, a small parachute to which a bag was tied. Inside the bag was a scraped ham bone. Around the shank the German tricolor of black, white and gold was painted in a band, and below on one side was inscribed lengthways, *"Zum Andenken an das ausgehungerte Deutschland,"* "A Memento from starved-out Germany." On the reverse side was a crude drawing of a Zeppelin dropping a bomb on the head of an elderly gentleman in a very high wing collar and a black tie. He was represented full face and was labeled, "Edwart Grey." Alongside him was written, *"Was fang' ich, armer Teufel, an?"*—"What shall I, poor devil, do?"

This cartoon was in keeping with the average German's picture of a frightened, cowed London, imagining " . . . with terror that one can already hear the beating of the screws of the Zeppelin cruisers," a beaten people ready to sue for peace.

The people of London were certainly frightened, and they expected the Zeppelin to return. But if the German High Command thought this the dominating result of "Murder by Zeppelin," as some of the papers were calling it, they were seriously mistaken. "The Germans," said *The Times* third leader on the morning of the 10th, "do not under-

stand human nature, and they have never understood it less
than in this matter." Frightened as he undeniably and understandably was at first, the average Londoner quickly became angry. "The Zeppelins," continued *The Times,*
"appear to cause wonderfully little panic at the moment of
murder, and no permanent panic afterwards. Their effect
is, not a demand for peace, but a demand of the whole nation to help in the war." Angry, revengeful, helpless, the
people of London turned upon the authorities and demanded immediate drastic action.

Any such action was the Navy's duty, as they were responsible for the defense of Great Britain against air attack.
Two days after the raid they appointed Sir Percy Scott, a
famous naval gunnery expert, as special controller of the
whole gun defense of London with direct responsibility only
to the Board of Admiralty and outside the control of the
Naval Director of Air Services. Admiral Scott, with the
vigor expected of him, immediately began a radical shake-up
of the feeble gun defenses, but surprised his sponsors by
coming out strongly in favor of the airplane as an equal part-
ner. He urged a very great increase in numbers of planes
and in the training of pilots in night flying.

The case of the airplane was considered by a subcommittee headed by the Director of Naval Air Services, Rear Admiral Vaughan-Lee, on September 16th. They concluded by
agreeing with Sir Percy's view, and tabled an increase to a
minimum of forty airplanes, twenty-four pilots, and four
new air stations in addition to Hendon and Chingford. But
before any definite action was taken the committee decided
to wait for the report which one of its members, Squadron
Commander Babington, was preparing on the air defense of
Paris.

Babington submitted his report on September 27th. The
committee was so impressed by the fact that the French capital, which had not been bombed, depended almost entirely

upon a powerful shield of guns and searchlights, with only a few airplanes, that they decided after all to leave things as they were, improving existing landing grounds as much as possible, but continuing to treat air defense as a second line duty using mostly inexperienced pilots and sending nearly all the fully trained ones to units overseas. On September 28th the Board of Admiralty discussed and officially approved these proposals.

But while the naval committee was talking and Mr. Arthur Balfour, recent successor to Winston Churchill at the Admiralty, was warning the House of Commons, "Do not let us ask too much of Sir Percy Scott, or the aircraft section of the Admiralty, or of the guns, even when they come in sufficient numbers," Lord Kitchener, Secretary of State for War, was taking strong independent action. Immediately after the raid of September 8th, he sent for the harassed and overworked commander of the Royal Flying Corps, Sir David Henderson, Director General of Military Aeronautics, and said to him abruptly: "What are you going to do about these airship raids?"

Henderson objected that the responsibility for the air defense of Great Britain rested with the Royal Naval Air Service, thinking uneasily of all the impossible demands already being made daily by the rapidly expanding Corps at the front upon his reserve training squadrons. The Secretary of State heard him out, then fixed him under the basilisk stare of the recruiting posters for the new armies, and said:

"I do not care who is responsible. If there are any more Zeppelin raids and the Royal Flying Corps do not interfere with them, I shall hold you responsible."

The Military Aeronautics Directorate worked in the same building but were independent of the four traditional departments of the War Office, and the Director General, dealing directly with the Secretary of War, had become used to his ambitious directives to the Army's Flying Corps. K.'s orders always had two things in common. They were impossible, and they were always carried out. There were no airplanes and no pilots available for home defense, but some would have to be found.

A month after the outbreak of war Kitchener had been forced to hand over temporary responsibility for the air defense of Britain to the Admiralty. Anticipating a short, sharp war, the Army had thrown every airworthy aircraft and pilot into the fighting. When the war dragged on after all, there were not even enough to replace battle losses, let alone form the new squadrons needed to support K.'s new armies.

General Henderson went to France to command the four Corps squadrons there. His deputy at home, Colonel Brancker, cut many corners to meet Kitchener's voracious demands, ordering new machines before the drawings were finished and casting his nets wide for volunteers. Somehow he managed to find a few machines now and then to assist the Navy in home defense.

In October 1914, the R.F.C. squadron at Brooklands was able to send two airplanes to Hounslow and two to Joyce Green, near Dartford, for temporary anti-Zeppelin duty, armed with rifles and hand grenades. At the end of the year, when it seemed likely that the Germans would send their new Zeppelins to England, training machines at Farnborough, Chelmsford, Joyce Green and Brooklands were kept standing by to go up against them.

Britain enjoyed a Christmas week free of Zeppelins, but on Christmas Day, when naval seaplanes operating from carriers were attempting to attack Nordholz,[1] a German seaplane appeared over the Thames Estuary and flew west as far as Woolwich. A Vickers fighter went up in pursuit from Joyce Green. The German turned east again and the Vickers closed and opened fire, but the observer's machine gun

1 Appendix C.

jammed. In his haste he had gone up without gloves and his hands were so numbed with cold that he could not clear the stoppage. Then engine trouble forced the machine to abandon the chase altogether.

No Zeppelins had come, but the threat was very grave on January 13th when Brancker informed the O.C., Administrative Wing, South Farnborough, "A certain proportion of war airplanes will be allotted to Reserve Airplane Squadrons as they become available; these machines are not to be used for the instruction of pupils; they are for the use of trained R.F.C. pilots, and are also available for the purpose of Home Defense and for training with other arms."

On the 19th occurred the first Zeppelin attack upon Britain, with no opposition from the air defenses. A week after the raid new War Office orders ran, "Stations west of South Farnborough will only be warned if it seems likely that the aerial raid is directed towards their neighborhood. . . . The senior officer at a station will order pilots into the air, if he considers from the local situation or from the information he receives, that such action is advisable; it must be recognized, however, that it will usually be difficult for an aeroplane to find an airship in the dark, and that, therefore, pilots should not be ordered to fly unless it seems very likely that the enemy can be found and engaged."

It seems a timid directive, even considering the great scarcity of men and machines and the urgent demands of training. The reason why its effect remained operative throughout the steadily increasing raids in the spring and summer of the year can probably be found in Kitchener's urgent preoccupation with other things, mainly the campaign in the Dardanelles.

In May, Mr. Churchill left the Admiralty and Mr. Arthur Balfour took his place. The new First Lord had nothing of his energetic predecessor's enthusiasm for the air and no experience or knowledge of aerial warfare. Furthermore,

the Royal Naval Air Service, with increasingly heavy com-
mitments in overseas operations, U-boat defense and work
with the fleet, was finding it difficult to find airplanes and
pilots for home defense. The Admiralty decided that it was
time for the War Office to assume the task once more, and on
June 18th, curiously enough the day on which the German
chief of Naval Staff's request for support in the removing of
restrictions on bombing London appeared on von Falkenhayn's desk, they requested the transfer.

Before submitting any definite proposals to the government, the two services met in committee to discuss the question. The War Office agreed in principle to the transfer but
were unwilling to take on the responsibility, knowing that
they did not have the means at that time to carry it out.

They did what they could to support the R.N.A.S. During the time of the German army airship raids on the
Thames Estuary in May, station commanders at the airdromes in War Office control, South Farnborough, Brooklands, Hounslow, Joyce Green, Dover and Shoreham, were
reminded that one machine was to be kept constantly available for home defense at each place. They were advised that
the best machine for the job was the Martinsyde Scout, a
tricky and rather unstable single-seater. Each machine was
to carry an armament consisting of six Carcass bombs, twelve
Hales naval grenades, 150 incendiary darts and five powder
bombs. Guns were not considered to be of any use, as it was
believed that the bullets then available were harmless to
Zeppelins. The envelope of a Zeppelin was thought to be
filled with an inert gas designed to mix with any hydrogen
released from the gas containers by lucky hits and prevent
an explosion.

On June 30th, a month after Linnarz had made his first
attack upon London, and a fortnight after Hirsch, flying
from Nordholz in the L10, the first of the new long-range
class Zeppelins, had bombed Tyneside heavily and shown

the potentialities of the new ships, three more flights were kept ready to go to Norwich, Dunmow and Hunton, "should occasion arise."

Raids continued, and airships came twice more to London. R.F.C. and R.N.A.S. aircraft bravely and blindly chanced the dark. In July representatives of the War Office and Admiralty met again to discuss the responsibility for home defense. The furthest that the Army would go was to forecast that the R.F.C. might be in a position to take over completely from the R.N.A.S. about the beginning of 1916, provided no other extra demands were made upon it in the meantime. As to who should take charge of the guns and searchlights, they had no opinion.

Then Kitchener experienced for himself Mathy's great curtain raiser of September 8th and sent Sir David Henderson to overhaul the Royal Flying Corps' arrangements for defense against Zeppelins. The Secretary's stinging words aroused resentment in his overburdened mind. . . . *What are you going to do about these airship raids?* . . . Kitchener made his grand decisions and issued his irrevocable edicts like an absolute monarch. Where were the means to carry them out?

Three successive raids on the nights of September 11th, 12th, and 13th made the question more urgent and immediate than ever. On the last of these attacks Mathy almost got through to London again, but a thunderstorm threw him badly off course and a shell damaged the L13 over Harwich. Landing at Hage, his ship was still further damaged. But repairs were effected in four days and she was ready to go to London again.

Two R.N.A.S. planes which took off from Dover missed him altogether. London would need all the defenses she could muster when the long, moonless nights of mid-October began. Before then, the Military Directorate at the

War Office would have to find, somehow, men and aircraft to form Kitchener's defenses of London.

There were no trained pilots or efficient airplanes to spare; they would have to come from the squadrons in training. Meanwhile, an equally pressing problem was the relocation of airfields. Places like Norwich, Dunmow and Hunton were too far out for the protection of London. Pilots taking off from these stations could not make the best use of any warning which might have been given, and to the hazards of interception and night flying would be added the worry of operating on a very extended line from the home field. They would not do. Equally, Brooklands and Farnborough were too westerly. It seemed likely that the next big raid would be launched from the northeast sector of the capital to avoid the concentration of guns along the Thames Estuary. In that case what was needed was a strong concentration of defenses there across its path. Accordingly, reconnaissance parties were sent out into that area to find areas suitable for new airfields.

Sir Percy Scott, in the meantime, had made a vigorous start in improving the gun and searchlight defenses of London. When he took over his temporary appointment he found to his disgust that after fourteen months of war the main defense of London against attacks by the Zeppelin fleet consisted of eight three-inch high-angle guns and four six-pounders with bad gun sights. In addition there was a collection of miscellaneous weapons, including six pom-poms and a Maxim, none of which could reach a Zeppelin. The ammunition supplied to the guns was of quite the wrong kind. The bursting charges were too small to do any damage and left large pieces of shell intact which were dangerous to civilians below, as were the pom-pom shells which exploded only on impact and were unlikely to reach a Zeppelin. Some damage and a few minor casualties, none of them fatal, had actually been caused on September 8th by shell fragments falling on the East End, chiefly from the Woolwich gun.

Sir Percy demanded, and got, an absolutely free hand in remodeling these meager defenses. He discarded the useless pom-poms at once and demanded 104 new anti-aircraft guns and a minimum of fifty more searchlights. He asked Admiral Jellicoe to let him have fifty subcaliber guns from the Fleet and began to set up his new gun sites before any of the guns themselves had even been promised. Three more three-inch guns were ready at Barnes Common, King's Cross and Dollis Hill early in October.

Most encouraging of all was the new French mobile 75-mm. anti-aircraft gun which Lieutenant Commander Rawlinson brought from Paris, where he had gone on Scott's orders to fetch a sample of the best weapon in the Paris defenses. This fine gun, on its special motor mounting, was made the nucleus of a London Mobile Section. Sir Percy also continued to urge the need for a strong airplane defense corps. He heartily approved the experimental project which the Royal Flying Corps was mounting on the northeastern fringe of the city.

The search for new flying grounds had yielded two good pieces of farmland. One was a ninety-acre piece of Sutton's Farm, near Hornchurch, owned and worked by Mr. Tom Crawford—an irregular slab of stubble land from which the corn had just been taken, obstructed by sheep netting and six haystacks, but in flat and well-drained country. The other, somewhat smaller, at Hainault Farm near Ilford, was a sixty-acre piece of grassland alongside the road to Chadwell Heath, owned by Mr. W. Poulter of Ilford. Both fields were officially requisitioned from the owners and designated temporary landing grounds Nos. II and III respectively.

With the addition of these two fields the R.F.C. would have machines for the defense of London at six stations, Hounslow, Northolt, Joyce Green, Dover, Landing Ground

No. II (Sutton's Farm) and Landing Ground No. III (Hainault Farm). Naval machines would be located at Chingford, Hendon, Chelmsford, the Isle of Grain and Maidstone. As well as all these main airdromes, two emergency landing grounds were to be marked out in Hyde Park, north and south of the eastern half of the Serpentine, one in the middle of Regent's Park between the Zoological Gardens to the north and the lake to the south, one at Blackheath, one on Wimbledon Common, and one in the grounds of Buckingham Palace. The Hyde Park, Regent's Park and Buckingham Palace grounds would be marked by red lights, the Blackheath and Wimbledon ones by flares.

Two more innovations included in the War Office scheme were a ring of observers on the ground in communication with them by telephone, and a cordon of thirteen-pounder mobile and anti-aircraft guns and searchlights round the key northeastern fringe of London.

Both the guns for the mobile column and the equipment and men needed for the Royal Flying Corps airdromes were to be drawn for temporary use only from units mobilizing for overseas. Working up at Gosport under the usual difficulties caused by acute shortage of trained pilots and efficient machines, was the newly formed 5th Wing under Lieutenant Colonel W. G. Salmond. On October 2nd Colonel Salmond received from the G.O.C. Royal Corps units in Britain instructions detailing arrangements he was to make "to bring machines to the vicinity of London for the period from 4th October to the 12th October inclusive."

O.C. 5th Wing was instructed to provide seven B.E.2c's with R.A.F. engines together with pilots, and one S.E.4a would be provided by No. 6 Wing. Two of the B.E.2c's were to go to Northolt, two to Landing Ground No. II, two to Landing Ground No. III, and one to Joyce Green. The S.E.4a would also be sent to Joyce Green. He was given the location of Landing Field No. II as "2 miles WSW. of Horn-

church" and of Landing Field No. III as "4 miles NW. of
Romford," and was to detail detachments to take charge of
them, to pitch portable hangars and look after the machines
there, the pilots being billeted in the houses which had a
telephone nearest the flying field, these houses to be detailed
later. Armament was to consist of R.L. electric tubes and
incendiary bombs, bomb racks and twenty-pound Hales
bombs, and R.A.F. cutting missiles if they were available.

One pilot was to be on duty each night at each of the airfields named. If a Zeppelin was reported approaching London the War Office would inform each of the grounds at
what hour a machine was to take off. This time would be
calculated so as to allow the pilot to attain a height of 8,000
feet before the Zeppelin approached. The pilot would
patrol at a height of 8,000 feet in the vicinity of his own
landing ground, unless he sighted a hostile airship, when he
would take any necessary action. If no airship was seen the
pilot was to land one and a half hours after the flight had
started. "It is essential," said the order, "that the engine
should be run previously, and that the machine should leave
the ground at the exact time ordered by the War Office." If
rain or one of the all too frequent Thames fogs were bad
enough to prevent flying, the War Office was to be informed
at once and the machine grounded. A searchlight would be
sited near Becontree Heath and another near Chigwell Row,
with the possible addition of two more near Buckhurst Hill
and Upminster. If no airship approached, at the end of one
and a half hours from the commencement of the flight these
searchlights would be turned on to the nearest landing
ground "for about a minute, to indicate its position." A
chain of observers was to be situated to the northeast of the
landing fields, and these would send up a rocket if they actually saw an airship passing over them. The rockets would be
of different colors according to the direction the airship was

taking. The key to these colors would be notified to pilots later.

As to detailed arrangements, O.C. No. 5 Wing was to detail detachments, with necessary transport, to put up hangars, look after machines, put out flares and perform all other necessary duties at Landing Grounds Nos. II and III. Three R.E.5 portable canvas hangars would be delivered by the C.O.O., O.A.S.D., at Romford station on Sunday morning, the 3rd, and one additional R.E.5 hangar was to be supplied by O.C. 5th Wing. Arrangements were being made by the Military Directorate for the delivery of two bomb racks and eight twenty-pound Hales bombs to Northolt direct, one bomb rack and four twenty-pound bombs to Joyce Green direct, and four bomb racks and sixteen twenty-pound bombs to Romford Station on the morning of the 3rd for collection by the detachments from 5th Wing detailed for Landing Grounds Nos. II and III. Racks were to be fitted to the machines at the various places as early as possible by the mechanics on the spot. As to lighting for the cockpits of the airplanes, the instructions specified, "The machines will either be fitted with duplicate lighting sets for their instruments, or the pilot will take up an electric torch with him, if only one lighting set can be fitted."

It was a stiff and complicated requirement, and the order left no doubt that speed was of the essence. It said specifically, "The hangars are to be put up on Sunday, the 3rd instant." That was the next day. At least the hangars were already in stores. That part could be done without too much breaking of hearts and backs. The other requirements would be more difficult to meet. "Dispatch the machines to the places detailed above," said the instructions, "so as to arrive before noon on the 4th instant." Seven B.E.2's had to be found, seven pilots selected from a batch of barely half-trained young recruits fresh from graduation.

There were two days in which to find them all and have

them transported, test the machines, brief the pilots and have them in position ready to go up and risk their lives and the valuable machines trying to find and destroy Zeppelins in the dark. It was more than a tall order, the squadron commander thought when Colonel Salmond passed his problem to them; it was impossible.

Major Louis Strange, well known as one of the daring handful of prewar aviators, had been posted to 5th Wing at Gosport on September 21st from France, where he had greatly distinguished himself, for the purpose of forming a new squadron, No. 23, from a nucleus of pilots drawn from No. 14 Squadron there, and work it up for overseas. When he arrived, machines were in very short supply. All he had in the way of airworthy and semi-airworthy machines at the beginning were a Blériot with a 50-h.p. Gnome engine, two Henri Farman box kites in a very broken-down condition, and the Avro No. 4741 which he himself had collected at Farnborough on his way to Gosport. With some guile he managed to persuade Major Barry Martin, who was struggling to form No. 22 Squadron in the face of similar difficulties, to part with one whole B.E.2c and another incomplete one in exchange for the two ramshackle Henri Farmans.

That was a start, but he found that to be sure of getting any more new aircraft he had to go and virtually live on the doorstep of the War Office and beg for them in person, and when he was allotted three new machines he thought it necessary to send three of his pilots to the factory itself to seize them the moment they were ready and stay with them until they were safely in his squadron's hangar at Gosport.

As to pilots, on paper at any rate he had approximately full strength, but all of them had come straight from their flying school and could not be regarded as fit to go on operations. "No. 23," said Strange, "taught itself to fly." Using his four best pupils as instructors he worked hard to bring the rest up to something like operational standard. He would have felt reasonably satisfied, knowing the general state of affairs, if he could have been allowed to keep the men he had until their training in the squadron was as near completion as could be hoped for. But the trouble was that in the first six weeks of the squadron's existence it was in its turn robbed of a whole flight to help to form another new squadron, No. 16 Reserve Squadron at Beaulieu, while trained pilots and mechanics were continually snatched away to replace overseas casualties or assist in the creation of squadrons.

It was the very efficiency of No. 23 Squadron which was its own undoing in this way. In the course of their training at Gosport some of Strange's pilots had been allowed to make flights in the dusk, to familiarize themselves to some extent with the weird and doubly dangerous world of night flying, and there were one or two other pilots in the wing who had done the same, either at Gosport or elsewhere. Naturally, when the order came through to provide pilots for use in the night defense of London against Zeppelins, it was from these men that the seven pilots selected in all were taken. These seven did not quite know how to treat the honor. On the one hand they did not want to run the risk of being left behind in England when "helmets, tropical" had appeared in the quartermaster's stores, but on the other the prospect of flying against Zeppelins offered obvious excitement and adventure to young men not very long out of school.

On Saturday, the 2nd, the erecting party detailed for Landing Grounds Nos. II and III received their orders and went into action. Captain Moore, with one light tender, one truck and twelve men from No. 23 Squadron, and Lieutenant Greene, with two trucks and twelve men from No. 22 Squadron, set off from Gosport for Romford Station, taking with them everything necessary for sleeping in the hangars they were to put up or in their trucks, as well as electric lamps, rations for one day and additional haversack rations.

Captain Moore had made arrangements to draw further rations at Romford. His orders were to supervise the erection of two R.E. sheds at Landing Ground No. II, two miles west-southwest of Hornchurch, and two at Landing Ground No. III, four miles northwest of Romford. Arriving at Romford station, he collected three R.E.5 hangars, four bomb racks and sixteen twenty-pound bombs, then took one hangar to Landing Ground No. II, two to Landing Ground No. III, and divided the bombs and bomb racks equally between the two fields.

On the same day, the O.C. No. 4 Reserve Airplane Squadron of the Royal Flying Corps at Northolt received notification that two B.E.2c's from 5th Wing would be accommodated there for the period 4th October to 12th October inclusive, and that the War Office was arranging for the delivery of two bomb racks and eight twenty-pound bombs to Northolt direct for the use of the two B.E.2c's.

By eleven o'clock on Sunday morning, landing T's had been put out at both Landing Grounds Nos. II and III, the second R.E. hangar for No. II had arrived at Romford station, been collected and erected, and Second Lieutenant H. MacD. O'Malley of No. 13 Squadron, flying to Sutton's Farm from Gosport in his B.E.2c, easily recognized his new field by the humpback shapes of the two canvas hangars on the skyline. At first arrangements were made for pilots to be billeted at the White Hart Hotel, a mile and a half away in Hornchurch, which had the nearest telephone, then a telephone was laid on at the farm itself and they were billeted there in the farmhouse.

At Landing Ground No. III, Lieutenant E. W. Powell in another B.E.2c flew in from Gosport. A telephone was installed at Hainault Farm House, on the opposite side of the road from the landing ground. The farmhouse stood empty and unfurnished, and arrangements had to be made for the officers billeted there to take their own bedding and creature comforts. At Northolt the O.C. was warned to expect two pilots to arrive by air with their B.E.2c's before noon on Monday, the 4th, and four air mechanics by road. O.C., Joyce Green, was told to expect one B.E.2c and pilot and four air mechanics by the evening of the 4th.

One pilot and a B.E.2c were already stationed at Joyce Green. On September 9th, the morning after Mathy's raid, Lieutenant R. S. Tipton of 5th Wing had been ordered to go by car to Farnborough and report to the O.C., Administrative Wing, there, to collect a 75-h.p. Renault-engined B.E.2c and fly it the same day to Joyce Green. The instructions were that in the event of no special orders being issued to him by the War Office, he was to patrol the air "within gliding distance of the airfield" between ten and eleven o'clock that night.

On the same day, Second Lieutenants Cooper and Morrison of 5th Wing had been ordered to collect a R.F.C. engined B.E.2c and take it to Chelmsford airfield, there to await further instructions from the War Office with regard to any Zeppelin attack which might develop.

6. BREITHAUPT

On Friday, October 8th, Second Lieutenant Yates of No. 23 Squadron and Lieutenant Jenkins of No. 14 Squadron relieved O'Malley at Sutton's Farm. On the same day Second Lieutenant John Slessor of No. 23 Squadron, who had just come back to Gosport after delivering a new B.E.2c to the R.F.C. Aircraft Park at St. Omer in France, where he had made unsuccessful attempts to attach himself to a front-line fighting squadron, was ordered to go to the Daimler works at Coventry to collect a new B.E.2c there and report to the new Landing Ground No. II at Sutton's Farm near Hornchurch to relieve Lieutenant Jenkins so that the latter could go to Hainault Farm and bring the flight there up to its full strength.

Slessor had left Haileybury at the end of the autumn term of 1914. For a short time he went to live at Haileybury House, the Stepney boys' club run by the college, as a cadet officer in A Company, the 1st Cadet Battalion of the Queen's Regiment, of which the N.C.O.'s and other ranks were provided by the club boys, a company headed in earlier days by Clement Attlee, who became Head of Haileybury House. Slessor's father, a man of doubly distinguished service to the country, both as a Regular Army officer and an Oxford don, had rejoined the colors on the outbreak of war, and his son, at seventeen, naturally volunteered as soon as he could for

the new armies. A boyhood attack of polio had left its mark
in the form of two game legs, and "a number of damp and
rather exhausting field days with the O.T.C." had made it
highly doubtful in his mind and anyone else's that he would
have any chance of getting into the Army as a fighting soldier. Through a friend at the War Office, however, there
seemed a slight chance he might find a place in the R.F.C.

He was lucky at his Selection Board. The officer in charge
was Lieutenant Colonel W. W. "Willy" Warner, an Indian
Army cavalry officer who had served with Slessors' uncle,
"a cheerful and unorthodox officer," says Slessor, "well
known in the Indian racing world, where, in the old days,
an unquestioning conformity with the rules had never been
considered essential to success." Shown into the office ahead
of a long queue of Regular officers, young Slessor confronted
Warner and Major "Ferdy" Waldron.

Warner said, "I don't see why this boy shouldn't perfectly
well be able to fly, do you, Ferdy?"

Waldron, looking a little doubtful, said, "Oh, well—I
don't know. Yes, I should think he'd fly all right." He
nodded at Slessor. "Let's see you walk across the room."

He was accepted and, being well under age, was told to
get his application form for a commission signed by his
father and the Master of Haileybury and be back in the War
Office by five o'clock in the afternoon for a medical exam.
His father was commanding officer of a battalion of the Ox-
fordshire Regiment in camp at Broxbourne, which was three
miles away from Haileybury. He never flew faster again
than he did that day. Luck was with him. Rushing out of
Broxbourne station he almost collided with a column of
marching men and had given up hope of finding transport
when he saw his father riding behind the band at the end of
the column. Within minutes he had borrowed his father's
horse and was galloping wildly up the road to Haileybury.
Jumping off in a flurry at the main gate of Quad, he col-

lected the Master's signature, and galloped off again in time
to catch the next train back to London.

But all this record-breaking was in vain. One look at his
medical history was enough for the doctors, who rejected
him as "totally unfit for any form of military service." However, the unorthodox Warner, who was not one to stand by
and see a keen spirit crushed for lack of an opportunity,
came to the rescue again and a few weeks later Slessor "received a nice eighteenth-birthday present in the shape of
orders to join No. 1 (Reserve) Airplane Squadron, R.F.C., at
Brooklands for flying instruction." He did his initial training on a Maurice Farman Longhorn, and recalls that it was
"a chancy thing—you didn't know whether you had control
or not." It was dangerous, but the aircraft were very slow
and there was a large cage of struts and wire to crumple
before the shock of a crash could reach the pilot. In the course
of thirty-five hours' solo on Maurice Farman Longhorns and
Shorthorns, on Henri Farmans with the Gnome engine, on
the Caudron, the machine notorious for having the "gliding
angle of a brick," on the old 50-h.p. Blériot monoplane, the
little Martinsyde Scout and the B.E.2b, he crashed four
planes and was very nearly thrown out of the course for his
bad record.

It was during the Battle of Loos in October 1915 that he
had been detailed from No. 23 Squadron at Fort Grange,
Gosport, to collect one of the first B.E.2c's to be produced
for the Corps squadrons in France and ferry it across to St.
Omer. He tried hard to persuade Major Newall, the C.O.
of No. 12 Squadron at St. Omer, to take him into his squadron, but the regulations against retaining ferry pilots in that
way were strict and Newall was firm. When he returned to
Gosport, somewhat cast down, Slessor was told that Colonel
Salmond had selected him to be one of the pilots to go to
the new landing grounds northeast of London to take part
in the first attempt at defending the capital by night. He was

selected as being particularly qualified in that he had made two "night flights," one of them in the dusk with the light still in the sky. He was ordered to collect another new machine from Coventry and join Yates at Sutton's Farm.

He collected the B.E.2c from Daimler's little flying field close to Coventry and blithely flew it at full throttle all the way to Farnborough, where he landed with his engine smoking and received the blistering remarks of an experienced sergeant pilot who had watched him come in. He left Gosport on the 11th but became lost in smog and just managed to land at Northolt. Here he was kept grounded for two days by the fog. It was on his second day here that the period of the experimental air defense round northeast London had originally been intended to cease.

The authorities had decided to maintain it a little longer. On the 13th air had cleared sufficiently for Slessor to be able to take off and make his way down river to Sutton's Farm, where he landed in the gathering dusk and found a thick Thames fog creeping up on the field. He touched down on a stubble of harvest just gleaned and came to a halt with his propeller a few feet from a patch of kale. In one corner of the field stood two old canvas R.E. hangars. A frustrated Yates greeted him. He had had a telephone message that afternoon to say that the thirteen-pounder gun on its way to the field from Shoeburyness had got stuck in a ditch en route and would be delayed. It had not arrived when Slessor landed, but he did not see any reason to worry, as it looked a bad night for Zepps, more like November than October, with the wisps of dank mist lying all over the flatlands bordering the river. Yates's B.E.2c had already been fitted with bomb racks and R.L. gear, but as it was getting dark, with the fog thickening badly all the time, and as they had no proper lighting arrangements he decided to postpone the fitting of this equipment, a fairly delicate business, to his own machine until the morning. He had an argument with

Yates, a fiery-tempered man, known as "Little" Yates in the wing, as to who should go on duty that night, Yates insisting that as he had got there first and had that much more experience of conditions at the field, he should take the watch, Slessor countering that as he had had no such experience at all it was only common sense that he should take the chance of getting some as quickly as he could. In the end they tossed a coin and Slessor won. Yates retired disgruntled to his billet at the farmhouse, Slessor to supper with the mechanics, all of them with their R.F.C. "maternity jackets" buttoned up high against the bitter cold of the evening.

At seven fifteen Slessor was lying on his camp bed with his boots off, under the wing of Yates's B.E.2c, the only operational machine, when the telephone by the side of the bed rang. He picked it up and recognized once again the cheerful voice of Colonel Warner, speaking from the War Office.

A Zeppelin had been seen heading south-sou'west toward Norwich, and anti-aircraft guns had been in action at Bacton, on the coast. Slessor was warned to stand by. At seven fifty-five the telephone rang again with another message to say that a Zeppelin had been reported passing due south over Thetford at seven thirty-five. Slessor was ordered to go up at once if the weather was suitable. But Warner was paternal in his insistence that he should not take off in bad conditions.

"Look," he said, "I don't want you to go up if you think it's too thick. It doesn't look at all good to me from here." At eight o'clock Slessor reported thick fog, making it quite impossible for a machine to go up. He was ordered to go into action immediately the fog cleared. For half an hour they waited, hearing Zeppelin engines overhead, running up the engine of the B.E. every few minutes to keep it warm, hoping that the fog would lift. Then the sound of engines died away.

At five minutes to nine Colonel Warner was on the telephone again to report that the anti-aircraft guns at Enfield were in action and to instruct them to light their flares at Suton's Farm for the guidance of a machine which had just gone up from Landing Ground No. III at Hainault Farm, to the north. At ten minutes past nine they were told that a Zeppelin had been sighted ten minutes previously about ten miles to the north of them and another over Waltham Abbey, twelve miles to the northwest, at a quarter to nine. It was at this moment that their long overdue thirteen-pounder put in its appearance, bumping on to the field out of the fog and causing a certain amount of confusion. The detachment was under the command of a very junior sub-altern who had apparently never been trained on anti-aircraft guns, and was understandably out of his element.

Men began falling over each other getting the gun cleared away for action and it and its small searchlight in position, as the throb of Zeppelin engines returned in the sky above. Then the racket of London's guns began. The fog looked as thick as ever, with visibility down to a few yards. Then, in the next twenty minutes, with the astonishing suddenness of Thames fogs, it rolled away. At nine thirty-four Hainault Farm reported that their machine had just landed, and two minutes after this Slessor was able to ring the War Office and tell Warner that he was about to take off. He was ordered to patrol for as long as his fuel would last at a height of 10,000 feet, then to land and ask for further instructions.

He took off down the lane of flickering gas flares to look for the Zeppelin and destroy it, his means of doing so four small oblong bombs full of gasoline, which the pilot pushed by hand down through a tube in the cockpit floor. In the tube an electrical contact ignited the fuse, whereupon the bomb burst into flames and a bunch of large fish hooks sprang out at the top. These were supposed to catch in the Zeppelin's envelope.

London had no blackout to speak of and when he had

climbed above the haze he saw the lights of the capital below
him. When he looked upwards into the dark he saw
straightaway the huge silver shape, quite silent, of the Zeppelin. It was apparently stationary and was clearly visible in
the glow from the lights of London, about 4-5,000 feet above
him. He stared, appalled at its vast size. It was like having
a cod's eye view of the *Mauretania*. Overcoming his shock
and awe he opened the throttle of the B.E. as wide as he
dared and began to climb toward the monstrous airship.

But the Zeppelin commander had already heard the drone
of airplanes in the night and had been waiting and listening, engines shut off, for attacking machines. He heard the
B.E. climbing towards him, then saw the machine caught
and held in the beam of its own searchlight from below. A
gun opened up and shrapnel bursts began to appear below
him.

When Slessor was about 1,000 feet below the airship he
saw a stream of fiery sparks spill out into the blackness as
its engines started up. The huge bulk swung round, cocked
its nose up at a sharp angle, and climbed rapidly away from
him. Slessor, with his throttle jammed wide open, was on
the edge of stalling speed and had no hope at all of catching
a Zeppelin climbing with all her engines full out. Finally he
lost her in cloud, then discovered with a shock that he was
lost himself. The airship, whose commander had thought
himself safe from further danger now that the London guns
had lost his range, was somewhat shaken, first by the appearance of the British machine and more especially by the shells
from the thirteen-pounder at Sutton's Farm, then by the
guns at Hainault Farm, Grange Camp at Waltham, and
Kelvedon Hatch, all of which opened fire on him as the ship
rose, shedding white vapor as her water ballast cascaded out
and froze in the cold night air.

It was not until the ship had passed some two or three
miles north of the latter gun and headed off east that her

captain, Lieutenant Commander Breithaupt, began to feel secure again. People heard her as she passed over Blackmore, flying slowly with her propellers making a great noise. About ten minutes past ten she flew close to Ingatestone, halfway between Brentwood and Chelmsford, heading toward the River Blackwater and Clacton, then she turned and headed northeast. At twenty past eleven she passed over Rushmere and was fired on by pom-poms of the R.N.A.S. *Rattler*. Breithaupt dropped the four high-explosive bombs left in his racks, which missed the guns and did no damage. Ten minutes after this he was fired on again at Woodbridge but this time made no reply. Flying on east of Wickham Market he was north of Orford at eleven forty-five, and just before midnight he passed out to sea just north of Aldeburgh.

Of five naval Zeppelins which had set out that night, he was the first to be steering back across the North Sea to Germany with his mission entirely accomplished, his own part in an ambitious tactical plan fulfilled, his target fairly and accurately struck, his brand new L15 unharmed. Two more of the original five had also carried out instructions and advanced on London in the wake of Breithaupt from different points of the compass. For this raid, more ambitious, more serious than ever before, all the new airships of Strasser's fleet had combined.

At seven o'clock that morning an anti-cyclone extended over Central Europe, with the barometer rising over France, Western Germany and Holland. A depression was approaching the western coasts of the British Isles from the Atlantic, but this the German weather forecasters could not know. Conditions looked very favorable to Strasser at Nordholz, and they remained that way, as the depression passed away northwest of Scotland during the course of the day and night, while the barometer steadily rose over England. The wind over the whole North Sea region was very light, its

direction mainly southerly, with westerly currents on the
East Coast of Britain. There was some mist on the East
Coast, but elsewhere the sky was clear with a few light
clouds. In this lagoon of German weather the Director's best
ships struck. Von Buttlar's L11, Mathy's L13, Böcker's L14,
Breithaupt's new L15 and Peterson's new L16 rose from
their German sheds, their objective London.

Mathy, Böcker, Breithaupt and Peterson reached the
vicinity of the English coast roughly together and waited for
one another between the Haisboro and Would Lightships.
Von Buttlar was nowhere in sight, and they gave him up,
crossing the coast at the same time, about half-past six, with
darkness covering England. A Maxim battery of the
R.N.A.S. at Bacton fired vainly at the shapes of airships
dimly seen, then there was silence as the droning monsters
made their way inland.

For a time they steered a course in close proximity to each
other. After reaching Norwich, two of them wandered off
the main course, uncertain of their position, following the
course of the River Wensum, then turned southwest again
and rejoined the others, and the four ships went on together
through the darkness, three in a group ahead and one astern.
On reaching Thetford, which they identified, the airships
opened out fanwise. Two ships, Breithaupt's L15 and Peterson's L16, continued on a direct course toward London, and
the other two, Mathy's L13 and Böcker's L14, laid their
courses respectively west and east of London, with the idea
of making their runs on the capital from directions different
from those of Breithaupt's and Peterson's attacks in the
aftermath of shock and confusion caused by the first wave.

Soon Peterson's ship became separated from Breithaupt's,
lagged behind and disappeared from view. The L15, a
brand new Zeppelin on her maiden raid, carried on alone,
steering steadfastly for the target. A flare thrown overboard
at Elvedon, west of Thetford, had shown Breithaupt his

whereabouts at seven twenty-five. Confidently he changed his course to the south, flew over Bury St. Edmunds, was seen at Halstead at eight o'clock and at White Notley, southeast of Braintree, ten minutes later. Here he changed course to the west and about twenty-five past eight dropped a fuel tank east of Harlow.

The other three ships were all behind the L15. Böcker's L14 had followed in her wake, about five minutes behind her, as far as Thetford, then their courses diverged until, at ten past eight, when the L15 turned west at White Notley toward London, Böcker's L14 was at Mark's Tey, eight miles east of her. South of Harlow, Mathy's L13 came up behind her and Breithaupt flashed his position to her. Following the line of river and railway past Roydon and Hoddesdon to Broxbourne, the L15 flew steadily on.

Here, at eight forty-six, she was sighted by ground observers and a mobile thirteen-pounder anti-aircraft gun fired eight rounds at her, estimating the height to be about 5-6,000 feet, immediately overhead, and a searchlight felt round the sky for her. The searchlight was too close to the gun to be of any use, but it helped Breithaupt, surprised by this unexpected fire, to drop four light explosives on the gun site. Three of the bombs fell within a hundred yards of the gun and blew the crew off their feet, causing no casualties, but wrecking a one-and-a-half-ton truck and a car attached to the gun section. Breithaupt passed over the gun position, turned in a half-circle to the west, then altered course to the south, toward London.

He did not approach the city immediately, but went off to the southwest. The L15 passed Potters Bar at ten minutes to nine, High Barnet five minutes later, and was over Elstree at a minute to nine, heading southwest. She passed south of Edgware at three minutes past nine and flew on in the direction of Wembley, cutting her engines to silence her approach and drifting in with the northwest wind. Turning east she came over London east of the Edgware Road and Regent's Park.

Upon the Strand, the great highway of Theaterland, the curtain of the London dim-out hung like a veil upon a deathless face. The lights were low on those pavements of gold, but behind the shutters they burned with a feverish, wartime brightness. *The Scarlet Pimpernel* was at the Strand Theatre, with Julia Neilson and Fred Terry. Milton Rosmer and Basil Gill delighted in *The Prodigal Son* at the Aldwych. At the Lyceum, Irving's Lyceum, which had continued its unflagging bill of drama through the first year of war, the timely revival of *Tommy Atkins* in August, 1914, and the violent and patriotic *In Time of War* which followed the 1914 Christmas Pantomime, had been succeeded by a run of plays by Frederick Melville. *Her Forbidden Marriage,* "a whirlwind drama of surprises," was followed by a revival of *Between Five Women*. It was this play, described as "a powerful drama of intense interest," which was running when Breithaupt came over the heart of Theaterland.

At the Gaiety, the glittering, immortal Gaiety, the hunger of wartime London for music and laughter was more than satisfied by the brilliant *Tonight's the Night*. The golden age of the Gaiety was past, the times of Seymour Hicks and Ellaline Terriss, of Rosie Boot and Ada Reeve, of Katie Seymour and Lionel Mackinder, of Lionel Moreton, the great era of the Gaiety Girls brought to a climax by the unsurpassed Gertie Millar in *Our Miss Gibbs* in 1908. The great George Edwardes, creator of the theater's greatest glory, had died only nine days before, on October 4th. The long unflagging run of brilliant and effervescent shows had faltered to a complete stop just before the war, while Edwardes was actually in Germany trying to recover from his mortal illness. But George Grossmith, one of his finest leading men, had stepped into "the Guv-nor's" shoes and had given the Gaiety back something of its old verve and glitter. War had created the need for the sort of delightful escape which he offered in *Tonight's the Night* and given the Gaiety a fevered, renaissance glow. No longer did the golden light stream out of the Grand Entrance across the Strand, but behind the shutters it warmed the hearts of tired, hurt men on leave from the subhuman horrors of the trenches.

On this autumn evening of October 13, 1915, the theaters were full, and laughter and gay chatter filled the rows packed with khaki and blue or made the bars alive with a determined gaiety as the curtain fell on the entr'acte. At twenty-six minutes past nine Bert Hammond, the house manager of the Lyceum, was passing through the Royal Rooms to his office with the evening's receipts when there was a series of tremendous crashes outside the theater. Some of the women attendants who were in the rooms screamed and shouted, "What on earth is that?" Hammond said, "I know what it is."

Rushing up to his room he dropped the money in his desk and ran through a private pass door into the auditorium. There he saw Frederick Melville exhorting the audience from the stage to "please keep your seats, there is no more danger." Fortunately, it was during intermission and the iron curtain was down, and most of the audience—there were about two thousand people in the building—were distributed in the bars, corridors and vestibule. There was no panic among the audience, and after the first shock the majority of them returned to their seats and waited to see what would happen next. Hammond went backstage to see if any damage had been done there or any casualties caused and found the stage covered with about two inches of broken glass, dirt and debris.

A conference with the stage manager and others was held at once. The orchestra under Mr. Sullivan Brooke went on playing in the meantime, and it was decided that they would have the stage swept up and continue with the drama. The curtain was raised on the third act of the play, but the audience had thinned considerably. The actors continued in a somewhat unreal atmosphere for about forty-five minutes, when a fire superintendent came through the pit door down to the stage and called for the stage manager. As Hammond was on the stage at the time he stopped the play and went to the footlights to see what the man had to say. A gas main which had caught fire in the middle of Wellington Street just outside "The Bell" public house could not be extinguished. Flames were leaping about eighteen feet in the air, and he advised that they should stop the play and ask the audience to disperse. Hammond did so at once, and asked them to leave quietly through the exits on the Strand side of the building, because most of the north and east side exits were badly blocked with debris and the doors had all been blown outward by the explosion in Wellington Street.

Breithaupt had reserved his bombs until he was well over the center of the city. It was at twenty-five past nine that he dropped his first high explosive at Exeter Street, off the Strand, killing one person and injuring two more. Immediately after the explosion the searchlights of the London defenses swung toward the L15, and the guns, almost doubled in numbers since Mathy's September attack by the efforts of Sir Percy Scott, began to fire at her. Over a river of bursting shells she steered on apparently unperturbed.

There were no casualties inside the Lyceum, but the bomb hit the dressing-room block at the corner of Exeter Street. The top of chorus room No. 23 was blown away and the side of the flies was perforated like a pepper box. The lantern over the stage was damaged beyond repair. The only physical damage to anyone was to the actress May Davis, who had been sitting in her dressing room knitting when the bomb exploded and the splintered glass from the window covered her face and hands and all the exposed parts of her body with thousands of minute cuts. An electrician who rushed from his workshop on to the stage escaped death by a fraction of an inch, as one of the heavy beam trusses from the roof of the stage fell just beside him, cutting a large piece of leather from the heel of his shoe but not injuring him.

Breithaupt's first bomb, which had fallen just across the way from the Gaiety, was immediately followed by a second high explosive which fell between the Lyceum and the *Morning Post* offices, in the midst of a small crowd of people who were watching the Zeppelin's progress in mingled awe and excitement. Seventeen people were killed near the Lyceum, twelve badly hurt and nine others slightly injured, some of the casualties being in "The Bell," public house on the corner of Exeter and Wellington Streets. In Exeter Street adjoining the theater and within twenty feet of where the bomb had dropped, two children were asleep in an upper room. Although the outside wall was perforated in many parts neither of the children were harmed. On the street corner, an old woman who had been on her pitch selling oranges outside the Lyceum Gallery for many years, was blown to pieces, but the Lyceum linkman, whose job it was to see theater patrons into and out of their cabs, was standing behind one of the portico pillars and escaped injury, although he was thrown heavily to the ground.

One of the electricians from the Gaiety was killed, and "Nelson," the theater's one-eyed messenger boy, also lost his life. Withers, the Gaiety cellarman, recovered after he had had his left leg and right heel blown off and his left arm so mangled that it had to be amputated. When the first bomb exploded, the world-famous ex-sergeant-major stage doorkeeper of the Gaiety, Jupp, was standing at his post talking to the actress Gladys Ffolliott. He pushed her inside and shut the door. The second bomb blew the door in and threw Jupp down backward. A huge fragment of white-hot, jagged metal smashed into the wall immediately behind the place where the girl had been sitting. Jupp got to his feet and stumbled outside, where he found Harry Powell, another member of the Gaiety staff, lying with a severe wound in the leg.

The L15's third high explosive fell in the road between the Gaiety and the Strand Theatre, at Catherine Street. Jimmy Wickham, the Gaiety's fourteen-year-old call boy, was out on an errand when the explosion flung him into the vestibule of the Strand. He was taken to Charing Cross Hospital with broken legs and a bomb splinter embedded in his chest just above the heart.

The fourth and fifth high explosives burst in Aldwych and killed four persons in the street there, seriously wounding five more and slightly injuring ten. The sixth and seventh fell between Aldwych and New Inn, then two incendiaries struck the Royal Courts of Justice, and the eighth and ninth high explosives dropped in Carey Street. The wooden buildings of the Belgian War Relief Committee's clearinghouse were wrecked and the new extension of the Law Courts slightly damaged by a small fire started there by one of the incendiaries. The tenth high explosive from the L15's racks exploded in the upper stories of two old houses in New Square, Lincoln's Inn, put up in the year 1697, not long after Lana had written of his aerial ship with such foreboding. The upper stories were wrecked but the rest of these two old buildings withstood the barbarian's bombs.

The next high explosive, the eleventh, fell on Old Square. When it burst, fragments chipped large pieces out of the stone and brickwork of the surrounding buildings and badly damaged the sixteenth-century stained-glass windows of Lincoln's Inn Chapel. The twelfth high explosive dropped on the roadway of Chancery Lane opposite Stone Buildings, accompanied by the third incendiary bomb, which fell in

Chancery Lane. The roadway was torn up badly, the water and gas mains shattered, the fronts of the buildings on the east side wrecked, and all the glass in Stone Buildings smashed. Flying fragments of stone did as much damage as the bomb splinters themselves. Three more incendiaries fell immediately after this north of Holborn, in South Square, Gray's Inn, followed by the thirteenth high explosive, which burst in the northwest corner of Gray's Inn Square. Four more incendiaries were dropped on or near Hatton Garden and one in Farringdon Road, before the L15 headed east over the City. In Gray's Inn the hall and some houses in the square were badly damaged, and in Hatton Garden and Farringdon Road several buildings caught fire when incendiaries fell on them.

Breithaupt left behind him what was to the people on the spot a scene from a nightmare. The shouts and cries from the streets, the smell of escaping gas, the water erupting from the torn water main, the glare from burning buildings, were like a picture of the San Francisco earthquake come alive, while the throb of the Zeppelin's engines and the vicious noise of the guns all around, flashing and banging like lightning, added greater terror to the shock and confusion. Breithaupt had caught the evening wartime crowds going about their stolen hours of laughter, trying to forget that the guns were thundering across the Channel and bloody Loos was exacting a growing toll of fathers, sons and sweethearts every day.

His next bombs fell in the road at Finsbury Pavement. The high explosives badly damaged buildings there, including one under construction, killed a soldier and three civilians, and injured ten people. Another fell on a small hotel in the Minories, partly wrecking it, and damaged houses near by in the Minories, Aldgate and Hounsditch. One person was killed and eight more injured. The next two high explosives straddled the London, Tilbury and Southend (Midland) Railway between Great Prescot and Royal Mint Streets. Tenement houses in Great Prescot, Chamber and Leman Streets were damaged and six people injured, Leman Street railway station being hit. The L15's last bomb on London, a high explosive, fell between Wellclose and Prince's Squares. A tarpaulin factory was wrecked and several other buildings damaged, but there were no casualties. The whole attack had lasted between ten and fifteen minutes. During this time the energetic fire kept up by the reconstituted London gun defense was enough to worry Breithaupt and to send him away without having dropped all his bombs. Although lack of practice by the gunners resulted in wild inaccuracy, this was a fault which it was obvious could be remedied without too much trouble.

The L15 went off over London and the West India Docks to Limehouse and there fire from guns at Woolwich forced her to turn sharply north. On leaving the Thames at Limehouse, Breithaupt steered directly north over Hackney to Leyton, then turned northeast. On his approach to the target he had been surprised to hear the sound of airplanes groping for him over the outskirts of London. Now, on his return flight over the same area he cut his engines and hovered, listening for the sounds of more attackers. It was then that he heard Slessor's B.E. and saw his exhaust flames below in the night. This was the first British machine he had actually seen and which he knew had seen him, and it was quite enough to send him climbing at full speed. But he was still not out of danger. The guns at Loughton, Hainault Farm, Waltham and Kelvedon Hatch opened up on him before the L15 left the northeastern fringe of the capital, and naval pom-poms and a Maxim shot at her as she left the coast of England for her home base.

On the last stage of the return flight the L15 began to run short of fuel, and by the time she was nearing Terschelling two of her engines were working spasmodically. Five hours later Breithaupt saw the captive balloon marking their base above the fog which lay thick below them. By then only one of their motors was working. Just as the Zeppelin was coming into land this motor failed. The ship immediately rose again to 1,500 feet and a strong southerly wind began to drive her back towards the sea. Breithaupt did the only thing possible and opened the gas valves for an immediate blind landing, as they had no ballast left, hoping that there were no houses below. The L15 struck the open countryside, landing hard. The lower part of her framework was forced down over the forward gondola, and there was other damage, but the airship was ready again for operations in a short time.

Three other Zeppelin commanders observed the furious shelling of the L15, and the effect upon them was striking. Mathy and Böcker, who had both brushed the outskirts of London, and Peterson were scattered at various points off the capital, preparing to make their own attacks in the wake of Breithaupt. Von Buttlar, who reached the coast an hour behind the others, penetrated no farther south than Norwich before he turned and went back to Nordholz.

Peterson in the L16 had shown signs of vacillation of purpose, whether from lack of heart or faulty navigation, from the start of the flight overland across England. Junior in rank to the other three captains, he was, for a Zeppelin commander, of an unusually nervous disposition, and worry over a sick wife in Germany did nothing to make up for his lack of the thrusting qualities which distinguished Mathy, Breithaupt, Böcker, Hirsch and the other leading captains. He had failed to play his part in the first phase of the attack plan, having lost touch with Breithaupt, who had nevertheless gone on alone and done his job successfully, and he was wandering half-heartedly about Essex when he saw the barrage open up over London and the L15 caught in the searchlights.

It was only two months since Peterson's new L12 had been hit by a shell and forced to crash-land in Belgium, where she had been totally destroyed by the R.N.A.S. When he saw the shells bursting below Breithaupt's ship he himself was hovering over Kelvedon Hatch. He immediately gave orders to turn around, and headed off due north. A burst of pom-pom fire from below, hopelessly short of range, lent wings to his flight. With motors running full out he steered at fifty knots for the coast.

At a quarter to ten, when he was near Sawbridgeworth, he saw away to the west the cluster of lights which marked the little country town of Hertford. Passing Much Hadham, going south of Standon and immediately north of Ware, he reached Hertford and unloaded the bombs which had been meant for London. After killing eight men and a child, injuring eleven men and four women, wrecking houses and shops, and damaging such important military targets as a hospital, a museum, a Conservative Club, a rectory, two breweries and a wine store, the Hertford Municipal Library and School of Art, and a stable, he made his departure. He was fired on by a solitary Maxim gun on Newmarket Heath, but left the coast over Mundesley about five minutes after midnight, and was last seen from the Haisboro Lightship at quarter past twelve, making in great haste for Germany.

The original tactical plan had gone adrift at several points by now. Mathy and Böcker had skirted London to the west and east respectively as planned, and Mathy in the L15 was near Watford when he saw Breithaupt drop his first bomb on the Strand and the guns begin firing on him. Böcker in the L14 had lost his bearings, having mistaken the estuary of the Thames for that of the Blackwater, and did not find them again until he had passed over Hythe and discovered himself over the Channel. As he turned back on to

a northerly course for London, he too saw the furious out-
burst of firing begin in the distance ahead of him.

The sight threw both these experienced and able commanders out of their stride. Neither of them made any
really determined attempt after that to reach their intended
target.

Even the calm-nerved Mathy was ruffled. Over Rick-
mansworth at about half-past nine, immediately after he
had seen the L15 under fire, he altered course to the south
and flew over the course of the River Colne past Uxbridge
and Staines. He was seen at Windsor, and crossed the
Thames at Weybridge about ten minutes to ten. Five minutes later he was near Effingham, then passed near Gomshall
and turned west to Guildford, passing over Newlands
Corner at five past ten. The L13 was now moving slowly,
apparently uncertain of her position, and dropped a flare at
Clandon at ten o'clock. Ten minutes later she appeared
over Guildford, hovered there for a few minutes, then flew
up the valley east toward Chilworth and dropped a second
flare there which lit up the surrounding countryside. The
one-pounder at the Powder Works opened fire on her and
she sheered off east, but in a minute or two Mathy brought
her back over the factory, then turned and headed back to
Guildford.

At twenty-five past ten he was over the town again, went
westward as far as Wood Street, and then southeast over the
Hog's Back to Atrington, St. Catherine's and Shalford. Here
he dropped a flare to mark the spot and released twelve
high-explosive bombs. There were no casualties, but a
great deal of minor damage was done to houses at St. Catherine's, and the line of the London and South Western Railway was damaged between the two tunnels south of Guildford. Two of the bombs fell in the River Wey, and one of
them killed a swan. Mathy turned off east and at twenty-
five to eleven passed over Chilworth, where he was fired

on by an anti-aircraft gun and soldiers with rifles. He went on without responding and passed Willingshurst, near Cranleigh, heading southeast, five minutes later. He continued on this course for a time, then turned northeast back toward London. About five minutes past eleven he passed over Tonbridge Camp, near Oxted, steering northeast. Then he sighted, to the north of him, another Zeppelin, and turned north to join her.

A rapid interchange of signals by lamp established identities. The northern ship was Böcker's L14, which had come up from the Channel, Böcker, rectifying his earlier mistake, had turned southwest over the sea and come overland again at Littlestone at twenty-five to ten. He passed Lydd about twenty to ten, Winchelsea a few minutes before ten o'clock, flew along the coast as far as Pett, near Hastings, then turned inland, having now fixed his true position, and established his course for London from the railway. It was misty, and he was not seen from the ground until he reached Frant, where at half-past ten he dropped seven incendiaries, none of which did any damage. Turning north, he dropped three high explosives at twenty to eleven on Tunbridge Wells, causing no damage except broken windows. By now the mist was so thick in this area that the Zeppelin could not be seen at all from the ground, but flying above it Böcker suddenly sighted the L13 south of him. The other ship turned towards him and they closed, being seen together near Tonbridge Camp at five past eleven.

After a short exchange of signals the two ships parted company again. Mathy headed directly north over Limpsfield and Böcker pursued his northwesterly course, heading directly toward London.

At this point, there was actually little to stop them both from steering over London and repeating Breithaupt's performance. Impressive as the sight and sound of the gunfire over the capital had seemed from a distance, its aim was universally wild and all the rounds were falling short. Many of the shells could not reach the 5–6,000 feet at which Breithaupt had flown.

As for airplanes, there were no more in the sky, nor were any more able to take off in the fog after this. At Northolt visibility was so bad that at quarter-past eight, when the general alarm had been sounded and Lieutenant Long was trying to get the cold, damp engine of his B.E.2c to start, the flare detachment reported that they could not even find the flares on the field. Fifteen minutes later Long was ordered officially not to go up as the fog was rolling up very thick from the east, and the War Office was informed that it was not safe for a machine to take off. By ten o'clock the fog was so thick that it was impossible to see more than three yards ahead. At quarter past ten the flares were, with difficulty, lit in case there were any other machines in the air, and a bonfire was started in the southwest corner of the airdrome. Long remained standing by his machine until quarter past two, when the order to dismiss came from the War Office.

Lieutenant Jenkins of No. 14 Squadron, the duty pilot at Hainault Farm, was ordered to go up at eight o'clock by the War Office. After flying for about half an hour he saw heavy gunfire north of London and headed towards it, but could find no sign of the enemy. He made a big circle south, and continued to make circles between his landing ground and London at between 8,000 and 9,000 feet. His engine, droning somewhere in the darkness, was one of the threatening sounds which Breithaupt heard as he made his run over London.

Jenkins saw nothing of him, and at the end of his patrol, about ten o'clock he came down. Fog over the landing field was very dense, and even when he was as low as a hundred feet from the ground on his half-blind approach he could not see the flares. Landing far short, he crashed through the top of a hedge and a barbed-wire fence, although the damage to his B.E.2c No. 2051 was only a broken propeller and a tear in the wing fabric which could easily be patched on the station, and he himself was unhurt.

A few minutes after he had crashed, the L15 passed right over the field, and the gun there opened fire on her. As soon as he came down the War Office had ordered another machine up, and as Lieutenant Wardle's No. 2053 was giving serious engine trouble, Jenkins ordered him to take up Lieutenant Porter's No. 4078, which had landed there for the night. After he had climbed to about 5,000 feet Wardle saw a single gun firing to the east and turned in that direction. Finding nothing, he climbed to 8,000 feet, circled for an hour and a quarter without incident, then, about quarter past eleven, headed for the airdrome. At about the same time, the only two other pilots in the air, Slessor from Sutton's Farm and Tipton from Joyce Green, were also completing their patrols and heading for their landing fields.

Like Jenkins before him, Wardle lost sight of the Hainault Farm flares about a hundred feet from the ground. Sinking in the direction of the field, but still some way up he stalled his engine and the B.E. nose-dived to the ground. Wardle was hardly shaken, but his borrowed machine was wrecked, with heavy damage to the right-hand lower plane, the right-hand V of the undercarriage struts, the axle, the front section of the right-hand lower longeron, and a wingtip skid.

Slessor lost Breithaupt in the cloudy darkness, then found that he himself had lost his bearings. Somewhere in the dark countryside below him lay Haileybury, where only a year before he had been sitting at the feet of Mr. Garland in the Classical Sixth. Slessor could not know what excitement his brush with Breithaupt had caused at his old school. The Sutton's Farm searchlight had shown excited boys and masters plainly the tableau of Zeppelin and attacking airplane

BREITHAUPT

in the night above them. Mr. Garland was reading in his study when a colleague burst in upon him and said:

"Come out and look quick—there's a Zeppelin right over the Quad!"

But Garland, the classical scholar, had seen a Zeppelin before—Haileybury lay directly in the path of the German raids upon London. "Aw!" he said. "If you've seen one you've seen the lot!" and returned to his book. Theocritus was forever new. "Perhaps," recalls Slessor, "if he had known that one of his very recent pupils was in hot pursuit of that Zeppelin, he would have come out and had a look; but I doubt it—he was a very sensible chap, was Toby Garland."

Eventually, "after some rather breathless floundering in the dark sky," he saw the Thames and followed it westward until he saw the faint L-shaped glow of flares below him. Now at 10,000 feet, he patrolled between the faintly gleaming markers of Tilbury and Chingford reservoirs, until his petrol began to get low, then came down. He discovered that in the hour and three-quarters during which he had been up the fog had become very thick again. He could see the flares through the fog below him, but when the machine sank into the fog they became just a blurred glow. As he made his final approach the searchlight operators, with the very best of intentions, turned the searchlight on to illuminate the flare path from the windward end, and blinded him just as he dipped into the fog. He crashed into the turnips at the edge of the stubble field, smashing a wing tip, an aileron and one V of his undercarriage.

It was quarter past eleven. Mathy and Böcker were still bearing north toward London, after their meeting over Tonbridge Camp. But London was spared the L14's bombs. When Böcker got as far as Croydon he unloaded them there, aiming for the lights of this important railway junction which were burning brightly. His aim was poor and most of the bombs fell on houses and small villas, killing nine people and injuring another fifteen. Böcker then turned east in the direction of Bromley, bent on returning home. Mathy, who had watched him bombing Croydon from a point to the east of him somewhere between Croydon and Farnborough in Kent, continued on his northerly course, and over Bickley, just south of Bromley, the two airships narrowly escaped colliding with one another.

A rattled and angry Böcker maintained his easterly course for the coast, then bore around to the northeast, aiming for the Thames near Erith and passing directly over Crayford, his mind framing the sharp complaint he intended to lodge against Mathy for faulty navigation when he returned to Hage. Mathy stayed in company with the L14 for a few miles, then, near Chislehurst, began to turn in an irregular curve to the west, toward London.

A few minutes after Slessor had put his nose into the turnips at Sutton's Farm, Tipton landed at Joyce Green, which was almost directly beneath Böcker's route as he left Kent. He was one of the two pilots out of five who flew that night to make a normal landing, after doing nearly double his scheduled share of duty. Landing originally at twenty-five to ten with a leakage of pressure, after an hour and a half on patrol, he went up again fifty-five minutes later after Captain L. da C. Penn-Gaskell's machine, which had taken his place, had landed again with engine failure. After a further fifty-five minutes fruitless patrol he flew toward London as far as Deptford but could see no sign of Zeppelins, although he saw frequent gun flashes. He landed at twenty-two minutes past eleven, and was instructed to put his machine away. Just as he was leaving the hangars he saw two Zeppelins above the airfield heading in a northerly direction. Rushing back into the hangar, he had his machine pushed out again and the engine run, but was ordered not to leave the ground as the guns had taken matters into their hands by opening an erratic fire upon both airships.

Mathy was heading toward London. Turning over Bexley Heath he steered west and passed south of Woolwich. But he went no farther. At quarter to twelve he turned back from London and approached Woolwich again from the southwest. Here was a solid military target which might provide some recompense for failing to strike the capital at its heart.

The L13 was picked up right away by the searchlight at Blackheath, and the gun there had fired seventeen rounds at her before the breech jammed badly. It was joined by the Honor Oak gun, which got off nine rounds. Unscathed, however, Mathy sailed over the whole length of the barracks and Arsenal. The barracks received three high explosives and fourteen incendiaries, but surprisingly little damage was done. The first high explosive hit the middle of the front parade and broke the windows of the Royal Artillery mess, the second fell on a barracks dining room in the East Square, destroying both it and a stable below, and the third blew in the back of a clothing store in Grand Depot Barracks. Four men were slightly injured, a horse was killed and nine more hurt. An incendiary fell in St. John's churchyard, causing no damage, and eight others dropped on streets and gardens close by, slightly damaging St. John's Church Schools and a house in Wellington Street, starting fires in Cross Street and Beresford Street, and burning out a shop in Thomas Street. Of those falling on the Arsenal, three incendiaries fell near the surgery, another in a new machine shop on Avenue G, another in 5th Street, and one high explosive on the main machine carriage shop, where it wrecked a crane and damaged a machine. Nine men were hurt in the Arsenal, and one of them died later. The last bomb, a high explosive, fell harmlessly in the magazine area on Plumstead Marshes.

From the German point of view, the attack was a poor second to Breithaupt's cool foray of destruction and terror. A good view of the Royal Albert Dock persuaded Mathy to claim later that he had heavily bombed the dock area.

Through the attack the L13 was under a ragged fire from the Woolwich anti-aircraft guns, and from the gun at Clapton. The shooting was poor in quality, but it was more than Mathy had expected to meet, and in fact one round had been more accurate than the gunners knew. Going off to the northeast, the L13 crossed the Thames at Barking Reach and was over Dagenham at five minutes to twelve.

Slessor was standing impatiently on the misty field at Sutton's Farm when the Zeppelin passed right overhead. With one machine damaged and out of action, and the other useless without its bomb carrying gear, all he could do was watch their gun firing hopefully at the airship. It got off ten rounds before the L13 disappeared, and achieved a good elevation, though it failed to get the measure of the Zeppelin's speed. After the explosion of the fifth round, which burst quite close astern, Mathy turned off at right angles, before resuming his northeasterly course. He was immediately engaged by the gun at Becontree Heath, which fired ten rounds at him.

Ground observers who had watched the progress of the L13 between Woolwich and this point had noticed a light suddenly appear in the darkened engine gondola toward the stern of the airship. A stray fragment of shrapnel from one of the London guns had struck one of the L13's propellers, and the light marked the efforts of the engine car crew to make on-the-spot repairs. Then the fourth shell from the Becontree Heath gun burst close under the airship's stern, and the light went out abruptly. Work was suspended in the car until the L13 could get clear of the guns which were sprouting up like mushrooms along her path. She carried on northeast past Brentwood, which she reached at ten minutes past twelve, and five minutes later was in the neighborhood of Ingatestone, south of Chelmsford. Here she was flying so low that watchers on the ground could see quite plainly that one of the Zeppelin's propellers was feathered and looked damaged. Mathy flew on, passed south of Chelmsford and Maldon, and approached the Blackwater Estuary at Tollesbury. He did not want to head out to sea as far south as this, so he turned northeast toward Colchester.

At this time the L14 was going home abreast of him, about six miles to the south, and crossing the mouth of the Blackwater Estuary near Clacton. Böcker did not go out to sea here either, but continued on a northeasterly course close to the coast. It was in their orders that they were not to quit the land until they were in the vicinity of the Orfordness Light, where additional markers were afforded if necessary by the Shipwash Lightship seven miles off shore and the Outer Gabbard fifteen miles further out to sea.

About quarter to one the L13 was seen from Mark's Tey, and was fired at by a Maxim near there. Five minutes later she was near Wivenhoe and turned up the line of river and railway to Colchester, where she was fired on by pom-poms and rifles. Flying slowly and erratically, she picked up the line of the railway to Ipswich and passed there about quarter past one. Then Mathy left the railway and went northeast to Otley, which he passed at half-past one, flying very slowly. Ten minutes later, having reached East Sohum, northwest of Wickham Market, he suddenly changed direction and went off at high speed due east over Framlingham and Saxmundham. Passing north of Leiston about five minutes to two, the L13 finally headed out over the sea for Germany at Dunwich about two o'clock, her crew rid at last of a

difficult and anxious action and very glad to see the empty
waters below them.

The departing raiders left behind them a London more
shocked, more stunned, more quickly moved to bitter anger than ever before. Material damage was considerably less,
but casualties were higher, than in Mathy's lone attack of
September 8th, and the feelings which the renewed on-
slaught stirred up were far fiercer and more immediate in
their expression than in the first great raid on the capital.

As early as the afternoon following the raid a public
meeting, organized by the *Globe,* was held at the Cannon
Street Hotel, and it was at this packed and angry demonstration that the word "reprisal" was first loudly aired.
Speech after speech hotly attacked the government for failing to protect the city against the activities of the Zeppelins,
and a resolution demanding "a declared policy of air reprisals for Zeppelin raids on London and other open cities"
was sweepingly carried, along with the corollary that a large
fleet of giant aircraft be formed at once under a separate
Ministry of the Air created solely for this purpose.

For years, said Mr. Joynson-Hicks, M.P., himself a member
of the coalition government, he had endeavored to call attention to the need for a Zeppelin fleet or an air fleet as a
preparation for contingencies which he had expected and
which had since arisen. The country knew now that our air
service could not keep Zeppelins away. Mr. Churchill had
promised that when the Zeppelins came there would be "a
swarm of hornets" to meet them. Where, he demanded,
was the "swarm of hornets" on Wednesday night, and where
had it been when the East Coast wanted protection in the
last six months? The men of the Air Service, he allowed,
were magnificent. They were more brave, more daring, and
more reckless of their own lives than those of any country.
Why had they not all that was necessary to enable them to

meet the Zeppelins before ever they reached the shores of this country?

Slessor had personal experience of the ugly feelings of many Londoners on the same day. After an hour or two of disturbed sleep he had set out for Farnborough early on the morning of the 14th in a Crossley tender pulling a R.F.C. flat trailer, with a corporal and two airmen, to collect a new starboard lower plane, an aileron, a wheel and an undercarriage V from the stores at the Administrative Wing. It took them a long time to get to Farnborough, a long time to collect the spares, and it was getting dark as they passed through the city into east London on their way back to Sutton's Farm. Like all service transport on operational duty they carried a blue light to show the police that they were entitled to use the headlights denied to civilians. As they turned into the Mile End Road with all their lights full on, there were angry cries and a crowd rushed at them and brought them to a standstill.

The wild stories of spies flashing motorcar lamps to guide Zeppelins to their targets which had started with the very first airship raid on England were in circulation everywhere, and helped to swell the hysteria of this mob. The uniforms meant nothing to them, and they had not heard of the air defenders of London, and Slessor had to get two policemen to stand one on either side of the driver's seat of the tender before they could get through.

In fact proposals for reprisals were completely academic at this stage. Britain did not have any of the equipment necessary to carry them out. There were no large, long-range bombers in British hands, and the bombing machines which were in use were inadequate. As for airships themselves, there were only a few tiny nonrigid ships which would be of no use at all. Sir Rider Haggard was one of those who went on record advocating a British airship fleet which

could actually attack the Zeppelins more effectively than airplanes.

In making such confident attacks people like Mr. Joynson-Hicks were assuming a great deal about the superiority
of the dirigible. Britain had built one big airship named,
typically, the *Mayfly*. The *Mayfly* had broken its back, and
this had been enough to convince the authorities that the
Zeppelin-type airship was not technically up to the demands
of long-range flight, even in the face of the loudly advertised
German Zeppelin fleet, and they had built no more *Mayflies*.
Now, from every side, critics of every caliber and political
color were telling the existing coalition government that the
Zeppelin raids had proved the former government utterly
and tragically wrong. If the government supported the belief at this time that the Zeppelins were vulnerable they were
going to have to prove it by swift action.

It was in any case far too late to begin building, almost
entirely from scratch, an airship fleet. If there was so strong
a case for the creation of an independent long-range bombing force of the kind which the air-minded Lord Kitchener
himself actually had in mind, and of a separate Ministry of
the Air to administer it, which the *Daily Mail* had been
urging for some years, something more than a mere notion
was needed now.

Last seconds of a German Zeppelin caught by searchlights and shot down over London.

Count Ferdinand von Zeppelin in the gondola of his L30, in 1916.

German Zeppelins crossing the North Sea in formation to attack London.

An early model takes off on a test flight.

Machine gun mounting on top of airship aft of rudder.

German exercise using a Blériot XI. About 1911.

Strasser, shot down in L70.

Mathy, killed commanding L31.

Böcker, commander of L14.

Breithaupt, much decorated raider.

Anti-Zeppelin B.E. 2C, painted black to make it invisible to raiders at night.

On the left, Lt. Leefe Robinson, first pilot to bring down a Zeppelin, with Lt. F. Sowrey, who destroyed L32.

Control gondola of L5, showing German Order of Merit received for its raids against London.

Close-up of electric bomb switches in the gondola of an airship.

Bomb damage in London, 1917.

Army technicians examine the rudder of wrecked L33, forced down near London.

7. KNOCK DEEP

Something had to be done about the Zepps. Everybody from the man in the street to the Secretary for War was saying so. Secure, as ever, from the sea, there was something rotten in the air defense of Britain.

It was the result partly of divided command, partly of lack of resources. The Board of Admiralty, which did not enjoy the responsibility, was actually charged with the job of defeating the Zeppelins, but their proper duties at sea were making exorbitant and increasing demands upon guns and airplanes, and they were no longer in a position to defend the country from German naval airships. The War Office, which was actually willing to take over full official responsibility from the Admiralty and was now pressing hard to be allowed to do so, was in an equally poor position with regard to equipment. Luckily, the waxing moon gave both parties time to come together and thrash out the problems and the question of transfer, and the winter weather too was at hand to give them a breathing spell and a chance to build against the renewed Zeppelin offensive which was sure to come with the earliest breath of spring.

The appointment of Sir Percy Scott, which was strong evidence of the Admiralty's preference for gun defense over airplanes, had caused the Army Council to agitate for the whole duty of air defense to be placed in their hands. The

Admiralty did not respond, but waited to see what further experience would bring. The raid of October 13th provided painful material for both Navy and Army experts to work upon, with press and public urging them to find a speedy answer.

The War Office wished to take over the air defense of London and to make the airplane the keystone of the defense, but still the Admiralty had not made known its mind on the subject. A knowledge of enemy reactions to the energetic London defenses might have helped them to come to some definite conclusions. In an interview with an American newspaper correspondent immediately after his successful raid of September 8th, Mathy praised the London guns and searchlights, saying, "As to an airplane corps for the defense of London, it must be remembered that it takes some time for an airplane to get up as high as a Zeppelin, and by the time it gets there the airship would be gone; then, too, it is most difficult for an airplane to land at night, while a Zeppelin can stay up all night, and longer if need be."

The London anti-aircraft gunners gave Mathy cause to respect them again on October 13th when they scored a hit on the engine car of the L13, and fear of them had made both him and Böcker abandon London. Breithaupt, too, was worried by their persistence. But this time the attention of the Royal Flying Corps airplanes from Hainault, Sutton's Farm and Joyce Green bothered him more. He reported afterward, "The L15 was caught in the beams of a large number of searchlights, the illumination, especially above the city, being as bright as day. Unusually violent anti-aircraft defense fire opened and the airship was soon surrounded by bursting shrapnel. Even more sinister was the appearance of another danger in addition to the anti-aircraft guns. Four airplanes, at first observed by the flames from the exhaust and then clearly shown in the beams of the searchlights, endeavored to reach the airship and shoot her down with incendiary ammunition—not until the L15 had dropped all her ballast was she out of reach of the enemy." But these "four airplanes," whose flaming exhausts in the night had worried Breithaupt, had only been filling in time before being sent about their official duty overseas, and on October 26th, Colonel Salmond reported "all the detachments have now returned to Fort Grange, Gosport."

A month later Second Lieutenant Slessor, who had been on that historic night of October 13th the first man to intercept a Zeppelin over Britain, was standing at the rail of the troopship *Scotian,* as she steamed into Mudros Harbor in the Dardanelles, having completed the significant first step in the career of a marshal of the Royal Air Force. The place where he had shown his mettle, Mr. Tom Crawford's little stubble field near Hornchurch village, was not, however, allowed to return at once to private ownership, neither was the other airfield at Hainault Farm.

After October 26th there was no more airplane defense of London. While the experts talked and weighed the evidence, the new airdromes remained empty, and Mr. Crawford's sheep roamed once more at will over the flying field at Sutton's Farm, finding the grazing, soiled with the excreta of machines, not as good as it had been. Eight days after this the Admiralty spoke. In reply to persistent War Office demands for action, they observed that, whereas at the time of the previous conferences in July, "it was assumed that airplanes were indispensable for the defense of London . . . it has been necessary to modify this opinion and it is not possible for the Admiralty to propose any definite arrangements for the transfer pending further experience." A conference was arranged, and it was eventually agreed, subject to notification by Lord Kitchener, that the R.F.C. should supply the air defense inland, the R.N.A.S. over the sea.

Gradually, the Army began to take over the London guns and searchlights, and at the end of December the Directorate of Military Aeronautics ordered that two B.E.2c's with pilots experienced in night flying were to be permanently maintained at each of ten airfields encircling London: Hounslow, which was the headquarters and depot for the establishment; Wimbledon Common, which had been in use, but only as an emergency landing ground, on October 13th; Croydon; Farningham, south of Dartford in Kent; Joyce Green; Hainault Farm; Sutton's Farm; Chingford—formerly a naval station at Hendon; and Northolt.

The detachments at most of these airfields were modeled upon those which had performed with such promise on October 13th. They were provided once again by various squadrons in training for overseas. Each unit included six mechanics and a Royal Engineer party with a searchlight. The pilots, as before, took it in turns to sleep on a camp bed under the wing of the duty machine in the hangar beside a telephone which communicated directly with the War Office.

As if to mark the renewal of confidence which the fresh development inspired, the Lyceum Theatre, closed since the bombing of October 13th, reopened on Boxing Day, December 27th, with the annual pantomime, "Robinson Crusoe." London squared her shoulders to meet the New Year, 1916.

The transfer was going ahead steadily when Lord Kitchener returned from the Dardanelles. His reaction to the *fait accompli* of the new move was a shock to the War Office. Perhaps piqued by action taken behind his back, as he felt, perhaps somewhat less of the supremely confident master of war since he had seen for himself the full scope of the Dardanelles disaster and studied the result of the bloody stalemate of Loos in September and October, he reviewed the new agreement in the middle of January and repudiated it. His main thought in doing so was of the drain which would otherwise result upon the already inadequate strength of the R.F.C. To support his new armies, now under training in

England, for the great offensive which the Allies were planning for the summer of 1916, he had decreed that no fewer than 120 squadrons would be needed. It was January, and the R.F.C. was far short of this huge target.

To establish a dozen permanent squadrons in Britain for home defense was, in his view, to undermine the new thrust before it started, so important had the cooperation of the corps squadrons become to the Army in the field.

And this was not all. In August the first of a new and powerful German fighter airplane, the Fokker monoplane, had appeared over the Western Front. Since then these machines had multiplied and the R.F.C. losses had risen in proportion to serious figures. The Fokker monoplane was faster and more maneuverable than anything else in the air, but its success was mainly due to its being fitted with special new interrupter mechanism which allowed a fixed machine gun to be fitted which fired in the airplane's direction of flight between the blades of the propeller as it revolved. The improvement in ease of aiming was enormous, and skilled pilots like Immelmann, who added a new maneuver of his own invention to the Fokker threat, were having a great success against the Martinsyde and Morane scouts of the R.F.C. and especially against the Farmans and B.E.2c's of the artillery cooperation squadrons.

Two new fighters, the F.E.2b and the D.H.2, both "pushers" which allowed a field of fire forward by having their engines behind the pilot between tail booms, were in production, but none of these had yet reached the Western Front. In the meantime a new idea of formation flying was evolved to combat the Fokkers. Unfortunately, although this gave some mutual protection to the British machines, it absorbed many more of them on any one duty.

In the face of the statistics even Kitchener of Khartoum lost his nerve. On January 18th the Army Council went back on its decision and wrote to the Admiralty withdrawing from the transfer. Those soldiers who had already taken over duties at guns and searchlights in London would remain there and come under Admiralty orders. But this fickleness in the face of obligations the Navy would not accept. They insisted that the Army "carry out an arrangement decided some six months ago for which a great many preparations have already been made and agreed to by both departments."

The Zeppelins struck again. Respectful of its defenses since October 13th, and wary of any additions which they had reason to believe had been made since then, they left London alone on this opening raid of the new year. This time they attempted to make good something which they had tried and failed to do in the autumn of the previous year, and deliver a heavy attack on Liverpool, a vitally important center of shipping and completely defenseless. Weather and the inexperience of some of the commanders combined to make the attempt a military failure, but heavily foreboding for the future was the large number of ships used. Nine naval Zeppelins crossed the North Sea on January 31st. They came over the Norfolk coast in successive waves and headed across the Midlands. The complete lack of defenses across their path promised to make this an ideal training flight for the new commanders, who had all the experienced captains—Mathy, Böcker, Breithaupt, Peterson, Buttlar and Loewe—to inspire them.

The misty weather, which hid them from British naval airplanes at the coastal stations, added to the blackout restrictions in force on the ground, obscured their route to Merseyside, causing even Mathy's navigation to go astray. Böcker, in the L14, penetrated farthest west, and even he did not go beyond Shrewsbury after eight hours' wandering about the Midlands. Loewe, in the L19, strayed as far south as Norwich, Buttlar as far north as Scunthorpe, where an uncertainly placed bomb load killed two men at the Redbourne iron works and slightly damaged the engine and boiler house. Mathy, in the L13, continued on course for Liverpool as far as Newcastle-under-Lyme, then suddenly turned away south past Stafford, Burton-on-Trent, Macclesfield and Buxton before leaving the coast over Skegness. A new commander, Dietrich, followed Mathy for some time but turned south near Derby and circled back to the coast at a point south of Lowestoft over Stafford, Wolverhampton, Walsall, Nuneaton, Market Harborough, Kettering, Ely and Thetford.

Stabbert reached Burton-on-Trent—which was unlucky to be bombed by three ships in the course of the night—then turned about and retraced his path homeward. Peterson and Ehrlich did not cross the Norfolk border, and Breithaupt in the L15 hugged the Wash most of the evening before turning for Germany. The airships unloaded their bombs wherever they found the biggest gaps in the blackout and killed seventy people in all, injuring another one hundred and thirteen.

All of the Zeppelins at their landfall and some in the meandering course of their return passed close enough to the London area to alert naval air stations and the ten airfields of the Royal Flying Corps ringing the capital. Thick ground mist lay everywhere over and around the city, but sixteen pilots in all went up in spite of it in a vain search for the raiders who were reported to have crossed the coast at the usual landfall near the Wash. Thirteen of them managed somehow to get down again without injury to themselves, three were unlucky.

When orders came from the War Office on the telephones of the R.F.C. airfields from Hounslow to Joyce Green for the machines on stand-by to go up whenever the fog permitted, it did not seem possible that any machine would fly that night, so thick was the fog at all points. At Northolt, where he commanded the training squadron, Major Penn-

Gaskell decided to try and get off to see for himself whether any of his pilots would stand a chance of operating safely in the murk. Penn-Gaskell, then a captain, had shared the flying with Lieutenant Tipton at Joyce Green on October 13th, and had landed without mishap in thick fog with a broken fuel pipe. The mist was very heavy when he took off from Northolt at a quarter to seven. His machine rocked down the line of flickering gasoline flares, then left the ground. As he did so an arm of mist must have encircled him. There was just enough visibility for the rest of the detachment to see his machine crash headlong into a tree. He was alive when they reached him, but so badly injured that he died five days later.

An almost exact repetition of the tragic accident happened an hour later when Major Unwin, taking off from Joyce Green, was suddenly blinded by the mist and also struck a tree. He was taken to the hospital critically injured, and died some days later. No pilot that night saw any sign of a Zeppelin. The one casualty in the raiding force fell a victim to the hazards of aerial navigation. This was Loewe's L19, which ran out of fuel at three o'clock in the morning near the home island of Borkum, crashed and drifted rapidly west. At half-past seven she was sighted in the water ninety-five miles east-by-north of Spurn by the skipper of the British trawler *King Stephen*. The crew of the airship were already half-dead with shock, exhaustion and exposure, and Loewe shouted to the trawler skipper through a megaphone, begging him to take them off, even offering him money to do so. Whatever his natural feelings the skipper decided that fifteen German sailors were too dangerous to have aboard his ship, and left them there clinging to the crippled airship on the black-icy water. It was not long afterward that she sank and all hands perished with her.

It remained to be seen what effect, if any, the results of this raid would have upon the War Committee when they

met again on February 10th. A really formidable number of
Zeppelins had appeared together over England, harbingers
surely of what was to come, and the defenders had only succeeded in repeating the sad story of the past. No official decision had yet been reached on the transfer. The affair was
still in the melting pot, even now.

However, the two services were sufficiently in accord for
the War Office to take one immediate and very important
step. On February 1st, the day following the Midland raid,
Major T. C. R. Higgins, the officer commanding the newly
formed No. 19 Reserve Squadron at Hounslow, was ordered
to take additional command of all the units on the airfields
scattered round London, and organize his unit for the defense of the capital.

Then, on February 10th, the War Committee met again
and this time they made up their minds. They gave their
official blessing to the forming of specialist squadrons for
home defense.

On February 16th Field Marshal Lord French, who had
been appointed Commander in Chief, Home Forces, on
December 19, 1915, having been superseded in command
of the army in France by Sir Douglas Haig, assumed responsibility for the defense of London, and shortly afterward for
the whole country.

At the same time a scheme of anti-aircraft defense already
drawn up was put into action as the equipment became
available. Centers of industry and population all over the
country were scheduled for special protection by being fitted
with concentrations of guns and searchlights, and by mobile
defenses mounted on motor trucks. For the protection of
London the War Office adopted Sir Percy Scott's original
plan, which had been based upon two rings of twin gun positions, one at five miles and the other at nine miles radius
from central London, and extended the plan to cover the
munitions and arms factories at Woolwich and Waltham

Abbey. There was also to be a third perimeter of search-lights, called "Airplane Lights" beyond the nine-mile ring for the particular use of home defense pilots in sighting Zeppelins. The experience of October 13th had shown that a plentiful number of accurate searchlights was vital if attacking airplanes were to find and hold the Zeppelins. When Colonel M. St. L. Simon assumed command of the anti-aircraft defenses of London he found that Sir Percy Scott had already formed a ring of gun positions to cover the central part of Greater London on a line through Kenton and Richmond. The center of this ring was covered by the guns in Regent's Park, at Tower Bridge, at Battersea and other places.

It was Simon's immediate job to extend this defended area to include the territory bounded by Hoddesdon, Potters Bar and Essendon. There were to be seven control centers in this area, with the ring of "Airplane Lights" outside it. The scheme called for eighty-three effective anti-aircraft guns. When Colonel Simon took over command there were sixty-five guns of various sorts in the London area, many of them, however, pom-poms, improvised six-pounders, three-pounders and two-pounders, none of any real value and all scheduled to be replaced by three-inch guns as soon as they became available.

Even after the ambitious Zeppelin raid of January 31st, scarcity of men and machines prevented separate units for home defense being detailed outside the London area at the time No. 19 Squadron at Hounslow was given its new role. The best that could be done was to send an extra three B.E.2c's to each of the training squadrons at Norwich, Thetford, Doncaster and Dover, and six to reinforce No. 5 Reserve Squadron to assist it in the defense of Birmingham and Coventry. Defense of Hull was temporarily provided by No. 47 Squadron at Beverley.

All these makeshift arrangements had been completed by

March 1st. Four days later three Zeppelins, the L11, L13 and L14, raided England. Yet again Mathy, who was making for Sheffield and industrial southwest Yorkshire, failed to reach his target, and on finding that a strong northeast gale was rising between him and Hage, went well south, left England over Deal, and found refuge in Belgium. But both Buttlar in the L11 and Böcker in the L14 bombed Hull in the intervals between snow showers. Seventeen people were killed in the city and fifty-two injured, and nearly all the damage was to civilian property. Once again the airships had deliberately avoided London.

The High Command, preoccupied with the new offensive at Verdun designed to break the French armies, which had been launched on February 21st, had lost interest in London, particularly the better armed city which now faced the Zeppelin threat with considerably greater confidence than before. But when the threat of a great new offensive by Kitchener's new armies to take the pressure off the hard-pressed French began to loom they turned their minds to the destruction of British war material and the disruption of war production in England, as well as to the importance of pinning down Royal Flying Corps squadrons in England which would otherwise be used against them in France. They thought in particular of the great munitions works in southern England, of Stowmarket and Waltham Abbey in Essex and of Woolwich. All these tasks called for the services of the Zeppelins.

Weather and a rising moon held them off for a time, and defense preparation in England went forward. It was decided, great as was the need for new squadron in France, with the French beginning to press for a large-scale British offensive there to relieve Verdun, that ten of the seventy fresh squadrons scheduled for the R.F.C. in December were to go to home defense duties. Some of these had been formed, some were in the process of organization, some ex-

isted only on paper. They were officially designated Home
Defense Squadrons. For greater efficiency in the London
area all the airplane defense units there were grouped together as a new Wing, the 18th, and Lieutenant Colonel
F. V. Holt, who had been brought back from France especially for the purpose, given command of it. All the new
squadrons of No. 18 Wing were still called Reserve Squadrons, and those already formed continued to fulfil training
duties, which included some night, or at least dusk, flying.
But there were not enough machines available to do any
systematic practice during the hours of total darkness. The
majority of pilots at Colonel Holt's outlying stations were
keen but very inexperienced young men.

Such was Second Lieutenant Alfred de Bathe Brandon,
stationed at Hainault Farm. When war broke out Brandon,
like most of the young men in New Zealand, rushed to volunteer. He was not called up until after the battle of the
Marne, however, and at that time it was generally thought
that the war would be over in three months, so when the
other partners in his law firm pressed him to get his release,
he did so. But by the time the New Year came it was clear
that the war would go on for a long time. Brandon's father,
seeing his restlessness and frustration, told him that if he
really wanted so badly to fight he had better take the boat
to England on his own initiative, and try to get a commission. It was the end of April before he could get a passage.
On the long voyage he decided to try for the Royal Naval
Air Service. He had a token qualification for the Navy in
that he and his cousin Wynyard Higginson had done a fair
amount of sailing in their canoes on Paremata Harbor and
on Lakes Rotorua and Rotaiti, and the thrill of flight drew
him strongly. When he arrived in Britain he lost no time in
applying to the Admiralty. But he was over age, and to his
intense disappointment received an answering letter saying

that His Majesty's Commissioners were unable to accept his services.

But Mr. Coates, who was on the London Board of the National Bank of New Zealand, made some inquiries on his behalf and found out that if he learned to fly privately he might have a better chance. He suggested that he should call on another New Zealander, Jack Carr from Auckland, who was in the R.N.A.S. at Chingford. Carr thought that Hendon was the most likely place to see about learning to fly. One night a little later Brandon was sitting dejectedly in a movie theater when he saw an advertisement for "joy rides" at Hendon airport. At the entrance he paid a half-crown to get in and found that he was about a mile away from the airplanes, but by the distribution of three more half-crowns he got to the side of the flying enclosure. The machines were taking off and flying right over his head, making a tremendous noise, and Brandon began to have tremulous doubts.

Then he saw a notice, "Passenger Flights Two Guineas." He paid, and was admitted into the enclosure itself. There was a small queue of nervous and excited customers—he wondered whether any of them were there for the same reason as himself—and it seemed to take a long time for his turn to come round. The machine was a Grahame-White Box Kite, which looked exactly what its name suggested. In front of this maze of struts and wires was a tiny wicker seat in which he had to sit holding on to two struts with his legs dangling into space. The pilot, who sat behind him, was strapped in. He thought, If anything goes wrong I'm going to be jettisoned. He did not appreciate that if the airplane crashed he would stand a better chance of being thrown clear for not being strapped in.

They moved forward. The unsilenced engine roared frighteningly and a 45-m.p.h. head wind tore at him. There came an unexpected bump as they went over the railway line. As the aircraft banked over in the turn Brandon thought to himself in wild panic that he only had to let go of the struts to do some unsupported flight on his own. He found himself moving round a landscape of tilting fields and houses with the wind on his face and a sickening lurch in his stomach whenever the machine sank in a patch of thin air. After what seemed like a few seconds—actually it was three minutes—came the silence of the throttled-down engine and the landing. As he was walking unsteadily away toward the gate a notice caught his eye which read, "Hall School of Flying, Hendon. Inquire within." He went inside as invited and found that it would cost him £75 (then about $330) to learn to fly.

He hesitated. "Would you take a check?"

The instructor rubbed his hands together. "Delighted." The check was handed over.

"When do I start, then?"

"Oh yes. Well, we'll start your instruction at four o'clock tomorrow morning."

The airplane was an old Caudron with a 30-h.p. Anzani engine. The pilot had to run this along the ground for about a mile, turn around a pylon and come back. A student went solo all the time, as the school did not own a dual-control machine. Some of them never got the hang of the machine, which was not easy to master. There was no throttle, and the engine had to be switched off and on to reduce speed or stop. To steer, a pilot had to get the right amount of wind, and with too much wind or rudder could easily find himself going in the opposite direction. Turning the greasy switch on and off hundreds of times was very tiring. After mastering this maneuver on the ground, Brandon was allowed to go faster, get the tail off the ground, and go along at about twenty miles an hour. Some got the tail too high, and the skids in front went into the ground, the machine turned over, and the would-be pilot usually packed his

things and left. The next stage was what was called
"straights."

One day the instructor said, "You had better take her off."
He started off, got the tail up, and this time left the engine
on. Suddenly the earth dropped away for what he thought
was about twenty feet. He landed immediately, very pleased
with himself, turned and came back to the sheds along the
ground.

"How high did I go?" he asked the instructor breathlessly.

"Oh, a couple of feet."

After this students usually became more ambitious, and
this was a danger point. Some got the nose too high, lost
flying speed and crashed. The machine went into the workshop for a few weeks and the pilot departed without his
license and poorer by £75. "Turns" were the next step, a
matter of taking the machine off, doing first a right-hand
turn, later a left-hand one, and coming back to the ground.
At last the time came when Brandon was promoted
to the big machine, a 40-h.p. Caudron, which was a very
much pleasanter machine to fly. On this he did circles and
figures of eight, and then the final test for his ticket, a landing with the engine off within a circle on the ground. This
had to be done from 500 feet, but most pupils went to 1,000,
which at the time seemed very high indeed. Brandon
climbed to 1,000, but lost himself in cloud and when he came
out of it could not find the field. Then he saw the railway
line on his right which should have been on his left.

There was no compass on the machine, and in the cloud,
with no landmarks visible, he had made a complete turn and
was flying away from the airfield. At 500 feet he opened
the throttle and crossed the railway line, but there was still
no airfield. He was lost, but kept on flying until he spotted
a suitable field and landed in it. He telephoned to the airfield and his instructor, Mr. Hill, came out and flew

the machine back. A little later he succeeded in qualifying for his pilot's license, which was dated October 17, 1915.

After Hendon he moved from his lodgings there, which the flying school had found for him, and into London. By now he had changed his mind about the R.N.A.S., as he had heard that they patrolled the coast and were not exactly in the middle of the world's first air war. He applied to the R.F.C., but had still had no reply at the end of November, when he chanced to meet a Major Brierley, who was impressed by the stubbornness of this volunteer from the other side of the world, pulled strings and got him into the corps. After much determined lobbying at the War Office by Brierley, Brandon received a telegram telling him to report to Northolt Airdrome at Ruislip.

Toward the end of February, Brandon and a pilot named Muir went to Salisbury Plain, stayed the night at the Prince of Wales Hotel at Ludgershall, and next day were orally examined in stationary and rotary engines, rigging, care and maintenance of airplanes, cross-country flying, Morse code, and the formation of troops. On the 26th they were granted their wings, and went on to the B.E.2c with the 70-h.p. engine, under Captain Bradley. A day or two later they passed their night flying tests and became qualified as night fighting pilots.

The "test" in fact consisted of two landings in the dusk. Brandon's took place at about half-past five and six, although it was fairly dark for the latter one. He was as anxious as anybody, and he never forgot the encouraging advice of their instructor, Lieutenant Collins, that "it isn't as bad as they say it is."

In the third week in March he was posted to Hainault Farm, for duty on the next Zeppelin raid, expected during the dark period at the end of the month. He was on stand-by there on the evening of March 31, 1916, when a Zeppelin warning was given over the telephone from the War Office.

Just before eight o'clock three Zeppelins had crossed the East Anglian coast. Two had come in over the suffolk coast, one south of Southwold, the other north of Aldeburgh. Another had crossed into Norfolk via the Would Lightship. From reports of their subsequent courses it seemed likely that they were heading for London.

The first two ships were the L13 and L15 with Mathy and Breithaupt in command. In the third, the L14, was Böcker, and somewhere close behind him over the sea was Peterson in the L16. It was the old and active quartet of veterans in ships which had come this way so often their crews swore they could find the way to London on their own. In their wake were the L7, L11, and L22. The weather favored this impressive squadron. The anti-cyclone which their meteorologists had found for them over northern France had spread north as predicted, and they had flown the North Sea against a dying west wind into a British sky deserted by cloud. South of the Wash the wind fell with the onset of night to a dead calm. In this lagoon of favorable weather Naval Airship Service headed for their targets, the great munitions factories at Stowmarket, Woolwich, Erith and Waltham Abbey.

Breithaupt was leading boldly in the L15, as he had done on October 13th, Mathy and Böcker following closely. She came in over Dunwich at a quarter to eight, dropping two high explosives in the sea as she came. Five minutes later she had reached Yoxford, where she dropped a fuel tank and an incendiary bomb, causing no damage. She dropped a flare at Framlingham at eight and at twenty minutes past eight dropped two high explosives and one incendiary on the docks at Ipswich. L15 kept on at forty miles an hour toward Colchester. At nine o'clock Breithaupt was able to see the course of the Thames and turned south-sou'west, passing over Orsett, with the river on his port beam, into the parish of No. 19 Reserve Squadron.

Mathy came in at Sizewell, passed Leiston at eight o'clock, and continued a southerly course. He turned northwest toward Kelsale and southwest again over Saxmundham, and at about twenty-six minutes past eight was near Charsfield, heading toward Ipswich.

His first objective was Stowmarket, which he approached from the southwest at quarter to nine, dropping two flares. His approach to the target was made easy for him when he picked up the lights of a train, the eight-fifteen from Ipswich, speeding below him in the darkness and followed it. The L13 was coming in for her run on the New Explosives Works when a searchlight and anti-aircraft guns there opened on her. Mathy immediately dropped twelve high explosives, which fell very close to the guns and the works buildings but scored no hits. Twenty-six rounds were fired by the six-pounder guns without effect. The action lasted about ten minutes, during which the Zeppelin, flying at a height of between 6,000 and 7,000 feet, was in the full beam of the searchlight for less than a moment.

Mathy sheered off to the westward. About a quarter past nine he came in for a second run over the New Explosives Works. Böcker, who was making for the same target, was at this moment some twenty-five minutes behind him, having difficulty with his navigation.

At this moment also Second Lieutenant Powell took off from Sutton's Farm, the first of the 19 Squadron pilots to get into the air. He was followed at nine twenty-five by Brandon from Hainault Farm, and five minutes after that Lieutenant Ridley went up from Joyce Green. Powell was at 8,500 feet, Ridley at 9,000, when they both saw a Zeppelin caught in a searchlight just north of Dartford and under fire from the guns.

As Brandon's machine left the ground, he swung to port off the line of flares, straightened up, and steered by a star. The B.E. went blindly on into the darkness, Brandon thinking, I hope to God the engine doesn't cut out. Getting his height he turned and there below was the airfield, well lit with flares. The engine was running beautifully, the machine climbing steadily, and the air was as smooth as a spring meadow. He thought of Lieutenant Collins. It isn't as bad as they say it is. . . .

The airship which Powell and Ridley had seen was Breithaupt in the L15. Powell was about a mile away and could do nothing for the time being, but Ridley, from Joyce Green, was close enough to attack. He fired twenty rounds at the airship and gave chase, but lost it in the darkness when the searchlights swung away from it. Below, Erith and Woolwich Arsenal lay exposed to Breithaupt's bombs. North, at Stowmarket, Mathy had dropped his second load of bombs. Little damage had been caused, however, and no casualties except one soldier slightly injured by a falling shell fragment, and the L13 was leaving the place as fast as she could, hit in one of her gas cells by a tracer shell. With only one balloon out of action she was by no means disabled, but a speedy withdrawal was called for. She dropped no more bombs after she was hit, but steered east-nor'east. She reached Stoneham about half past nine and was losing gas by that time to the extent that Mathy ordered three large petrol tanks to be jettisoned. The L13 was not seen again until she was near the coast, flying very low.

Meanwhile, Breithaupt, having lost Ridley, continued across the Thames. The London lights felt for him all round the sky and suddenly one of them stumbled across the long shape of the airship and held it fast. Immediately the other beams swung upon it and in a moment the L15 was caught in a pool of light from Erith, Dartford, Abbey Wood, Purfleet and Plumstead. The blinding deluge of white light was followed by the explosion of shells as the guns at Purfleet, Abbey Wood, Erith, Erith Marsh, Southern Outfall,

Plumstead Common and Plumstead Marsh opened a heavy
fire.

Breithaupt swung the great ship north to avoid the smoke
and stink of near misses from the accurate shooting of the
Purfleet battery, and at nine forty-three dropped twenty
high explosives and twenty-four incendiaries, meant for
Erith and Woolwich, on open fields at Rainham. As the
Zeppelin passed over the Rainham-Wennington Road at
quarter to nine jubilant gunners and ground observers saw
a shell burst so close aboard her that it must have hit.
Whether as a result of a hit in particular or the general effect
of the barrage, the L15 went off in a northeasterly direction
over Upminister. She passed over Brentwood at 9,000 feet.

Brandon had taken off from Hainault Farm at twenty-five
minutes past nine, and circled round the airdrome, climbing. At twenty to ten he had reached 6,000 feet when he
saw a Zeppelin high up on his right caught in the searchlight
beams. It was the L15. She appeared to be heading toward
a point directly in front of him, so he continued in that direction. He was keeping his mind strictly on his flying until
a "flaming onion" glowed in the sky. It seemed to go well
above the Zeppelin and looked like a near miss, but before
the shell had finished its course the Zeppelin had passed its
line of flight, and he saw that the near miss was an illusion,
for the airship was about three miles away. This shell had
probably been aimed at the Zeppelin but was a signal to the
pilots that she was about.

With his mind back on his airplane, Brandon realized
with alarm that he had been pulling back on the stick in a
heavy-handed way. After four or five minutes the Zeppelin
escaped from the searchlight. Shortly afterward, a single
powerful beam flashed across her twice but failed to hold
her. A second or two later Brandon picked up the Zeppelin.
She was growing larger and larger as they approached each
other, and finally passed over his head six or seven hundred

feet above him. He turned and followed and got underneath her, thinking what a magnificent sight she was against
the stars. He was climbing as hard as he could when suddenly he felt the airplane wallowing, with little or no power
left in the stick. He shoved the stick forward and sighed
with relief when the machine slowly put her nose down and
regained flying speed.

Finding himself passing the Zeppelin, he went on climbing on a wide circle to starboard, never losing sight of the
airship. Ahead of the huge nose, he turned in a wide circle
and came toward her. Suddenly she became gigantic below
him, and he found himself about to pass over her amidships.
The twin yellow flames of his exhaust and his identification
lights, which in his excitement he had forgotten to switch
off, were seen by some of the Zeppelin crew in the after engine gondola, and the word *"Flieger!"* (aviator!) passed
quickly round.

At about three or four hundred feet above the airship's
broad back Brandon released his first batch of Rankin incendiary darts. He strained his ears to hear above the noise
of his and the Zeppelin's engines, heard something like three
reports and thought he had made a hit. Then he heard
more reports, which sounded like bursts of machine-gun fire,
and began to feel doubtful of a hit after all.

The machine-gun fire was from the gun platform high on
the L15's back. As Brandon's B.E. had shown up above
them, one of the petty officers there had called through the
speaking tube connected to the captain's position in the
for'ard gondola fifty feet below, "Airplane just over
the ship!" Breithaupt, anxiously watching his dials, saw that
the ship was losing height from serious damage to her gas
containers. He left the control car and climbed the vertical
ladder inside the vast, swaying hull, the stench of escaping
hydrogen in his nostrils. He made out the lights and exhaust

flames of the attacking machine soon after he had reached the upper gun platform.

The gun crew there told him that bombs from the British airplane had straddled the ship, but it was very difficult to see anything clearly, and impossible to tell whether the damage to the ship had been done by shell splinters or unexploded bombs from the airplane or both. The vital facts were that the airship was losing gas from several balloons and the attacking airplane was following her, obviously preparing for another attack.

Brandon circled round the nose of the Zeppelin once more and turned round to get to its tail. As he passed down its looming flank streams of bullets came toward him. This fire was surprisingly accurate and he suddenly remembered that he still had all his lights on. He switched them off quickly and the fire began to fall off. He flew on for two or three hundred yards, then turned and maneuvered into a direct line with the course of the Zeppelin, about five hundred feet above it. The huge ship was dimly lit up below him by the stars. Closing his throttle he glided toward it at sixty miles an hour, the B.E.'s nose pointing just off the tail of the airship.

Trying to keep the machine on course he fumbled at the same time for an incendiary bomb. He found a bomb and tried to put it into the tube. It was pitch dark inside the cockpit nacelle and he felt blindly for the tube, getting more and more rattled. The thick British sweater which he had put on underneath his leather flying coat to keep out the intense cold seriously impeded him. He could not find the tube, and to his further alarm found he had to take his eyes off the Zeppelin for a moment. He peered and fumbled about with the bomb but still could not get it into the tube. Shooting a quick and frantic glance over the side to see where he was he was aghast to see that in a very few seconds he would have overshot the Zeppelin.

In his fluster and inexperience—he had only thirty hours' flying time to his name—he concluded that the airship had turned completely round and was in fact now coming toward him. Dumping the useless bomb in his lap, he hastily let off the third and fourth batches of incendiary darts, opened up the engine and turned right back on his course, heading in a southerly direction.

Experience would have told him that during the brief period when he had taken his eyes off the enemy—too brief for the airship to have turned round—either he had unconsciously pulled the nose of his machine up enough almost to have hidden the Zeppelin under his wing—a very common thing to happen, even with an object as huge as a Zeppelin—or the airship itself was diving, or, more likely, sinking away from him with leaking gas-bags. As it was, the Zeppelin had not turned about, and Brandon and Breithaupt were now flying on diverging courses. For some time, as he flew on south without sighting anything, the New Zealander was able to tell himself that the Zeppelin must have got a good start on him. As time went on this became more and more impossible to believe, and the truth began to dawn upon him. Angry with himself, he switched his lights on again and saw that he was at 8,000 feet. He cruised around at this height for a time and saw nothing, then dropped to 6,000 feet in the hope of further action.

It was five minutes to ten when Brandon dropped his first load of incendiary darts upon the L15. Five minutes later German radio operators listening on the Zeppelin wavelength picked up the following message:

"Have bombarded battery near Stowmarket with success. Am hit, have turned back. Will land at Hage about 4 a.m.—L13."

Almost on top of this signal came another, which ran: "Have been hit. Request Ostend keep watch on Airship wavelength—L15."

The most immediate effect of these two signals was upon Böcker in the L14. After losing his way for a time he had eventually picked up the main line of the Great Eastern Railway and followed it past Diss to Houghley, where he lost the line and continued on a south-sou'westerly course. He was east of Elmswell at ten o'clock when his wireless operator intercepted the distress signals from Mathy and Breithaupt. He continued on his course for a short time, then, at twenty-five past ten he picked up another message from Breithaupt:

"Require immediate assistance betweeen Thames and Ostend—L15."

Breithaupt was obviously in serious trouble. Five minutes after he had heard this message Böcker was over Sudbury. Whether in momentary confusion or in error, thinking he had reached Stowmarket, he dropped eight high explosives and nineteen incendiaries on the town as he passed over it from east to west, the first bomb actually falling just after the church clock had climbed the half hour. Three men and two women were killed, and one man wounded, all of them indoors. An inn and two houses were demolished, and many houses lost all their windows. Böcker then flew southwest past Bulmer and Halstead, and passed over Braintree at five-past eleven. Here he dropped three high explosives, killing four people, wounding three, and demolishing or partly damaging several houses.

Böcker was not the only one seriously influenced by the second message from the stricken L15. Peterson had been over an hour behind the leaders and had not crossed the coast until twenty-five past nine. An hour after this he was at Wroxham, and it was then that he too picked up Breithaupt's signal of distress. The significance of the news made him break off his course. He turned south-sou'west over Thorpe and Stoke Holy Cross to Long Stratton, turned west to New Buckenham, then at five-past eleven swung southwest to East Harling and North Topham, where he dropped a fuel tank. He passed Ixworth at twenty-five to twelve and was soon over Bury St. Edmunds. It was over this peaceful town, and not on Stowmarket or Erith or Woolwich that Peterson, who had bombed defenseless little Hertford on October 13th in similar circumstances, dropped his cargo. As he approached the town he was fired on by a mobile pom-pom section of the Royal Naval Anti-Aircraft Corps.

He aimed bombs at the guns and the town, twenty-one high explosives and five incendiaries in all, killed six people and injured another six, wrecked two cottages and badly damaged nine others. It was not a very fine night's work. He turned north and eventually went out to sea over Lowestoft at five past one, dropping one heavy high explosive, which damaged a streetcar shed and caused no casualties, and was fired on by a Naval twelve-pounder at Pakefield and six-pounder at Lowestoft in return, whereupon Peterson rose out of range and made for Germany at high speed.

If the radio signals from Mathy and Breithaupt had in fact shaken Böcker's nerve, he rapidly regained it. Flying on toward London, he passed Great Waltham at a quarter past eleven and Highwood Quarter at eleven twenty-five. He was fired on when over Doddinghurst by a pom-pom at Kelvedon Hatch.

This rattled Böcker again. He continued on course for a mile or two, then, as searchlights suddenly swung upon the L14, circled to the south and turned rightabout, passing right over the Kelvedon Hatch gun, which again fired. He aimed two high explosives at the gun, and nine more at Blackmore, but did no more than smash windows.

He flew steadily back northeast over Chelmsford, past Terling to a point between Braintree and Coggeshall, where he was sighted at ten past twelve. Then he circled round to the south of Castle Hedingham, went north and turned round from northeast to southwest over Great Yeldham.

He had changed his mind about running for home. The distress signals, plus the attentions of the Kelvedon Hatch gun, had thrown him out of his stride, but the lapse was only temporary. Now he had recovered something of his resolution and was pressing south again. At twenty to one he was over Braintree again, at five to one he dropped one high explosive at Springfield, a mile and a half east-nor'-east of Chelmsford, causing no damage, passed Chelmsford, turned south-sou'west at Stock, and was heard passing over Brentwood soon afterward.

Böcker was looking for a good target, but he could not face the London guns, so he headed south-sou'east, making for the oil storage tanks at Thames Haven. At half-past one he found it and dropped five explosives and twelve incendiaries. The Asiatic Oil Company had a very narrow escape when his bombs hit two empty tanks and started a small fire on the pier, which was soon extinguished. There were no casualties.

Under fire from Thames Haven, Kynockstown, and Pitsea, Böcker dropped a flare, which failed to ignite and fell on Canvey Island. He passed Rochford at forty minutes past one, Southminster ten minutes later and then Mersea. At five-past two he flew east of Colchester, passed between Mistley and Stratford St. Mary, and on to Wenstead and Ipswich.

He was sighted near Saxmundham at quarter to three, at Thelverton five minutes afterward, and finally flew out to sea south of Dunwich. There had been no further signals from either the L13 or the L15.

The L13 had been less seriously hit. Ten minutes after he had sent his warning signal from a position over Suffolk not far from the coast, Mathy sighted the headlights of the cars of a machinegun section of the R.N.A.S. at Wangford.

He dropped eleven high explosives and five incendiaries, aiming for the battery, and afterward seven high explosives and twenty incendiaries on the airfield at Covehithe, all from a height of only 2,000 feet, to which loss of gas had reduced him. None of the bombs caused any casualties or damage, but the loss of them enabled the crippled ship to rise to safer heights and make good speed for Germany. She reached the shelter of her shed at Hage at two o'clock, after hugging the Dutch coast all the way.

By three o'clock in the morning all the airships which had crossed the English coast, except one, had got clear again and were back over the sea steering for home. The L22, with *Kapitan-Leutnant* Dietrich in command, had carried out the usual feint on targets in the north. Over Cleethorpes at the mouth of the Humber he dropped six high explosives and had the luck to hit a chapel which was in use as a billet by the 3rd Manchesters. The chapel was completely destroyed, twenty-nine men inside it killed and fifty-three others badly wounded. One army Zeppelin, the LZ90 or 93, made a timid probe as far as Ipswich, then returned without result. Another approached the Suffolk coast but turned back short if it. Of the other naval airships, Buttlar in the L11, not surprisingly, once again turned back before reaching England, and so did the old L7, which was virtually on a crew training flight and not intended to raid.

After twenty-five past ten no further signals were picked up from the L15. At some point between the accurate attention of the East London guns and the end of Brandon's attack Breithaupt had decided that the damage done to the L15 necessitated making for Belgium. Three containers in the midships part of the ship were punctured and pouring out gas. The ship was losing height fast, and Breithaupt lightened her as much as he could, throwing over board two machine guns and every nonessential movable object.

The detritus fell in fields at Stock, South Hanningfield and Woodham Ferrers. By this time he had picked up the River Crouch. Slowly and with great difficulty the L15 followed the left bank of the river, passed Althouse at twenty-five past ten, at which point Breithaupt sent his second and last distress signal for help, flew between Burnham and Southminster and reached Foulness.

It was encouraging to see the gleam of water below the control car at last, but Breithaupt now had to decide whether his ship was sufficiently under control to risk crossing it. The Zeppelin, a few hours before the invincible dreadnought of the air, aloof and secure in the buoyant altitudes, able to face a thousand miles of ocean if need be, was a crippled thing now, and the little span of water across to Belgium as daunting as the great Ocean Sea to the earliest navigators.

Breithaupt circled twice over Foulness, trying his rudders, then pointed the airship's nose toward Belgium, fairly confident that he had about enough gas to keep him airborne as far as one of the army sheds. But he had underestimated the effects of the damage upon the delicately balanced structure of his ship. The finely wrought structure of aluminum girders had been so severely tried by the collapse of the three central balloons that the L15 broke her back and from a height of 2,000 feet fell into the sea at the Knock Deep about eleven o'clock, twenty miles from Foulness Point to the west, fifteen from Margate immediately to the south, the two outermost arms of the Thames.

Breithaupt had ordered all the men who could be spared up into the ship, and only he and two helmsmen remained in the forward control car. He was now thrown violently to the floor of the car, which quickly became completely submerged. He could feel his body "being tossed around like a cork by the masses of water which roared in." Somehow he managed to struggle out of the car and reach the surface, and the crew hauled him up into the airship. One of the two helmsmen also reached the surface, having lost all his teeth in the crash, but they never saw the other helmsman again.

The L15 was obviously sinking slowly, and they all huddled together on top of the ship, the broken midships section of which was completely submerged.

At half past three, four and a half hours later, one of the ship's company of the armed trawler *Olivine*, Lieutenant Mackintosh, R.N.R., sighted the broken monster riding on the sea. The night was very dark and there was a slight haze, but the sea was smooth. Mackintosh brought the *Olivine* near and estimated the situation. The Zeppelin was clearly in a sinking condition. The crew, who must be far gone from fatigue and exposure, clung to the top of the envelope, waving their arms feebly in surrender. There seemed to be about fifteen of them, but Mackintosh, knowing that there were other naval vessels close at hand, decided to risk taking them on board. He rescued the fourteen survivors of the L15's crew, then transferred them to a faster ship and resumed his patrol.

Captain John Bells, a Tyne sea pilot of South Shields, who was bringing the Danish steamer *Svanholm* from the Tyne to the Thames, was watching the sea ahead at quarter past six, when the ship was about a mile south of the Kentish Knock Lightship, when he sighted "a great commotion on the water." The weather was fine and clear, the sea smooth. The *Svanholm* steamed on toward the scene and about a quarter of a mile from her Bells could make out a small fleet of assorted destroyers, mine sweepers and patrol vessels maneuvering around a large object floating in the sea. A few moments later he saw that the wreckage was that of a disabled Zeppelin, the figures L15 painted in large red outlines on her port quarter.

The airship was broken completely in half, and there was

a big hole or vent in her envelope near the stern. She was about fifty feet out of the water aft and twenty feet for'ard, and her cars were submerged. Bells saw a man come out of a manhole door in the side of the Zeppelin and crawl along the envelope, trying at the same time to hold up his hands in surrender. Then another came out, and others followed. The airship, gray in color, seemed to be floating very buoyantly, and as the *Svanholm* steamed by efforts were being made by the encircling warships to get a tow rope on board her.

About seven o'clock word passed round Chatham Dockyard that a destroyer was bringing in the crew of a Zeppelin which had been brought down in the sea during the night. The dockers waited with excitement. Women in the rope factory who had just finished the night shift stayed on to see the Germans.

The destroyer berthed, and fourteen German sailors, the first Zeppelin aviators to set foot on English soil, came down the brow on to the dockside. The dockers gaped and some sensed the unreality of the occasion. These were the Zeppelin murderers, the worst of the bestial Huns.

The airship commander—someone whispered that he was a cousin of von Hindenburg—said in English, "I take all the responsibility upon myself. My men are not responsible." He expected them all to be shot as soon as they landed. He was a tall young officer, and at some time during the night he had managed to put on his full naval uniform for the occasion. On his right breast was the Iron Cross. He was handsome, and bore himself stiffly and proudly.

His men were less imposing, and looked far more the mechanic type than seamen. A few of them wore their own uniforms of navy blue serge, but eight or nine of them had no shoes or socks, three or four were in shirt sleeves, and one had no trousers. Some had been given blankets, others tarpaulin jackets. They stood about on the dockside for a few minutes, then those barely clothed and barefoot or needing medical attention were helped into a naval motor ambulance and driven to a barracks outside the dockyard. Nine of the more serious cases were transferred to Fort Spit Hospital.

There some of the men talked freely. They told the hospital staff that lots had been drawn in the airship as to who would remain behind to blow it up when retreat was found to be impossible. A junior officer had drawn the suicidal mission, but when the time came for Breithaupt to give the signal it was found impossible to carry it out.

The remainder were marched under a Royal Marine escort to a preliminary place of detention. Breithaupt, who had put on his long sealskin coat, walked impassively at their head, but some of the others looked cast down and bitter, and obviously felt deeply the ignominy of their position—eagles with broken wings. It was April Fool's Day. There were no scenes of public jubilation as they marched. The dockers and Royal Navy men watched them in silence, and most of the route lay over ground closed to the general public. A little later, however, a small number of neutral journalists were allowed to talk to them.

All the men were young, between the ages of twenty-five and thirty-five. Breithaupt himself said he was thirty-three. They seemed strong and healthy, and were quite cheerful. All were obviously feeling a certain amount of relief. As the men who had bombed theatreland they had all expected to be shot as soon as they reached English soil. Questioned about the action of the previous night, some of the men said that they had been hit as many as three times before they could drop any bombs, and the radio operator said that signals of distress had been sent out at twenty-five past ten and at ten to eleven, just before the airship hit the sea, but they seemed to know little of the details of their flights. Two or three of them said that they could see only land or water on dark nights, though their officers knew where they were.

"We do not know," said one man, "what our officers may see through the glasses; we could see nothing." Asked about their feelings on killing women and children, another man said, "We do as we are ordered." Only one man, a mechanic, would admit to having been on a raid before. He said that he had twice been over England.

The officers were not very communicative. Lieutenant Kuhne, the Second Officer of the L15, spoke English fluently and said that he had spent some time in England before the war. Asked what his business had been, he smiled and said, "That I cannot tell." He refused to express any opinion on the military effectiveness of the raids.

Breithaupt said: "You must not suppose that we set out to kill women and children. We have higher military aims. You would not find one officer in the German army or navy who would go to kill women and children. Such things happen accidentally in war." When told, he would not believe that the Zeppelins had so far only hurt civilians and damaged civilian property, but had damaged no worthwhile military target at all. "It is obvious," he said, "that you are being deprived of the truth."

Someone said, "Were you at five thousand feet when you were hit?"

Breithaupt said, "I wouldn't think of flying so low over England."

A journalist asked, "Is it true that you signaled to the patrol ship for rescue?"

"No, no," Breithaupt said quickly. "I would never dream of doing that. We would rather take the risk of losing our lives."

By this time the L15 was no more. Determined attempts had been made to tow her into port, but she eventually foundered off Westgate as dawn came over the water, and her secrets went with her.

The Times, though saluting the shared triumph, was, as ever, cautious. "Just as gunfire is a protective measure," it said, "so are airplanes when boldly and skilfully handled; and it is a combination of the two methods, together with development of searchlights, which will some day make it far more difficult for Zeppelins to raid our shores."

With British action in support of the French Army imminent in France, London could not expect to be free of further German frightfulness for very long. The pilots of No. 18 Wing, who obviously needed all the night flying practice they could get, would have to look to their recent shared laurels.

8. 39 SQUADRON

There was some cause for optimism. The very Zeppelin which had made the October 13th attack upon London was at the bottom of the sea off the pleasure coast of Kent; Breithaupt was in custody at Donnington Hall. The first of that quartet of veterans who formed the heart of the Zeppelin offensive was out of action. Those engaged in the air defense were encouraged and the people of London gratified, if not exactly transported with joy. A Zepp was down, but then these victories, though infrequent, had been reported before, remote triumphs of heroism on the overseas fronts. It was at home, in the dark skies over London, that the people waited to see their ordeal avenged. If our gunners and airmen were to knock down Zepps now that things were better organized, it must be where it would be seen by the greatest number, a torch in the frightened London night.

April Fool's Day for the German airship arm was followed up by a further breath of spring for the defenses. First, there was a promise of more effective armament for the airplanes of the home defense units. Warneford's activities against Zeppelins had been a mixed blessing. In his attack on a Zeppelin on May 17, 1915, he had used "flaming bullets," a type of incendiary. Warneford was certain he had hit the airship with them, yet the hydrogen in the gas-bags did not ignite. The failure was mistakenly put down to the use of an inert gas between envelope and gas-bag skin which prevented the incendiary charge from burning, and the machine gun was abandoned in favor of the bomb. It was with a bomb, dropped from above, that Warneford subsequently destroyed the LZ38, and this success proved a similarly misleading example in arms and tactics. The bombs then in use, which exploded so luckily for this gallant airman, were not normally so reliable, but his success with them resulted in their being retained along with the corollary that only an attack from above an airship guaranteed any chance of success. In fact, the whole method was altogether too uncertain.

It was not understood, first, that to ask a pilot untrained in the little-known science of night flying to bring a machine, the performance of which was far inferior to that of a Zeppelin, into position above the enemy at night, to juggle an incendiary into the R.L. tube, to keep the airship below in sight, and to maintain a generally unstable airplane, with no such later refinements as trimming tabs to keep it steady, in a good position above the target, was to ask for a miracle. Further, Warneford's bullets had failed—if they really had hit the Zeppelin's gas-bags—because there had been insufficient air to combine with the hydrogen and allow the incendiary charge to ignite. It needed no protective gas to swamp them, and this theory was in fact pure myth.

The clumsiness and general unsuitability of the R.L. tube was realized soon after the B.E.s of 5th Wing had taken off with it on October 13th, and it had already been scheduled as obsolete before Brandon's attack upon the L15. The poor results of his persistent and courageous performance that night finally showed up the unreliability of bombing from above. His explosive darts did not go off, and he had such difficulty in making his attack that he misjudged the behavior of the Zeppelin and finally lost it altogether. It was

not by any means entirely a case of inexperience. Brandon
was let down badly by his weapons and by his tactical training.

Successful techniques of this kind are evolved only by
hard and dangerous practice, but dissatisfied pilots now felt
that the old unwieldy method of attack should be scrapped.
Experiments had been under way since the beginning of
1915 in the development of an incendiary-plus-explosive bullet which could be fired from a machine gun. The general
idea was for an aircraft to carry armor-piercing, explosive-
incendiary, and tracer bullets mixed alternately in its
drums. The machine would then attack from below the
airship, and between them the armor-piercing bullets and
the explosive charges in the incendiaries would blast
through solid structure, envelope fabric and gas-bag skin so
that air could flow into the gas-bag on the heels of the bullets and allow the incendiary charge to work and ignite the
hydrogen.

A special luminous "tracer" bullet first developed at the
Royal Laboratory at Woolwich to help the pilot's aim by
showing up in the dark was in use by home defense airplanes. The tracer bullet produced in the Royal Laboratory tended to go off dangerously in the gun and there were
so many failures that it was dropped in 1915 when the pressure of other work prevented the Laboratory from carrying
out the further exhaustive tests necessary. But when the
new Ministry of Munitions was formed they took over the
firm of Messrs. Aeromotors and gave them the task of pro-
ducing a good tracer bullet.

At the beginning of April 1916, experiments were still in
progress there using different tracing mixtures. At that time,
there were no explosive-incendiaries in service and only
some of the old, volatile tracer. It was an alarming state of
affairs, with the threat of a spring Zeppelin offensive. Then,
on April 12th, there was some progress. The Director of

Air Organization sent out the following letter to headquarters units of the home defense airplanes:

"It is proposed to issue shortly an explosive bullet for use against Zeppelins, and in this connection, I am directed to inform you that its use is strictly restricted to firing from an airplane against an airship."

There were three separate types of explosive-incendiary bullets under development for the Navy and Army air services, and one of them was actually in production. This was the Buckingham .303 bullet. Its existence was owed to the foresight of its inventor, J. F. Buckingham, the owner of a Coventry engineering company, who had studied the structure and potentialities of airships, and in January 1915, had taken out a patent for an anti-Zeppelin bullet, based upon phosphorus for its incendiary mixture.

His first bullet, a .45 caliber, impressed Admiralty representatives so much when it set fire to balloons at a range of four hundred yards in April 1915, that he was encouraged to apply the same principles to the standard .303 caliber. Samples of these reached the Admiralty in October 1915, after Breithaupt's raid, and were judged successful enough for an order to be placed immediately. The R.N.A.S. began to receive the Buckingham bullet in December, and the R.F.C., with the urgent task of home defense looming, became very successful. They decided to issue the bullet to the new home defense units as soon as it was available. Experiments with two other explosive bullets, the Brock and the Pomeroy, were also promising well, and were in their final stages.

On April 15th there came another important step in home defense. All the units detailed for home defense in the London area recently gathered for administrative purposes under Major Higgins' No. 19 Reserve Squadron were officially designated No. 39 Home Defense Squadron, with Major Higgins as its commanding officer. With the creation of this unit, London's own anti-aircraft squadron, came a new policy of concentrating its strength upon airfields northeast of London on the model of the temporary detachments of the previous October 13th, using the two fields which had been taken over at that time.

No time was lost in moving men and machines to Hainault Farm and Sutton's Farm. The scheme was to maintain a flight of six airplanes at each airfield, and to locate a third to house another flight, which for the time being remained at Hounslow, the squadron's headquarters and depot. There all training and organization were carried out, and from there the two outlying stations were supplied and administered. Hounslow became a center of incessant, excited activity, as Major Higgins began the job of building his new squadron.

Night flying was organized for all new pilots reporting for duty with the squadron, and experiments began there into new methods of operating at night. The new order came into being just in time for the Sutton's and Hainault Farm pilots of 39 to meet the next Zeppelin attacks, which were made by both the Imperial navy and the German army airship services with renewed determination.

Zeppelins appeared over England again on April 24th. It seemed a good day for them from the weather point of view. The British Isles and the western half of the North Sea were coming under the influence of a depression approaching from the west. The wind over the central North Sea was southerly to southwesterly, its velocity at about 1,500 feet about 40 to 50 miles an hour. Further west it was even greater, and rain was falling as far east as Nottingham. But the German weather forecasters could see none of this. Their prognostication was colored by the anti-cyclone seen to be extending its influence westward as far as Holland and Belgium. The wind was light from the south and the sky cloudless. With a rising barometer and an absence of reports from the British Isles they predicted fair weather, and ten naval Zeppelins left their sheds with confidence.

Bombing England was, however, a secondary consideration this time. For some time the German High Command had been in touch with the leaders of the Sinn Fein movement in Ireland. Speaking in the United States in 1914, John Redmond had said, "Not an Irishman in America today would not rejoice to hear that a German army was marching in triumph across England from Yarmouth to Milford Haven." Now the German navy was to synchronize a bombardment of the British coast with a rebel rising in Ireland on the 25th, and the naval Zeppelin service was ordered out in force to support it, with some airships detailed to make a diversionary raid on targets a little way inland as they reached the English coast on the evening previous to the bombardment. Accordingly, eight Zeppelins left the north German coast on the 24th in conjunction with a fleet of four battle cruisers, six light cruisers and a torpedo flotilla. The old Zeppelins L6 and L7 accompanied the ships part of the way. Later that evening six airships crossed the East Anglian coast. One made for Lincolnshire, four for Norfolk, and one for Suffolk.

Peterson, in the L16, crossed the coast at quarter past ten, felt his way to Thetford, having dropped a bundle of illustrated German newspapers by parachute at Kimberley on the way, circled to the west, turned back northeast, and when he was fired on from Newmarket Heath at half past twelve, dropped eighteen high explosives in a line across the middle of Newmarket, damaging houses in the center of the town, injuring one man and killing the champion racehorse Coup-de-Main in its stables on Bury Road. He dropped another high explosive and an incendiary outside the town, then made off at high speed to the northeast. When he returned to Germany he reported that he had bombed Cambridge.

Dietrich in the L21 made for Stowmarket, but mobile guns of the Royal Garrison Artillery at Badley Park and Thorney Green and two fixed six-pounders at Stowmarket gave him such a hot reception that he retreated in a hurry, having wasted nine high explosives. He crossed the coast about the same time as Peterson, then joined the cruisers. Schubert in the L23 followed the line of the Broads, dropped nine high explosives near Ridlington, which broke the windows of a church and a farmhouse and damaged a cottage, then a further six near the R.N.A.S. station at Bacton, as he was leaving the coast, displacing the searchlight there. *Korvetten Kapitan* Schuetze dropped almost the whole of his load, nineteen high explosives and twenty-six incendiaries, over the village of Dilham. There were no casualties except an unfortunate woman who died of shock. At Bacton he was fired on by three-pounder guns of the R.N.A.A.C. and one gas-bag was hit and collapsed. He barely regained his base. Two other airships appeared overland, Proells in the L13 and Ehrlich in the L17, but the net result of their activities was one window broken at Alford.

This feeble demonstration completed, which can hardly have paid its way, even as a feint, the airship squadron took up its main job of scouting for the bombarding ships. The old L6 and L7 had brought the squadron as far as 4° east, and had returned to Germany at four o'clock on the morning of the 25th when the naval attack had reached its objective. Stelling in the L9 remained with the ships for the whole operation, and was sighted off the St. Nicholas Lightship at ten past four, when the German warships were beginning their fire. L21 was well on its way home when Dietrich turned round about two o'clock, joined the fleet, and along with the L16 scouted ahead of it as it approached the coast. The three airships—the L11, 13 and 23—were watching its northwest flank, the L17 and L20 its southern, as it made the coast, then the L17 went off northwest to the Lincolnshire coast to watch for any counterattack from the Humber. Covered by their watchful eyes, the German cruisers threw their shells into Yarmouth and Lowestoft.

There was no interference from the air with the Zeppelin squadron. One machine had gone up from Thetford at midnight, one from Dover just before three and another at four, and none of them saw anything of the raiders. But it was to be a long day.

Flying weather improved on the 25th. Neither of the fronts observed by British and German weather forecasters on the previous day developed as expected. The depression over Britain did not spread far east and the wind had moderated considerably over the North Sea in time to give the German naval airships easy flying conditions on the 24th, though wind and cloud over the coast hampered them. On the 25th the anti-cyclone centered over Germany and the Baltic extended its benign influence over the southern part of the North Sea, southern England and France. Conditions were not affected by depressions in the vicinity of Ireland and Iceland, and the barometer continued to rise. The wind, which earlier in the day varied from 25 to 30–40 miles per hour over East Anglia, diminished to less than 15 over the North Sea during the evening. The sky was then cloudless south of the Wash.

It had been almost a year since the German army airship service had made a serious attack on London. On this April evening of fair weather they came again in strength. *Hauptmann* Linnarz, their best and most daring commander before, led the attack again in a brand new Zeppelin of the latest type, the LZ97. With him were the LZ81, LZ88, LZ93, and the ZXII, one of the oldest army Zeppelins.

Oberleutnant Lampel, Linnarz's second in command, afterward described the progress of the L97. The airship's crew had only landed at dawn from a long cross-country training flight. They refreshed themselves with a short sleep

in the forenoon, then worked all-out in the afternoon preparing their ship for the raid. As evening drew on the ship
left her shed and took off for England.

"We cast one brief glance round our home airdrome," says
Lampel, "which lay flooded in the light of the setting sun,
and then started the engines. Every man was filled with an
inexpressible joy; we were off to England!

"A long journey lay before us, the first section being over
conquered Belgian territory. After a short time Brussels had
been passed, and darkness drew on apace. It was well into
the night before we reached the coast, and for hours after
that we cruised over the English Channel, which could be
seen dark green, almost black, beneath us. Night pressed
down menacingly upon us, only millions of stars glittered in
the heavens, and reflected their light in the waves. But here
and there beneath us were red flecks which we knew were
not the reflected images of stars. They were lookout vessels
and patrol boats, through whose funnels we could see, deep
down, the glowing furnaces. Except for these there was no
light at all; everything was shrouded in unfathomable darkness and silence.

"Over England at last! Our hands are drawn to the bomb
release lever like iron to a magnet: but the time has not yet
come. London is our objective, and there still remains a
good two hours' flight before we arrive at our journey's end.
We lean out of the gondola portholes once more, and pick
out landmarks and locate them on the map as well as we can
from that height in the bright moonlight. Below us everything is as still as death, and the country is perfectly darkened. Not a gun is fired, not a searchlight directed at us.
The English naturally do not want to give away prematurely
the positions of their defense batteries and the towns which
they protect.

"At high speed we steer for the city, the Commander
standing ready on the bombing platform. The electric lamps

which he has now switched on glow with a dull, vari-colored light. His hand is on the buttons and levers. 'Let go!' he cries. The first bomb has fallen on London! We lean over the side. What a cursed long time it takes between release and impact while the bomb travels those thousands of feet! We fear that it has proved a dud—until the explosion reassures us. Already we have frightened them; away goes the second, an incendiary bomb. It blazes up underneath and sets fire to something, thereby giving us a point by which to calculate our drift and ground speed. While one of us releases the bombs and another observes results, I make rapid calculations at the navigation table. Now the second incendiary hit is also visible. The flames have scarcely leapt convulsively upward in a shower of red sparks before we hear the shattering report of an explosion, so loud that it is plainly audible above the roar of the propellers. At the same time on come the searchlights, reaching after us like the gigantic spiders' legs; right, left and all around. In a moment the bright body of the ship lies in the beams.

" 'Hard a-port!' The steersman spins his wheel, and in a moment the great ship obeys its helm. We are out of the dazzling rays and once more in the depths of night. But it is no longer pitch dark. The countless beams of searchlights fill the sky with a vivid light. They have lost us—strike, as it were, wildly past us, catch us once again, go on over us; one remains still, the others hunt around, crossing it or searching along it for the objective, while we steer in quite a different direction."

But Lampel's navigation was not as accurate as he imagined, and the bombs which he thought had hit London had actually fallen to the northeast of the city. About ten minutes to eleven forty-seven incendiary bombs had fallen from the LZ97 in a line between Fyfield and Ongar, and the only damage done was to a shed. Twenty minutes later Linnarz dropped twelve high explosives along a line curving from

the southwest round to the southeast between Forest Farm
and Aldeborough, just west of 39 Squadron's field at Hainault Farm. Linnarz was running into danger. After he had
dropped a thirteenth high explosive at Newbury Park he
began to encounter very heavy gunfire from below, and
turned off sharply northwest. He reached Seven Kings with
the anti-aircraft fire increasing in intensity all the time, and
here he was attacked in succession by two B.E.2c's of 39
Squadron.

Lieutenant W. Leefe Robinson had taken off from Sutton's Farm and had reached 8,000 feet when he sighted the
Zeppelin about 2,000 feet above him and opened fire, but his
tracers fell away short and the airship soon outclimbed him.
Captain Arthur Harris, from Hounslow, also got to within
2,000 feet of the LZ97 and had opened fire when his gun
jammed and could not be freed. Two other of the 39th
Squadron pilots went up from Sutton's Farm, two more from
Hounslow, and two from Hainault Farm, but the raiders
all got clear.

Linnarz and his crew were severely shaken by the fierce
gunfire and the airplane attacks. A year had made a great
difference to the London air defenses, and the Army airships
had received a welcome which sent them back once more
into obscurity. Linnarz lost no time in running for home
after Harris' attack. All the way to the coast the LZ97 had
to run the gauntlet of the guns. Lampel says:

"This mad frolic continues for hours on end. We lose all
idea of the passage of time as we fly on, every half a minute
releasing another bomb. Every explosion is observed and its
position pin-pricked on the map. It is difficult to understand
how we manage to survive the storm of shell and shrapnel,
for, according to the chronometer, we have spent a good
hour under that furious fire. When London lies far behind
us, we can still recognize it distinctly; the searchlights are
still stabbing the darkness—more than sixty of them—looking

for the bird that has already flown. Silence closes in around us, and everything beneath seems stricken with death.

"The English coast lies behind us, receding farther and farther into the distance, and the foam on the crests of the waves beneath shimmers in the moonlight as though it is phosphorescent. A vague twilight envelops us. It is pitch dark inside the gondola, with the exception of the very faint spots of light from the pointers of the instruments. Many-colored stars still dance before our eyes, the results of the dazzling searchlights. We are over the sea. The man at the elevating wheel rubs his eyes, blinks, quickly slides open the shutter of his lamp, and flashes its rays on his instruments. The gondola is lit up, as the light gleams on the aluminum. Then hell is let loose! They have long lain in wait for us down below there, and now the little dot of a gondola light has betrayed us. In a moment the searchlights of the warships in the Thames Estuary have caught us and hold us fast. Again a withering blast of fire is directed against us. 'Put out that light!' The Commander reaches over the steersman's shoulder and switches it off. But the ship, once caught, cannot get away from the searchlights. Shell after shell shrieks up at us, among them incendiary shells; they burst dangerously near. After ten minutes the light grows fainter, and the firing dies away. Again we travel through the gloom and silence, hour after hour."

The LZ97 was the only airship which came near to success that night. The LZ93 dropped her bombs at Harwich and at Shotley, near the naval camp there. A 240-pound bomb which fell at Parkeston Quay sank through the new soil into the mud below and could not be found, even at a depth of twenty feet. Guns at Shotley gave the Zeppelin a hot send-off and she departed dropping her remaining bombs near the Sunk Lightship. The LZ81, *Oberleutnant* Barth, made a brief appearance off the Downs, dropped eight high explosives all round the little steamer *Argus* in Deal Harbor, was fired at from Walmer and retreated seaward. The LZ88 came in over Herne Bay, wandered over Whitstable, Sturry, Preston, Canterbury, Wingham and Chislet Marshes, and went out to sea again, having scattered her load about the open countryside. The old ZXII did not make England at all. Chased by a French plane off Ostend shortly before three o'clock, she was lucky to escape. A single army airship returned on the following night, but came only a little way inland over Kent and retreated after dropping her bombs in the sea off Deal.

On May 2nd the spring offensive of the Zepplin services was brought to a close by a sprawling combined raid of eight naval airships and one army, extending from Cromarty in the north of Scotland to the Wash. Seven ships were ordered to reconnoiter and bomb the naval bases at the Firth of Forth, the Tay and Cromarty, the army ship, the LZ98, to attack the Humber, and the remaining navy ship industrial targets in Yorkshire. None of the airships fulfilled their missions, and the success of the whole operation was symbolized by the three Zeppelins which wasted their bombs upon a patch of burning heather at Danby Moor, set alight by a previous incendiary bomb. Stabbert in the L20 spent so much time over Scotland that he could not regain his base, and his ship finally blundered across the Norwegian coast and crashed into the Hafrsfjord, where she broke in two. There was a further disaster on May 4th when the L7, coming out to attack the British fleet which was supporting a R.N.A.S. raid on the Zepppelin sheds at Tondern, was hit by a six-inch shell from the light cruiser *Galatea* and fell in burning ruin into the sea. The submarine E31 rescued seven survivors and sank the floating wreck of the Zeppelin. After this loss the Zeppelin services did not venture over England again until they began to take delivery of a new and very much improved Zeppelin, the L30 class, in the summer.

As they awaited their new ships and made plans for a greater offensive than ever before, in England the air defenses of London worked hard to improve their technique. Although half the machines at Hounslow were constantly in use for ordinary training purposes, night flying was carried out whenever possible. There were some bad accidents. Second Lieutenant Frederick Sowrey, the first flying officer to join No. 39 Squadron on its formation, who had been selected by Major Higgins to become Assistant to the Squadron Adjutant, Captain Jim Annsley, was standing with Higgins by the hangars at Hounslow one very black and dirty night watching M. M. Tomlinson, one of 39's flight commanders, taking off for a night practice. On the take-off, Tomlinson, who was short-sighted, had trouble. Horrified, they saw his navigation lights go out as he crashed into the ground at the edge of the field. Tomlinson was alive, but he lost the sight of one eye. A particularly gruesome fate was that of a pilot, Binden-Blood, who spun a S.E.4 into the ground and stumbled from the wreckage covered in flame from head to foot to run wildly about the field until he collapsed and died.

The system of lighting by flares was greatly improved under Major Higgins' direction. The old type of flare, simply a bucket containing half a gallon of gasoline, was wasteful and burned only for half an hour. Higgins introduced the new Money flare, an asbestos wick in a wire container, which used kerosene and burned steadily through mist and fog. The actual number of flares was increased so that a pilot took off with a single line of five flares arranged at intervals of one hundred yards on his left-hand side. One more flare was placed at right angles to the far end of the long arm to form an L. Various methods to aid a pilot in judging height when coming in to land at night were tried out at Hounslow. One of those thought well of by pilots was that of a red light mounted on a pole near the end of the flare path, known as a "gliding light," but this was never adopted.

Rather more dangerous were the experiments with new weapons. Still lacking a good incendiary-explosive bullet, the squadron made tests with the Le Prieur rocket in use in France against kite balloons. This impressive weapon was fitted into a tube, of which there were three mounted on each outer pair of wing struts on the B.E.2c's, and touched off electrically by the pilot operating switches in the cockpit. The rocket was unreliable and dangerous to operate, however, because separate rockets took very different lengths of time to leave the tube after the pilot had made his switch and often did not leave it at all, but went off aboard the aircraft. At the end of April, however, a firm order was placed for supplies of the Buckingham bullet, and in May two further types of explosive-incendiary bullet were ordered for use against the Zeppelins.

Sharing the mistaken belief that the exhaust gases from a Zeppelin's motors were piped between the envelope and the skin of the gas-bags to form a layer of inert gas which would prevent an incendiary bullet from burning, Commander F. A. Brock of the Intelligence Section of the Air Department at the Admiralty had experimented with an explosive-incendiary bullet which would blow a path through both skins for the air to mix with the hydrogen and allow the incendiary mixture to ignite. Tests and experiments were made against balloons until the bullet was judged effective at a range of 800 yards, and an order was placed for half a million of the bullets.

An order of the same size was given to Mr. John Pomeroy, an Australian, who had been turned down when he first submitted an explosive bullet to the Admiralty in August 1914, but whose invention was eventually sponsored by the Munitions Inventions Department in December 1915, tested and found effective, though volatile. It was basically a better bullet than the Brock, but for a time was prone to far too many premature explosions. In June an improved form of the Buckingham bullet went into production, and by the end of July the trouble with the Pomeroy had been largely cured and the bullet was officially approved in August. These new anti-Zeppelin bullets, which seemed so promising, began to reach the Home Defense Squadrons of the Royal Flying Corps about the same time as the new L30 class Zeppelins occupied the hangars of the German naval airship service.

With fair flying weather predicted for the ripening summer and the autumn, a clash of new weapons could soon be expected. With France already convulsed in the great holocaust and slaughter of the Somme Battle, the offensive which the British Army had launched to relieve the cruelly battered French at Verdun, England had reason to look forward with uneasy fear to her own time of trial, to the battle for London.

9. ZEPP SUNDAY

In June and July important things happened in England and in Germany which foretold the seriousness of the coming struggle for the mastery of the English sky. Early in June two young pilots named Frederick Sowrey and Wulstan Tempest joined B flight of No. 39 Squadron at Sutton's Farm, where the flight commander was that William Leefe Robinson who had dueled briefly with Linnarz on the night of April 25th. There were a number of pilots at the three airfields administered by No. 39 who now had some experience of attacking Zeppelins, including Brandon at Hainault Farm, who had come the closest of all to actually bringing one down.

During June the War Office decided that the practice of combining ordinary training with anti-Zeppelin patrols did not work. Machines were being too roughly handled by trainee pilots to be of any use against the Zeppelins, and the experienced pilots were being overburdened by having to combine the duties of instructors by day and those of Home Defense pilots by night. Flying training was removed from the duties of the Home Defense squadrons and on June 25th they were formed into a special, independent Home Defense Wing, under the command of Lieutenant Colonel Holt, with headquarters at Adastral House. The new wing comprised, besides No. 39 Squadron, Nos. 33 at Bramham Moor,

36 at Cramlington, 38 forming at Castle Bromwich, 50 at Dover, and 51 at Norwich. A searchlight unit of six lights was attached to each Home Defense squadron.

In the middle of July the new Zeppelin L31, second of the new line, with improved bomb load and performance, came off the stocks—and was given to Heinrich Mathy. A fortnight later she was flying over Lowestoft as one of a raiding force of ten naval airships which were prevented from causing more than slight damage to targets in England by thick mist and fog.

The naval Zeppelins returned in force on the 31st. Of the eight ships which crossed the coast, the L16 reached Newark, bombing as she went, but caused no casualties. Mathy in the L31 broke some windows at Thanet, the rest meandered at a cautious height over Norfolk, Suffolk and Cambridgeshire, and the damage their random bombs created was negligible. Again, pursuing airplanes saw nothing in the thick mist which lay over East Anglia and had great difficulty in getting down safely.

These timid raids were followed by two more in early August. On the 2nd, six Zeppelins were over England. The L21 bombed Thetford airfield with no effect, and three other ships covered the same area, with similar results. As it dropped its bombs over Harwich, the L11 was hit by a shell and reached home with difficulty. Mathy spent some time over Thanet again, then flew over Deal and Dover but was given such a rough passage by the guns that he hurriedly retreated and dropped all his bombs in the sea. Naval pilots flew close to some of the Zeppelins, but none was able to get in an attack.

On the 8th, nine Zeppelins raided various targets from Norfolk to Northumberland.

A thick mist shrouded most of England. The L24 bombed Hull and killed ten persons, the L11 raided Whitley Bay, the small seaside resort north of Newcastle-on-Tyne, injur-

ing a man, a woman and three children, and was chased unsuccessfully by Flight Lieutenant De Roeper in a B.E.2c
from Redcar airdrome. Courageously, he held on to the
Zeppelin until she disappeared in the fog twenty miles out
to sea.

These were all tenative, ineffectual raids. Commanders
were getting used to the feel of their new ships, and waiting
for the bad weather to break and give them a chance to show
what the L30's could do. On August 24th Mathy, now beginning to get his hand in with the L31, gave a foretaste to
the uneasy citizens of London. Alone of four ships which
crossed the coast he got through to London, and history repeated itself almost twelve months to the day. This time he
came toward the capital up the Thames Estuary. Passing
Canvey Island and Barking, he turned south, crossed the
river at Millwall, skirted Woolwich, went back over the
Thames and returned to sea over Shoeburyness. His bombs
fell on Millwall, Deptford, Greenwich, Blackheath, Eltham
and Plumstead in the early hours of the morning, killed
nine persons, injured forty, and did much damage to houses
in all these districts.

Fifteen airplanes were up in the starless gloom of that
night. Four pilots caught glimpses of Zeppelins through the
clouds, but only Woodhouse of No. 50 Squadron at Dover
got close enough to attack one. About quarter past two
Dover's warning whistles went off. People heard the throb
of Zeppelin engines above them and went to their windows,
even wandered out into the streets in their night attire, to
see what could be seen. There were cheers and a wave of
excitement as they watched the searchlights flicker rapidly
round the sky, then pause, retrack, and splash the huge
shape of the Zepp with white light. Woodhouse saw her and
strained for height, holding his B.E. on the lip of a stall.

Peterson in his new L32, blinded by the probing light,
saw him as he flashed across the beams. The searchlights

were alert and accurate and made the veteran Zeppelin commander anxious. The solitary B.E. did not worry him. He
knew his airship could easily outclimb the panting airplanes,
but he was thrown off his stroke. Sidestepping the searchlights he turned off over the Channel, rising out of reach of
the frustrated Woodhouse.

Woodhouse climbed after him and managed to keep him
in view for a while. Then thick cloud hid the Zepp like a
tiger in the brush. When the B.E. came out of the cloud
Woodhouse saw her again. He was at 7,000 feet, and quickly
estimated that the Zepp was a good 2,000 feet above him, but
he thought it was worth a try and emptied a drum at her.
The red-yellow dotted lines curved up into the darkness
from the hot muzzle of his Lewis and fell away below the
vanishing gas-bag.

While Woodhouse was struggling to reload, one hand on
the stick, the other pushing the heavy drum into place on
the gun above his head, the Zeppelin disappeared into another cloud bank and he never saw her again. He plunged
into cloud himself and lost his bearings. Only a dim haze
of yellow light in the heart of the gloom, where the searchlights still fingered the clouds seeking Peterson, led him
home.

It had been Mathy's night. His alone of the twelve naval
airships to begin the raid had got to London, the first Zeppelin to penetrate her growing defenses since the October
13th raid of the previous year. Of the seven R.F.C. machines
to go up none came within miles of the master bomber and
not a single bullet was fired at him.

The raid crowned the successes of the summer raids and
enraged Londoners. The Germans had got away with it
again. The people were told that R.F.C. pilots went up
against the Zepps, but the only aircraft they ever saw in the
threatening night above them were the arrogant, casually
cruising Zeppelins. The press demanded action. Angry

questions were asked in the House. Sir David Henderson, Director General of Aeronautics at the War Office, came under a hotter fire than Mathy. The burden of outraged protest was always the same. *What was the R.F.C. doing?*

At Sutton's Farm people had smiled indulgently when the dashing flight commander, Lieutenant Robinson, or his number two, Second Lieutenant Fred Sowrey, brushed roof-tops with their spinning wheels, loosening tiles with the rush of air. Farmer Tom Crawford had managed to control his feelings as he looked over his hedge and watched the two black-painted planes score streetcar lines across what had once been his best grazing land and stain the emerald grass with oil and exhaust dirt until it was nothing but 500 square yards of scorched earth and stubble. When Leefe Robinson looped the loop six times in succession over the farmhouse he even made jokes about it "curdling my cows' milk," shook his fist in mock outrage and threatened to "have the law" on him.

It was all in a good cause. Better to have Lieutenant Robinson zooming over your head than a Uhlan lancer swinging his boots up on your kitchen table. When they looked up and shaded their eyes and saw the two biplanes chasing each other across the sun the people of Hornchurch grinned and said, "It's Robby again. He'll break his neck one of these days." Sometimes Farmer Crawford's patience with the continual racket and smell of airplanes wore unavoidably very thin, and his pretended air of disgust became real, his complaints hot and genuine. He gave expression to his feelings one day to Leefe Robinson. Equally exasperated, the flight commander, who was busy fixing something inside the cockpit nacelle of his B.E., slapped the Lewis gun in front of him, and shouted:

"If you don't clear off I'll turn this gun on you!"

To all appearances without a care, neither young airman was quite so clear of conscience as he seemed. Both pilots knew very well that the Zepps were getting away, literally, with murder. They knew that they, as the flying and fighting part of B Flight, 39 Squadron, Home Defense Wing, had been sent to this field on the rim of London to do more than give German airship commanders a few uneasy moments and a laugh in the mess at Nordholz afterward. They were here to kill Zepps. And so far the bag was empty.

They had read the papers. They had read the long columns of names in *The Times* that made the eyes ache and broke so many hearts this summer of Verdun and the Somme. Many of those names were of men they had flown and trained with, men who were dying in the sky over Flanders in their dozens, the price being paid by the Royal Flying Corps for mastering the German air force.

The men at the lonely listening stations on the East Coast began to wonder whether their faithful, unspectacular, unsung drudgery was worth it after all. The volunteer observers, the keen mobile anti-aircraft gunners of Commander Rawlinson's crack force, the cryptographers at the Admiralty, all the links in the chain of air defense began to feel much as a hard-working halfback line feels when its forward cannot score and the crowd is yelling for scalps.

Saturday, September 2nd, had been a dull, rainy day in London and the home counties. At Sutton's Farm the rain had been heavy enough to prevent flying. Robinson and Sowrey had spent the afternoon in the hangars tuning up their machines. Robinson had passed the remark, "Doesn't look like Zepp weather today."

In London soldiers on leave and their girls were buying tickets, if they could still get them, at the Globe Theatre for Moya Mannering and A. E. Matthews in *Peg O' My Heart;* for Harry Gratton's new revue *Some* at the Vaudeville, with Bea Lillie and Lee White; and, of course, for *Chu Chin Chow* at His Majesty's. Very few went to the Scala to watch the official War Office films, blurred and jerky, of life at the front in Kut, Salonika and the Somme.

In Room 40, Old Building, at the Admiralty the afternoon had dragged on to the usual accompaniment of the pneumatic cylinders thudding into the waiting basket, bringing up intercepted enemy coded messages from the telegraph office in the basement. The noise was a persistent irritation which jarred the tired nerves of Sir Alfred Ewing's cryptographers and code experts. Maskell, the garrulous old messenger from Naval Intelligence, had just marched off with the second delivery of decoded German messages from all parts of the war front locked in his shiny black tin box.

Ewing, a short, thick-set man with a large head and very keen, alert blue eyes, sat drinking a cup of tea. His preoccupation these days with the department was largely formal. He had so thoroughly trained his staff that the vital and secret work which went on day and night behind the locked door marked 40 and the complex of rooms behind it hummed along on its own with no more than an occasional touch of the oil can from him or from his leading code expert, Fleet Paymaster Rotter. "The Japanese," as Lord Haldane called them, were men from every part of service and civilian life. They included peers, publishers, diplomats, dons, landowners, lawyers, linguists, schoolmasters and scholars. There was even a clergyman.

The "crosswords" which they deciphered with unfailing swiftness were mostly secret enemy messages picked up by our radio listening stations. "The Japanese" were of war-winning importance. Already they had deciphered a message which had led directly to the Dogger Bank victory. Room 40's greatest glory was to be reached on the day when Lieutenant Rotter, fetched from a sickbed, decoded in three hours the infamous Zimmermann telegram, but at this moment, a little before five o'clock on Saturday afternoon,

September 2nd, 1916, the department was on the brink of a tense enough few hours.

The first message for urgent treatment came down the pneumatic tube from the listening station at Hunstanton, on the Wash, the scene of the first Zepp raid on Britain eighteen months before. The code, a simple substitution cipher, was a comparatively easy job to break. But before the first message was fully decoded others had come thudding down the tube from listening stations all over the eastern counties and France. They were all radio signals from Zeppelins leaving their bases. Most of the airships gave their identification letters. Message after message was decoded and checked to see if any particularly indiscreet commander had mentioned specific targets. Incredible though it seemed in the light of the famous German "thoroughness," this had sometimes happened.

There was no luck of this kind, but Room 40 quickly discovered the general objective of the gathering armada. Several of the Zeppelins included in their signals the words, "Only H.V.B. carried."

When he was told, Ewing raised his bushy, unkempt eyebrows. "We're in for it again." When a Zeppelin commander left his most confidential code books behind him and carried "Only H.V.B.," the simplest cipher, Room 40 knew for certain that he was steering for England.

Shortly after five o'clock, thanks to the inscrutably Oriental minds of "The Japanese," Admiral Hall, Director of Naval Intelligence, knew that eighteen Zeppelins had left their bases and were heading for Britain.

There was even more significant news. While most of the messages came from German naval airships, several had been sent by army Zeppelins. The airship services of the German army and navy, forever playing politics to score off each other, had never seriously combined before. That, and the size of the combined fleet—more Zeppelins than had ever attacked together—pointed to the opening of a new phase in the Zepp terror, a giant raid. Intelligence considered these facts and added to them an estimate of the sort of weather the Zeppelins were likely to meet.

The Zepps did not like heavy rain, which clung to the envelope and weighed down a ship already loaded to capacity with bombs and fuel. Strong winds could blow the lighter-than-air craft hopelessly off course. On the morning of the 2nd an anti-cyclone of moderate intensity was centered over Germany and extended its influence over the Low Countries, bringing light rain. There was a slight depression in the Channel, but a rising barometer in East Anglia showed that there was little chance of this spreading northward. The only effect, in fact, had been to cause a little rain in southeastern England.

The wind over the North Sea was light from the westward, its velocity averaging about twelve miles per hour to start with but now decreasing to under ten miles per hour and to about five between Flanders and this country, giving light opposition to the huge gas-bags, especially to the army Zepps flying the short haul from Belgium. The weather was generally fair, but there was a good deal of cloud and some mist, especially in the London area and in Norfolk. There would be no moon. Conditions were therefore very favorable for an air raid everywhere along our eastern and southeastern coasts as far north as the Humber. It was a good guess that the coming night's work would make or break the air defense of the British capital.

In Room 40 the pattern of the raid began to emerge. From the spurt of direction-finding signals intercepted from the airships as they nosed their way across the North Sea dodging rain squalls it gradually became obvious that the original concentration was loosening.

Commander Rawlinson's mobile column of guns from London had now dug in a few hundred yards from the Nor-

folk coast near Bacton. This site was next door to the coast-
guard station which had a convenient telephone line to the
Haisboro Lightship anchored eight miles out to sea. The
lightship was a customary landfall for Zeppelins nearing the
coast after their flight from Germany, and her lookouts were
alert tonight watching for the valkyries to muster overhead.

At 9:15 came the order from G.H.Q., Home Forces, "Take
air-raid action."

Just before ten o'clock two Zeppelins approached the
lightship and hovered about its masthead, waiting for the
rest to come up and combine in a concentrated lunge across
darkened Britain. Rawlinson, waiting anxiously by his guns
for further news, was brought an urgent message that the
captain of the lightship insisted on speaking to him person-
ally at once. When he arrived breathless at the telephone,
expecting to be told that at least a dozen Zeppelins had
foregathered, an angry voice crackled in his ear:

"Is that the commander of the guns ashore?"

"Yes."

"Look, I can't have this damned telephone on board here
just now. I'm going to cut it off."

"I'll be damned if you'll do anything of the kind! What
the devil's the matter?"

"I'm going to cut it off, that's all."

"If you do anything of the kind I'll send a boat and have
you brought ashore under arrest. Good God, man, the
whole country is waiting for information from your ship."

"I'm the captain of this ship. . . ."

"Your orders are that the telephone *must not be touched*.
I warn you. You do so at your peril."

The captain, slightly subdued, huffed and puffed. "But
I must shift my anchors, they're not holding properly. I
must cut off the phone. The wire might get broken before
I can get the ship firmly anchored again in the proper position."

The anchors were not shifted. More Zeppelins moving
on the rendezvous cut short this conversation until seven of
the gray monsters hovered above the lightship. They
waited briefly together for stragglers which never came, then
headed for the coast.

At ten minutes to ten Rawlinson heard five explosions
about ten miles south of his camp. His three-pounder at
Bacton immediately confirmed that they were bombs. Five
minutes later the Mundesley gun reported three bombs
about ten miles to the west-nor'west of them. At five-past
ten two bombs exploded about five miles to the north of
Rawlinson's H.Q. Five minutes after this the Bacton gun
reported that they had been hearing the hum of approaching Zeppelins for three minutes. At twenty past ten, four
bombs fell about three miles to the southeast of H.Q., followed by four more a few minutes later and three more
shortly after that. At twenty-five past ten the H.Q. gunners
heard a Zeppelin coming in from the sea.

In the rain and the thick, low cloud the airship passed
right over them unseen, crossing the coast from the northeast, making perhaps 33 to 45 miles per hour at a height of
5,000 to 6,000 feet. Rawlinson tried both his searchlights,
but they could not pierce the clouds. The guns remained
silent. At forty minutes past ten the dying throb of the
Zepp's engines faded out toward the southwest. Rawlinson
switched off his lights.

At exactly this moment a solitary airship was sighted by
ground observers crossing the Foulness sands twelve miles
north of Southend on the Thames Estuary. She did not, as
watchers expected, head for London, but steered northwest
in the general direction of Chelmsford.

At all points round the coast Zeppelins were now coming
in from the sea, at Skegness, over the Wash, at Wells, at
Bacton, at Cromer and at Mundesley, and there were more
Zepps still over the sea. At ten past eleven Rawlinson heard

bombs again. Explosions now continued steadily to the south and out at sea. The long, broken night of violence had begun.

On the lonely field at Sutton's Farm Lieutenant Robinson sprawled on his camp bed beside his aircraft in the canvas hangar. William Leefe Robinson, at this time twenty-one years old, was born at Tollidetta, South Coory, Southern India, on July 14, 1895, the youngest of a family of seven, whose father, Horace Robinson, was in the Indian Service, and whose grandfather, W. C. Robinson, had been Chief Naval Constructor of H.M. Dockyard, Portsmouth. They were a family deeply rooted in the English upper-class tradition of service by leadership.

At the age of fourteen he was sent to St. Bees School on the Cumberland coast, where he was a popular and outstanding house and Rugby captain. He entered Sandhurst ten days after war had broken out, having crammed at Bournemouth in company with a son of Rudyard Kipling. By the end of the year he had been commissioned and assigned to the Worcester Regiment. Transferring to the Royal Flying Corps, he was wounded in the arm over Lille while flying as an observer and turned his convalescence into a successful attempt at gaining his wings as a pilot. He had been a Home Defense pilot ever since. After his frustrating fight with Linnarz in May he had sworn that next time it would be "either the Zepp or I."

Leefe Robinson was a little too good, those who envied him might have thought, to be true. He was a young man of great charm, tall, athletic, handsome, with the kind of good looks associated with that figure of fun and tragedy, the Edwardian blade. It was easy to imagine the gay airman—"Robby" to his acquaintances, "Robin" to intimate friends—in straw hat and striped blazer punting down the Thames or the Isis, less easy to picture him in the smelly cockpit of a B.E. He had fair, wavy hair. His mouth was rather feminine, his chin far from craggy, and his mustache no better than a good try. But his eyes gave a better clue to his character. They were blue and clear and very steady. He could have been a playboy and nothing more, except for his enthusiasm for what was to him the splendid game of flying; except for his habit of laboring with the mechanics in the hangar; except for his unusually detailed practical knowledge of his airplane; except for the brilliant and instinctive touch he showed in the air, which even the oldest sweat in the ground staff at Sutton's Farm admitted was "top-hole."

At eight minutes past eleven the telephone beside Robinson's bed tinkled and a drawling voice at the Horse Guards gave the order, "Take air-raid action."

No. 39 Squadron's standing order was for each flight of two aircraft at its various fields to send up one machine at two-hourly intervals. Tonight Leefe Robinson from Sutton's Farm, Brandon from Hainault Farm and Ross from North Weald had first trick: Robinson to cover Sutton's Farm–Joyce Green; Brandon, Hainault–Sutton's Farm; and Ross, North Weald–Hainault. It was a system arranged to throw as wide a net as possible across the path of Zeppelins making for London.

Leefe Robinson's machine, B.E.2c No. 2092, was quickly trundled out of the hangar and positioned for take-off. Robinson himself, an enthusiast to the last detail, supervised fuelling and final engine and airframe checks in the clammy, drifting ground fog that covered the tiny airfield.

The fog was quite thick and for a moment he wondered whether to inform Horse Guards and beg off, but he thought that the air was probably reasonably clear a few yards off the ground and decided not to telephone. Around him in the shrouding mist he could see mechanics lighting the new, more efficient Money flares along the flight path. These wicks of asbestos and kerosene devised by the C. O., Major Higgins, burned longer and far brighter than the old buckets of gasoline and shone through mist and fog. They would show him his landfall when he came down again. Still very cold, he flapped his arms vigorously across his chest and climbed stiffly up into the cockpit of the B.E.

He switched on the cockpit lighting. That was another new device for the night fliers. Not only were the dials lit up but the figures on them were daubed with luminous paint in case the lights failed. He checked the Lewis pointing up to the dim stars above and in front of his helmeted head, and saw that he had a full quota of drums. They all contained the new explosive-incendiary bullets mixed alternately with tracer for aiming in the dark. He had all the gadgets tonight, he thought. If he couldn't do something with these marvels of science he ought to be sent back to the trenches.

He was ready. He pulled his goggles down over his eyes, and coughed, feeling the gritty fog in his mouth and throat. He stuck his head over the side.

"Gas switches on."

"Gas switches on." The mechanic echoed him hollowly through the vacuum in the mist.

"Choke out."

"Choke out."

"Contact."

"Contact."

The mechanic swung the heavy prop. The engine was cold and it took three attempts to start it.

He warmed up the engine, checked his instruments, then —"Chocks away."

"Chocks away." Mechanics jerked the blocks away, Robinson opened the throttle, and the machine was bumping down Tom Crawford's grass. In a few minutes he was clear, and the mist had fallen away below him.

As Leefe Robinson was climbing out of the mist to begin his lonely watch under the stars the single Zeppelin which had crept in unheralded and crossed the Foulness Sands was over Coggeshall, halfway between Chelmsford and Colchester. Soon afterward she turned west, passed over Saffron Walden, groping her way uncertainly on, and near Great Chesterford went round in a circle to try to find her bearings. Then she resumed her course west, picked up the Great Northern Railway line at Royston in Hertfordshire, and followed it as it bent southwest to Hitchin, to Luton, to the northeast fringes of London.

Luton heard her drone in the night about one o'clock. She was turning toward the capital all the time now, the first of the raiders to approach. At London Colney, south of St. Albans, she dropped three high-explosive and three incendiary bombs to get her sights set and at the same time give her the extra buoyancy she would need to outrange the London guns. Five minutes later, heading due east, she dropped two high explosives and two incendiaries in a wood at North Mimms. At one twenty-eight she dropped an explosive and two incendiaries at Littleheath, where she cut a gas main and damaged two houses, then turned fast north, then northwest, dropping three more bombs as she went.

At one thirty-five she dropped two explosives and seven incendiaries on the Stud Farm at Clayhill, where a row of stables was set on fire and three valuable yearlings destroyed. She then steered westward and dropped three incendiaries at Cockfosters, near the Enfield Isolation Hospital. At one forty-five she crossed the Great Northern Railway line south of Hadley Wood, dropped two bombs, and turned and recrossed the railway, going east. At ten minutes past two she dropped three bombs in a field at Southgate and turned south over Wood Green, then east.

As the lone airship passed just south of Alexandra Palace she was picked up by the Finsbury Park and Victoria Park lights. The Finsbury Park gun at once opened fire on her and other guns in the North and Central London defenses followed. The guns were so accurate, especially the Temple House gun, that they forced her to turn off to the northeast over Tottenham.

At twelve minutes past two she was over Edmonton and dropped six high explosives there. One of these fell in the grounds of Ely's explosive plant but it did not go off. Two minutes later, retreating north, she dropped two high explosives at Ponders End, where she broke streetcar and telephone wires and badly damaged the roads and a water main. She bombed Enfield Highway and had just released twelve high explosives at Forty Hill and Turkey Street when an aircraft dived upon her, coming from the southeast.

At ten minutes past one Leefe Robinson's lonely, uneventful watch had been suddenly and dramatically relieved. Somewhere southeast of Woolwich he had spotted an airship caught by two searchlights heading northeast toward the Gravesend-Tilbury area. The clouds had gathered and thickened in that part and he saw that the searchlights were having a difficult time keeping up with the raider. By this time he had managed to climb to 12,900 feet and he steered in the direction of the Zeppelin and the few scattered shrapnel blossoms in the sky below it.

He flew on for ten minutes, slowly gaining on the Zepp. He judged it to be about two hundred feet below and decided to hold his height advantage rather than risk a fast dive at the target, knowing he could never outclimb a Zepp once he had fallen below her. A moment later he was regretting his caution. A thicker belt of cloud rolled up, the Zeppelin plunged into it, and airplane and gunners were all left groping blindly. They never picked her up again and after another quarter of an hour Leefe Robinson returned to his patrol, chagrined at losing the Zeppelin, but too generally cold and cramped to feel very angry at his error in tactics.

About ten minutes to two he noticed a fiery glow in the northeast. Thinking that where there was fire there might be a Zepp, he headed for it. He had been flying for fifteen minutes when one of the searchlights flicking to and fro out of the blackness below him halted and fixed on the long, dark shape of the Foulness Zeppelin as it came nosing out of a smudge of cloud like an Ouse River chub from the shadows of a mudbank prowling for food. Robinson had had one lesson, and he did not make the same mistake again. Engine full on, he put his nose down and steered straight for the Zepp. As he drew closer he noticed that the night tracer shells were all curving either too high above or too far below the airship's limelit hull.

A special constable standing on high ground in southeast London thought that the Zepp caught in the searchlights looked like a bar of polished steel about the thickness of a piston rod. For a time it seemed to hang there motionless while the shells burst all round it. Then it made to turn as if in the direction of the coast but a shell exploded near its nose and it swung round in the opposite direction. Its tail dipped and it made to climb, and a shell burst right over it. It sank lower, and three shells burst below, behind and in front of it. The Zepp seemed to wriggle from side to side, unable to escape. Then it seemed as if a black shadow passed between the constable's vision and the brilliant light so far up in the sky. Then he looked again. The Zepp was gone and the little shining rod of steel had disappeared. The firing ceased and the searchlights swung round the sky.

As the lights appeared to lose the Zeppelin there was a moment of intense silence in all the streets of London, then a great sigh of disappointment.

In this lull, when a second raider seemed about to escape, and her captain probably thought he was clear, Leefe Robinson's B.E. bucked and cavorted in the fierce blast of shrap-

nel near misses as he dived for the bow of the airship.
Mackay of the second patrol from North Weald, who had
taken off at one o'clock, had seen the Zepp held in a searchlight when he was at the Joyce Green end of his patrol and
given chase. When he was within a mile of the airship he
caught a brief glimpse of a B.E. heading at full speed for
the bows of the Zepp.

In the early days of the air defense, when the defending
pilots' lack of success had first caused a great outcry from
press and public, a dramatic instruction had appeared in
the orders of one squadron, running thus, "If the airplane
fails to stop the airship by the time all ammunition is ex-
pended, and the airship is still heading for London, then
the pilot must decide to sacrifice himself and his machine
and ram the airship at the utmost speed." The B.E. that
Mackay saw fleetingly was going so fast to the bull's-eye
that he thought the pilot meant to ram.

Leefe Robinson was diving to position himself beneath
the giant hull. Blind attacks from above had been proved
useless. The new idea was to rake the underbelly of the
airship with bullets. He leveled off 800 feet underneath the
nose and flew straight and level the length of the Zeppelin
immediately beneath its control and engine cars, spraying it
with explosive-incendiary. He used up one drum on this
pass, then looked behind him but could see no apparent result. When he had changed drums he climbed, turned, and
flew right down the great looming flank of the roaring
monster, emptying another drum into it. Still no flame
or flicker of fire upon her. She plunged on like some huge
Moby Dick trailing the toothpick lances of her attackers.

When he had reloaded again he tried a different tactic.
This time he positioned himself behind the stern of the
airship. He was only about five hundred feet from her and
concentrated the whole of the third drum on one spot on
the belly near the monstrous tail fins. He saw the incan-

descent tracer hitting the hull. She seemed utterly invulnerable. The last round left the muzzle and the Lewis fell silent.

Just then he saw a sullen red glow inside the envelope of the Zepp in the spot he had been firing at. In a few seconds the whole after part was ablaze. Flame a hundred feet high whooshed up in front of his eyes, roaring and furnace hot.

In a street in Dulwich heads were popping out of all the windows. People were moving about in the street, calling to each other.

A man called out, "It's half past two, dear!"

Then a woman screamed, "Look, look!"

High up and miles away in the sky a tongue of fire had appeared. Like a firework at a carnival a lick of flame ran round the sausage shape of a Zepp. Its body shone silver in the light.

In Walthamstow they saw the searchlights blink out. There was no need for them. The whole capital was illuminated by a vast, elongated, yellow flaming torch. In one narrow street a woman cried, "Thank God. She's done for!"

A child's voice shrieked, "We've got her!"

In East Ham a boy of twelve stood among gaping men and women in pajamas and nightgowns and saw what seemed like a furnace door suddenly opened in the night and a mass of red-hot coals exposed. Flames burst out all round the lighted body of the Zepp. There were loud cheers. Railway engines blew eccentric shrieking salutes on their whistles. He thought it was just like Children's Empire Day.

All over southeast London they watched the ball of fire burning in the sky to the north. The ball swelled in size. Suddenly there was a great white burst of fire. The whole of London was illuminated as if being photographed by a giant flashlight. The dome of St. Paul's, the towers of Westminster, the silver serpent of the river, all stood out, and for the brief second of that awful flash a ghastly panorama of London was thrown on to the black screen of the night.

From Staines to Southend people gasped at the terrible vision in the sky. Then cheering broke out like a great forest fire spreading over the capital. In many a street voices began "God Save the King." Children screamed wildly, men and women danced and shouted hysterically. A spontaneous upsurge of something like New Year's Eve and Mafeking Night put together and multiplied many times gripped London.

For a moment the doomed Zepp retained straight and level flight like a great bar of iron fresh from the furnace. Then it could be seen descending slowly in a shallow dive, nose down.

Below it Leefe Robinson fought the controls in a desperate effort to dodge the vast blazing mass which everywhere filled his vision. He managed with only a second to spare to sideslip out of harm's way. The crackling, roaring thing fell past him and it was like feeling the terrifying heat of the flames of hell on his face. He was not cold for a long time after that. Stunned and shaken he watched the awful wreck sink slowly away out of the sky forever.

Exhilaration surged through him. In a burst of joy he grabbed his Very pistol and fired off round after round of red cartridges, dropped a parachute flare, and put the B.E. into a wild loop. It was just like stunting over Tom Crawford's house, only this time there was something to celebrate. The people below saw the little red stars of victory and the brilliant snowflake falling and cheered their unknown champion.

Sowrey, who had taken off from Sutton's Farm half an hour after his flight commander, saw a small yellow flame in the sky and thought immediately that Robinson's engine had caught fire. Then the distant flame turned red, glowed, and grew larger, and he knew it was a Zepp burning. Mackay in his B.E. a few hundred yards away had time to notice that the whole vault of the sky from horizon to horizon was bathed red with fire, and the clouds below glared an unpleasant flesh pink. He afterward chased a departing Zepp himself northeast of Hainault and was about to open fire when she disappeared in cloud. Hunt from Hainault Farm got even closer to Leefe Robinson's victim than Mackay, so close in fact that he was about to fire into her when he saw her begin to burn. He broke off, and in the spreading pool of light sighted another a short distance away, well illuminated by the flames. But the glare was so fierce that it blinded him and when he had recovered the second Zeppelin had left the zone of light. Later he chased a third airship but lost her too.

The wild relief at seeing a nightmare Zepp destroyed in flames purged Londoners deepest fears of the menace. It had the reverse effect upon the other airships pressing in from the rim of London.

The army airships from Belgium crossed the coast farther south than the naval Zeppelins from Germany, like the Foulness Zeppelin, and came in singly and uncoordinated. One army ship came over the coast at Frinton about eleven o'clock, began to curve westward toward London, but at half past twelve gave up the idea and retreated over Yarmouth, where Lieutenant Cadbury of the R.N.A.S. chased her out to sea. Another army Zeppelin crossed the coast at Littlestone at midnight, steered over Ashford, Maidstone and Sevenoaks and on to Gravesend, where she dropped her bombs, under pressure from the Dartford guns. Here she was chased unsuccessfully by Leefe Robinson in his first attack and driven north by more gunfire until she finally left the coast over Saxmundham.

The L22 from Nordholz came in over the Wash and turned north, zigzagged over the Humber and dropped a few bombs ineffectually. The L13 came straight in over the Humber from the sea and eventually bombed East Retford in Nottinghamshire, where the glare from the gasworks was her marker, before leaving again over the mouth of the Humber.

These were light feints, and the main attack came in over Norfolk and Essex on London.

The L16 was steering for London in the wake of the Foulness Zeppelin and only a short distance behind her. When the L16's commander saw the ship ahead on fire he turned at once and steered north at his maximum speed. Hunt in his B.E. saw him and gave chase until he lost him in the clouds.

When Captain Ernst Lehmann arrived over the London suburbs in the LZ98 the continued din of bombs and gunfire told him that several other Zeppelins were already in action. He saw the spectacle as an endless sea of houses lying under a silvery fog pierced by the flashes of bomb bursts and blazing fires. The other airships were hidden, and the searchlights were groping about the sky, their conical rays passing through each other like bodiless ghosts.

He felt as if he were sitting in a theater box, with the brightly lit stage before him and the darkened auditorium below. A whole hour went by before he ventured to come over the city. Steering from one cloud bank to another to avoid the guns and lights, he dropped his bombs on the docks. Over the Thames, searchlights picked him up and shrapnel drove him away to the northeast.

He was in the chartroom bending over the maps to plot their course home when he heard his staff officer, von Gemmingen, cry out wildly. Lehmann looked behind him and saw a bright ball of flame in the sky. He knew that the blazing meteor on the farther rim of the city could only be one of their ships. He, too, lost no time in heading for the coast.

Peterson in the L32 had just fixed his course by the reservoir at Tring and was heading for London when he saw the great fire in the sky some miles ahead of him near the city. The captain, who had been worrying about his wife's failing health and was in a highly nervous state, burst into tears when he saw the flaming wreck, thinking that it must be Mathy, who was always first over the target. He did not know that Mathy had not reached London that night. The sight knocked the heart out of him and he very soon turned away and steered for home, unloading his bombs on Hertford as he fled.

The light-headed crowds watched the Zepp, hanging in the heavens like an enormous serpent writhing in a framework of erupting flame, continue to fall away northward. Sometimes the crimson flame took on a bluish tinge, sometimes it became streaked with yellow. The whole of South London stared until its eyes ached. When the glowing mass finally sank out of sight behind the rooftops people fancied they could smell burning wood and fabric. In Dulwich a man with a pedantic turn of mind rushed into the house and brought out a copy of the *Daily Mail* which he triumphantly proceeded to read in the street by the glare in the sky. He was fourteen miles away from the dying Zepp.

The whole of Chiswick, even farther away, was lit up as if by a gigantic bonfire. The blazing airship was seen distinctly at Gravesend, thirty miles away. The glow in the sky shed its light on places forty, even fifty miles distant.

Harry Shepherd, a Stock Exchange broker, had taken his friend Sam Lambert for a quiet weekend with the family at their country cottage in the little village of Cuffley, six miles north of Enfield. About twenty minutes past one on Sunday morning Mrs. Shepherd awoke and shook her husband. "What's that droning in the sky?" she said. Shepherd, climbing out of a deep sleep, heard the noise too. She said, "I believe it's the Zepps."

He said, "They're probably doing something down at the farm. Go back to sleep." But in the cottage next door they could hear the people talking and moving about, and the noise in the sky was like a train thundering along.

Shepherd sat up. "It *is* the Zepps."

They were trying to get to sleep again, and Shepherd was thinking, It doesn't seem possible, Zepps at Cuffley, when they heard a bomb go off somewhere. There was a heavy *boom*, then a great flash in the window at the foot of the bed, lighting up the whole room.

Presently they heard the droning coming back, louder than before, until the sound of it was all round them. The guns had stopped. There was nothing but the awful droning. Then they heard the popping noise of a machine gun somewhere overhead. It must have been about three minutes after that that a reddish light suddenly appeared in the sky.

"What's that, what's that?" they kept asking each other. Shepherd said, "Incendiary bombs or shrapnel, most likely. We'd better keep under cover."

Then the whole sky lighted up. Lambert said, "My God, that was a pretty bad hit."

The night was on fire. Shepherd said suddenly, "I can't stay in here without knowing what that is." He threw open the front door and ran out.

He saw the thing on fire up there in the heavens, white flames shooting out of the top of it. He yelled, "It's all right, it's all right! They've hit it! Come and see it!"

The others rushed out and they stood there looking at it. They heard it crackling and saw all its twisted framework collapsing.

It was falling toward the triangle formed by Castle Farm, the Plough Inn and St. Andrew's Church, its white-hot girders folding inward, flames and sparks trailing it like the tail of a comet.

At Castle Farm little Kathleen Holloway stood on the broad step outside their kitchen door. She could not move, could hardly breathe. She did not know whether she wanted to stay there or rush inside to her mother. The thing in the sky was all on fire and turning over. The fire was running all round it and straight up into the air. She did not know whether it was a Zeppelin or the airplane she had heard first, and she started to cry.

The burning thing got hotter and hotter, and bigger and bigger, like a house. Her father shouted, "It's coming down, it's coming down!" and pulled her inside. They all clung together, the house as bright as day, all the pots and pans in the kitchen gleaming.

She wanted to see it. Breaking away from her father's grip she ran outside again. It was much farther down now, right on top of them, burning hot. It looked like a very big half-moon. It was blowing over across their fields toward them. Something was spilling out of it. She saw some dark things fall from it. Fire was dropping off it. It looked to her as if it had made up its mind to come straight at them. It came lower and lower, crackling and very, very hot. She had to look straight up in the sky to see it. It went right over the pond and over the branches of their oak tree, and the leaves all turned red. It was very hot.

She heard it hit the ground with a big crunching noise. "Oh dear, it's hit the Plough!" she cried out as her father came out of the house. She wanted to go and see but he held her back.

Harry Shepherd and Sam Lambert saw the fire shooting up behind the Plough. Shepherd said the first thing that came into his head. "Come along, Sam, we must get a bit of it!"

He and Lambert started running toward the Plough and met the pub keeper and his wife in the road.

"Where is it?" they shouted. It was foggy and difficult to

see anything. Then they saw the dull glowing mass on the other side of the fence. They climbed the fence into the field. The fire was lighting up the whole inn. Ammunition was exploding with a noise like jumping squibs, and they rushed back to the road. There they met the pub keeper again. He said, "A special's just come—gone in through that gate."

They ran back—if the constable could get through, so could they. He met them as they came. "Keep back, keep back!" he shouted. "Ammunition! Something's dropped off further down the field. Go and see what it is!"

They found a huge propeller blade which had torn through the hedge and embedded itself in the ground like an Indian totem pole. When they got back to the fire the constable was pulling things out of the fire with a long iron bar. They saw bodies tangled up in the mass of glowing wire, flames running all over them. Sam Lambert found himself staring in surprise at a broken thermos flask lying some yards away from the wreck. A thermos in a Zeppelin. It seemed very odd to him.

People were rushing over the fields toward the burning wreckage. The special constable first on the scene had summoned help. Acting Sergeant Jesse White of the Metropolitan Police came along and saw three bodies lying near the propeller which Shepherd had found. The bodies were burning and pinned down by the wire. They managed to put out some of the flames with buckets of water and pull the three dead men out. The first man had his legs burned off and his arms up to the elbows, and was the only one recognizable as a human being. They laid the three bodies under the hedge.

The Zeppelin burned for two hours after it had crashed. It was not very much of a wreck for a Zepp, Sam Lambert thought when he saw it at dawn, only about twenty-five square yards of it. He had a sudden fear that it might have been one of our own smaller airships after all. And Kathleen Holloway could not believe that this was the big thing that roared down on them like a burning house falling out of the sky.

As it smoldered, more and more firemen, police and R.F.C. men arrived to take charge and explore the wreckage. The airship seemed to be burning away to nothing. An officer said, "It's funny. There doesn't seem to have been any aluminum in the thing at all. They're making them of wood. They must be short."

Some of the firemen jumped on to the smoldering rubbish and hoses were rigged, but no one was saved alive. All human remains were put together under the hedge with a tarpaulin over them. Charred swords, revolvers, and three Iron Crosses were picked up. One of the charred bodies had been found with one hand gripping the remains of the airship's wheel. These were taken to be the remains of the airship commander and placed separate from the others.

At daybreak a violent thunderstorm broke and brought torrential rain and vivid lightning to the scene. But the downpour did not stop the great pilgrimage which began before first light.

Local people came early and in droves, and the police and soldiers had to form a cordon round the wreckage. At dawn Cuffley was packed with sightseers from all the home counties and beyond. "The place!" was the cry. "We must see the place!" The narrow lane running alongside the field where the wreck lay became blocked with cars, buses, traps, donkey carts, farm wagons and gaping pedestrians. Farther out, the main roads were choked with cars, taxis and motorcycles. All London had got up before sunrise, and before that the northern roads too had glittered with the hooded headlights of hundreds of cars. Streams of bicycles followed in their wake.

Very soon new arrivals found it impossible to get anywhere near the Zeppelin. People squelching along the yellow, muddy, sandy road from the streetcar terminus to the field were met by shouts of, "Go back. You won't see anything!" But they still tramped on under the shrapnel rain toward the Place Where It Fell.

At dawn the wreckage was still smoldering. In places heaps of hot cinders gave out clouds of steam as tired firemen pumped doggedly at the handle of the little local fire-engine, and there was the sort of sour smell which always arises from a wood fire quenched by water. Admiral Hall, head of Naval Intelligence, was one of those who arrived at this stage, and he was disappointed to find that the airship had practically burned itself out.

There was very little to see, a mass of wire, blackened and twirled up in rings, much charred wood, a round metal disk discolored like dirty silver, some scrap iron and bits of steel. R.F.C. mechanics, soldiers, police and Red Cross nurses poked about among the debris. Men piled bits of wreckage into boxes and the boxes into trucks. A straggling cordon of soldiers surrounded the proceedings. Beyond them in dense crowds stood the pilgrims.

They stared at the black, wet tarpaulin under which the bodies lay. A leg and an arm could be seen sticking out, and several daring and morbid onlookers tried to get close enough to lift a corner of the rain-soaked shroud. But they were all pushed roughly away by the soldiers, and one of them found himself sprawling in the mud from a purposeful kick. Motor ambulances stood by to take the bodies to the church when the final search of the wreckage had been made. At the Place, hardly anyone spoke, but worked or stood mostly in silence.

They stood all day and watched the mechanics rolling up the tangled wire until all that was left of the great Zeppelin was a scattered trail of ash and innumerable tiny splinters of wood, metal and fabric which lasted souvenir hunters for several weeks.

At nightfall hundreds found themselves stranded under the teeming rain. Many of those who walked to Gordon Hill and Potters Bar found it impossible to get trains and walked on to Barnet, a further seven or eight miles. Girls who had come out expecting a summer afternoon's excursion were exhausted, silk stockings torn and muddy, blouses soaked. The stream of homeward-bound cars, bicycles and traps went on into the small hours. Cars lay crippled and ditched by the roadside. Motorists who had miscalculated the mileage and the unforeseeable detours appealed desperately to others for gas. Every telephone in the district was besieged by the pilgrims begging taxi proprietors in London to send out cabs. But the stream of people coming out had already created a famine. At night the Place was nothing but a piece of soaking grass, broken hedges and churned mud.

So ended Zepp Sunday, which some people called Leefe Robinson Day.

Great honors and rewards lay ahead for the man who had killed The Great Fire Raid—the Victoria Cross from the hands of the King, a total of £4,250 in prizes offered to the first man to bring down a Zeppelin on British soil, but what he prized most on Zepp Sunday was sleep.

When he had fired his last red Very cartridge the victorious flier, at the limit of his and his machine's endurance, with very little oil or fuel left, picked up the airfield flares with difficulty in the mist and landed at Sutton's Farm at quarter to three. Utterly exhausted and so cold and stiff he could hardly speak, he went with Sowrey into the little office, made out of an old airplane crate, which was the only building of four walls which B Flight possessed. Here the clerk was ready, as he always was when the flight commander returned from a patrol, with a mug of hot cocoa. He was sip-

ping it when Colonel Holt came through on the phone
from Adastral House with congratulations and a demand for
an immediate report on the night's action.

Robinson mumbled some irritated objection. He was very
tired and still very cold.

Holt said urgently, "You've *got* to write it!" Robinson
finished his cocoa, wrote the report, then at last collapsed
on his camp bed in the hangar. He slept, while away at
Bacton, Commander Rawlinson was listening to the last
badly shaken Zeppelins of the defeated armada droning out
over the coast, and while the world and his wife were beginning their trek to Cuffley. He was belligerent when Sowrey
shook him at dawn to take him out to the scene of the crash.
He said, "For God's sake, can't a fellow get some sleep on a
Sunday morning?"

He went to Cuffley and strolled on the field briefly in the
morning. In the afternoon he went there again and was
standing watching the damp ashes of his victim when he
recognized a girl he knew.

He said, "I say, please don't give me away. I've already
had one dose of popularity this morning and it very nearly
killed me. My back's black and blue with the thumps the
crowd gave me. Won't you take me away and hide me
somewhere?"

The girl said, "Mr. Robinson, you're hopeless, really."

The Zepp slayer laughed and stroked his little mustache.
"Well, anyway, did you enjoy the fireworks?"

"I should just think I did."

"So did I."

On Monday evening, in the tea room of the Plough, a
formal travesty of an inquest was held on the bodies pulled
from the wreckage of the Zeppelin. Security forbade all but
the barest details, and the jury took less than an hour to
reach the verdict:

"That on the 3rd day of September, sixteen unknown German airmen were found dead in a wrecked German Zeppelin airship in a field near the Plough Inn, Cuffley; that the Zeppelin was brought down by the fire of a British airplane manned by Lieutenant Robinson, of the Royal Flying Corps; the cause of their death was injuries, the result of the destruction of the Zeppelin."

In a brief discussion with the R.F.C. officers attending the inquest as to the manner in which the verdict should be phrased the coroner said, "You need not be afraid of the jury finding a verdict of murder."

Little sympathy was expressed in any quarter for the dead men in St. Andrew's Church, these wretches scorched, scalded or suffocated to death. On the same day as the short, grotesque proceedings in the tea room at the Plough, another inquest was held in a Hertfordshire village on "two young persons killed by a bomb from a hostile aircraft."

Two sisters, aged twelve and twenty-six, had been killed in this place and had been found by their father, after the Zeppelin had passed, with terrible injuries. The doctor who examined them gave as his evidence that "the younger girl had a dozen wounds on her left side, and her left leg was so badly injured that I had to amputate it. She died, however, early this morning. The elder girl had been struck in the stomach so badly as to cause her death."

In the light of facts like these, the news that the German dead were to be given a military funeral was badly received by many of the ordinary people of Britain, and it seemed likely that the funeral itself, arranged to take place that Wednesday at Potters Bar, would give rise to some ugly scenes. Angry people, especially in London, said that coffins of best pine were too good for "the baby killers," as Zeppelin airmen were universally called, that it would be more fitting for their remains to be thrown together into a hole in the ground.

Only at the entrance to the cemetery was there, in fact,

any incident. As the coffins were being borne through the gates a middle-aged woman threw two eggs at one of them, which spattered on the black shroud covering it. The ceremony was very short and admission to the cemetery was restricted to parishioners. Whatever these people thought when they saw Royal Flying Corps officers who had carried the coffin of the dead German commander salute him as he was lowered into the grave, they kept silent. Then the sounding of the Last Post gave these dead, who had everywhere been denounced as murderers, the formal designation of soldiers.

By this time the last pilgrims and journalists had left Cuffley. They returned to their homes greatly heartened by seeing with their own eyes what a new St. George had made of the terrible Zepp, the symbol of their deepest fears. Instead of awaiting their nights with terror, they looked forward to them, to see what he and his colleagues would do to the ones that got away.

10. THE GIANT KILLERS

Life at Sutton's Farm after Zepp Sunday was never quite the same. The place was a scene of heroic endeavor to the public, particularly to the people of Hornchurch, to whom it was "our airdrome," and for the airmen all the monotony that was intrinsic to their routine was temporarily gone in place of a general excitement and exhilaration.

It was the end of anonymity for Leefe Robinson. His photograph appeared in the newspapers and he was recognized and acclaimed wherever he went. The scene in Windsor town after the King had presented him with the Victoria Cross and promoted him to captain, when his car was overwhelmed by cheering crowds determined to shake his hand or at least touch his tunic or the wings on his chest, was repeated over and over again. His favorite London restaurant, the Piccadilly Grill, was never the same comfortable haven of relaxation, and if he went again to hear the lovely high voice of Violet Essex singing his favorite "Oh For A Life In Bohemia," he shared the attention of the audience with the star of the show.

On duty both he and Sowrey, close friends in private, were very much the professional soldier, and orders were given and carried out with the efficiency and punctilio found only in the best regular units. No careless work was tolerated in the flight. If Robinson noticed so much as a scratch on

a piston, it was, "What's this? Get that seen to right away."
His paper work, which he did not enjoy, was nevertheless
immaculate, and his handling of an aircraft or his running
of the flight alike bore the stamp of conscientious thoroughness. Away from the airfield he broke out frequently.
On his first trip in the new Prince Henry Vauxhall bought
out of his prize money he sighted another car with a hunts-
man's relish, shouted, "There's a Ford! Let's ram it!", put
his foot to the floor, and gave the other startled driver the
shock of his life. Off duty he could be a madcap, on duty
never.

He was ably and keenly supported by his flight, by his
friend Fred Sowrey, Lieutenant Bowers, the searchlight
officer, Flight Sergeant Church, the rigger sergeant, Sergeant Gunter, the fitter sergeant, Sergeant Pike, who looked
after all the guns, and all the others, and was respected,
liked, and a little hero-worshiped, for he had all the qualities
looked for, and so rarely found, in the man of the hour. He
was the perfect answer to the public craving at that time
for a symbolic figure of the young English officer who was
coming forward light-heartedly to fight and die so gallantly
in the grimmest, most ghastly war so-called civilized man had
ever inflicted upon humanity.

He inspired a particularly close study of Zeppelin fighting in B Flight. Putting their heads together, the pilots
decided that by far the most important rule in attacking an
airship was to get as high as possible first, well above the
10,000 feet which was about the maximum reached so far.
This they could not do in their B.E.2c's, as the machines
stood at the moment. The B.E.s were anything but streamlined, and a particular nuisance was the air suction set up in
flight by the empty front cockpit, so it was cowled over and
sealed off, and the performance of the aircraft at once improved. A heavy millstone around a pilot's neck was provided by the very weighty collection of outmoded arma-

ment with which the machines of Home Defense Squadrons were by official order decked out.

B Flight decided to risk the wrath of the high brass and scrap it all. Rankin darts, Carcass bombs, Le Prieur rockets, all useless, were removed and dumped, and they relied henceforth entirely upon their Lewis guns and new explosive-incendiary ammunition. They soon found that the decrease in weight added several thousand feet to the operational ceiling of the B.E.s. Some extra weight was saved at the expense of armament by taking up only partially filled drums of ammunition.

These half drums carried only forty-seven rounds each, arranged in the pattern armor-piercing, Brock, tracer (called "sparklet") in the drum. There were only three drums, and the Brock bullets were still imperfect. They still tended to explode in the gun and would even go off if dropped on the ground. But they had now proved themselves better than the bombs and darts, which were of no use at all, and the unreliable and dangerous rockets, one of which had gone off on the ground and chased Leefe Robinson across the airdrome for several yards. They practiced shooting off their stripped-down Lewises at the old gravel pit near the field, and put in as much flying in the hours of real darkness as they could. Nearly every time they wanted to take off or use the tender they still had to boot some of Mr. Crawford's sheep out of the road.

Neither Robinson nor Sowrey were hell-raisers. It was mostly unfledged trainee pilots who poured beer over their heads and bawled,

> So drink up your glasses steady,
> This world is a world full of lies.
> Here's a health to the dead already,
> And hurrah for the next man that dies!

Both were handsome, dashing young men. Both enjoyed

female society and were much in demand, but there were no wild orgies on leave, no bevies of chorus girls. Neither Robinson nor Sowrey drank or smoked more than occasionally. When they did strike a light they would both flourish elongated cigarette holders which they affected. The feeling was encouraged in the flight that physical fitness was important to an anti-Zeppelin pilot. Few pilots engaged in normal duties realized the special dangers of Home Defense. Pilots of No. 39 Squadron found themselves looked upon sideways at the R.F.C. Club in Bruton Street if they let fall that they had been night-flying, still almost an unknown practice, regarded as a pursuit of cranky lunatics and exhibitionists.

In the "Dark" periods they were on parade at eight o'clock, trained hard all forenoon and afternoon, and stood by in turn by the War Office telephone at night. On mornings after a patrol a pilot would be allowed to sleep until about ten o'clock in the morning.

There was an alarm on Saturday night, September 16th. It was Robinson's turn for first trick that night. "Some of us," says Mr. Charles Perfect of Hornchurch, "were waiting to witness his ascent, but instead, we suddenly saw a bright light on the airfield and concluded that something untoward had happened."

It was indeed "something untoward." Leefe Robinson, taking off in the machine in which he had made history on the night of September 2nd, crashed into the boundary hedge and the machine caught fire. The B.E. was a total wreck, but Robinson managed to scramble out unhurt. It was not until the night of the 23rd that there was another alarm.

Now the moon was hidden in the autumn sky, and on this particular day the weather had looked encouraging to Captain Strasser at Nordholz. The Naval airship commanders were not so perturbed by the fate of the Army ship on the

2nd, which so many of them had seen with their own eyes, that they were reluctant to try again. Mathy in particular was determined to set the record straight again by demonstrating that the loss of the wooden-framed Schütte-Lanz had been the result of the usual army carelessness.

On the 23rd an anti-cyclone which had passed slowly eastward across the British Isles during the preceding days was centered over Germany, a beckoning sunshade of fair weather. The system extended its influence over England and the greater part of the North Sea. Scotland and the northern part of the North Sea were experiencing the effects of a depression centered between Iceland and the Faroes. In the southern part of the North Sea the wind velocity at 1,500 feet was low, between ten and fifteen miles an hour, blowing from between south and southeast. The weather was fair generally, with some morning mist or fog at inland stations in England. During the night conditions became quieter, and the wind was reported as calm on the east coast of Britain.

Eleven naval Zeppelins left their sheds in Germany for England. Eight of these were ordered to attack targets north of the Wash, between there and the Humber. Three others, Mathy in the L31, Peterson in the L32, and Böcker in the new L33, which was making her maiden raid, were to make for London and deliver the greatest blow which the Zeppelin service had yet dealt the British capital. The general intentions of the raiding squadron were not long hidden from Admiralty Intelligence.

At four o'clock in the afternoon Sowrey and Robinson were having tea with Major Morton and his wife at Woodford when Morton was called to the telephone. He came back. "You'd better be on your way," he said. They returned to Sutton's Farm and about nine o'clock were ordered to stand by, with Sowrey having first trick.

An hour later Böcker in the L33 came over the Thames

Estuary north of the Black Deep Lightship, the first of the London-bound Zeppelins to cross the coast.

At twelve minutes past ten he was fired on by a destroyer in the Edinburgh channel, but was not hit, and at twenty to eleven this big, brand-new airship, the pride of the German naval airship service, was following on the ill-fated course of the SL11 over Foulness. Böcker went straight inland, steered between Southminster and Burnham-on-Crouch, passed South Farmbridge at eleven, and flew on slowly straight for London.

About this time Mathy and Peterson were crossing the coast in company. Unlike Böcker, however, they had approached along a route intended to take London by surprise. The two ships had come overland together from Germany across Belgium, passed through the Straits of Dover between nine o'clock and half past ten, then felt their way along the coast to Dungeness. Peterson dropped six high explosives as soon as he saw the coast beneath him. Two fell in the sea and one wrecked a house. Then, in his inimitable fashion, he began to wander about the countryside, hovering, picking up, hovering again, making his reluctant and irresolute approach to London, perhaps with the spectacle of the burning Schütte-Lanz still before his eyes.

He was afraid to follow the bold, unflinching dash which Mathy now made upon the capital. The senior captain of the German naval airship service came over the coast at Rye at eleven o'clock and maintained a steady course over Hawkhurst, Horsmonden, Tunbridge Wells, Brasted, Oxted, Caterham, Coulsdon, Carshalton and Mitcham to London, reserving all his bombs for the city.

Mathy, ever thorough and thoughtful, had expected serious opposition from the British ground defenses, and had made special preparations to deal with them. When the guns of the southeastern defenses of London opened on him, he turned the tables this time by dropping flares which blanketed the searchlights and made them useless. Only the four-inch quick-firer at Croydon came into action, and one minute later even that was silent. Keeping at the unusually great height of 12,000 feet and flying fast, Mathy went straight on. At Kenley he dropped four high explosives at twenty-five past twelve, which wrecked two houses and injured two persons. These were his trial bombs, aimed at the first light to be seen. At half past twelve the L31 was over the Purley defenses, but the searchlight there had a defective mirror and was useless. It was now that the Croydon light picked up the Zeppelin for a moment, but two flares from Mathy drowned it. After dropping two high explosives and two incendiaries on two farms at Mitcham, he began the bombing of London.

Flying straight on north, he dropped ten high explosives and twenty-two incendiaries on Streatham. The Croydon searchlight picked him up again briefly but another flare doused it. The Dulwich and Streatham searchlights did not find the airship at all. The Dulwich gunners saw her for a second in the Croydon searchlight but she had escaped the beam before they could open fire. The Streatham Common railway station was hit, the permanent track torn up, and rolling stock and a signal box badly damaged. Four houses were wrecked, and ten other houses and ten shops severely damaged. Seven persons were killed, six of them in a street-car hit by fragments of a 660-pound bomb on Streatham Hill, and twenty-seven more injured. The Streatham Hill railway station was also damaged.

Mathy had now picked up the main line of the road through Streatham and Brixton Hill to Kennington, and he followed it accurately as far as the latter. On Brixton he dropped six high explosives, including one of 220-pounds, and seventeen incendiaries, wrecked a house, damaged a garage, twenty-one houses and twenty-one shops seriously, another forty houses slightly, and killed seven persons and injured another seventeen. Finally, at Kennington, he dropped one high explosive, which only shattered windows. Now he flew over the Thames east of London Bridge and was seen clearly from the Embankment about twenty to one. Six minutes after this he dropped ten more high explosives on Lea Bridge Road and Leyton. Twelve houses were badly and many others slightly damaged, eight persons were killed and thirty-one others hurt.

It had been a bold, brutal, successful attack, and out of it the L31 emerged unharmed. By now thick mist had arisen and the guns in the northeastern sector could not see her as she droned over them. Mathy went east of Chingford at ten to one, and was seen briefly between Buckhurst Hill and Waltham Abbey at a minute to one. At three minutes past one the Chingford searchlight picked up the airship and held her for four minutes, but Mathy then eluded the beam without trouble. Flying over Nazeing and Harlow to Takeley, east of Bishop's Stortford, he passed Haverhill, Bury St. Edmunds, Diss, Bungay in Suffolk, was seen north of Beccles at ten past two, and five minutes later flew out to sea south of Yarmouth. The L31 passed unscathed through a hasty barrage put up by guns at Fritton, and by naval guns on shore and aboard a warship off the coast, and passed over the Cross Sand Lightship, going very high and very fast to the east and home.

Mathy's skill and finesse had rewarded him, but luck had not favored the reckless course of the L33. On her way toward London, she had reached Billericay in Essex at twenty-seven minutes past eleven. Böcker then flew south over Brentwood, and about twenty to twelve dropped four sighting incendiaries on Upminster Common. Ten minutes later the inhabitants of Hornchurch heard six tremendous explosions as he released a batch of high explosives, aimed at the Sutton's Farm airfield but badly placed. At five to twelve Böcker dropped a flare south of Chadwell Heath and was picked up by a solitary searchlight. He shook off the beam, however, and no other lights managed to find him, the guns remaining silent. When he was over Wanstead a few minutes later he suddenly turned southeast and at six minutes past twelve altered course again to go southwest between the Becton and North Woolwich guns, almost at once turning again northwest towards West Ham. At ten past twelve he passed over the West Ham gun and met the first shells of the London barrage. At the same time he began to drop his bombs on East London.

Hurriedly, under a thick and increasingly accurate anti-aircraft fire, he began on Bromley, where he dropped one 220-pound high explosive and five incendiaries on St. Leonard's and Empress Streets, wrecking four houses, killing six persons and injuring another eleven, and went on to drop several bombs on Bow.

But Böcker was by no means getting things his own way. In fact by now he was in some trouble. The shooting of the East London guns had been good from the start. The West Ham gun had got off the very impressive figure of eighteen rounds in two minutes, and the Victoria Park gun seven in one minute, before they both unfortunately jammed. Better still, one 4.7 inch shell from the Becton gun had burst very close to the airship, and hits were claimed on her nose and tail. The Wanstead gun fired off eleven accurate rounds in three minutes, the last three of which were observed as "range." One or more shells from either or both of these two guns must have hit the L33, for from here onward she began to lose gas slowly.

Badly rattled, hit in at least one gas-bag, Böcker turned off north-nor'east. At nineteen minutes past twelve he was over Buckhurst Hill, and people there could plainly hear that the airship was in trouble. Her engines were running badly, making the sort of pounding noise which suggested to trained observers that a propeller had been hit. The L33 was picked up then by the Kelvedon Common searchlights, and two minutes later came under fire from the gun there, while she was at a height of about 9,000 feet.

One propeller had been damaged, a shell had passed clean through the hull, and the airship was losing gas through splinter holes, though not especially rapidly. To wriggle free of the Kelvedon Common searchlight, Böcker tried to climb fast, and watchers saw the "smoke cloud" spill out of the Zeppelin's underbelly which was actually water ballast being released. Böcker was making slow progress when, at half past twelve, he was attacked by an airplane.

It was Brandon. At twenty-seven minutes to twelve he had taken off from Hainault Farm with orders to patrol between Hainault and Sutton's Farm. He first saw the Zeppelin in the searchlight beams some distance away and made for it. Before he could close it, the airship had eluded the beams and he lost it. But a good estimation of its probable course in the darkness enabled him to pick it up again. He went on climbing and put a drum of ammunition on the gun. He had intended to give it two drums at long range and two at short range, but when he came up from behind the Zeppelin and raised the gun to open fire it jerked out of the mounting. As it fell he managed to drag it back across the cockpit nacelle and just saved it from falling overboard. He had no hope of getting it back in position and very nearly let it go after all, but made one desperate attempt to fix the heavy Lewis on again. By unstrapping himself and standing upright in the unstable cockpit he managed to get the gun back.

By the time he had strapped himself in again he had overshot the Zeppelin. Turning the machine right round, he saw the airship coming towards him. He elevated the Lewis to fire a burst but the two antagonists passed each other too quickly for him to get a shot in. Once again he turned right round and this time came up upon the airship's stern. On

this pass he fired a whole drum, most of it into the vulnerable stern and the rest all along the hull as he passed. It was
impossible to miss such a gigantic, elongated target, but he
was astonished at his apparently poor shooting. The Zeppelin must have been hit by all his bullets, except the few
which burned out before they reached her, but there was no
apparent result.

He turned round again, put on a fresh drum, and came in
from the stern once more. This time after about ten shots
the gun jammed. Owing to the danger of premature explosions and fire from the Brock ammunition they had been
ordered not to try to correct a jam in the air, but he gave the
gun one jerk on the cocking handle, with no result. The
gun was out of action, but at Hainault Farm, unlike B
Flight at Sutton's Farm, they had retained their authorized
armament, and Brandon's machine carried Le Prieur rockets
on its outer wing struts. With the idea of using these he
turned to the rear and climbed to get above the Zeppelin.

The ease with which he had picked up the airship several
times from below misled him. He should not have taken
his eyes off it. When he turned this time there was no sign
of the Zeppelin. Either it was invisible against the gray
band between the lower stars and the earth, or it had turned
off its original course. He saw no more of this Zeppelin.
Shortly afterward his engine cut out and Brandon tried the
only thing possible. With the engine switched off and the
throttle wide open he dived the machine to get a pull on a
possible choked line. He switched on and the engine picked
up, but every time the aircraft slowed up at the top gliding
angle, the engine would cut out again. He continued his
patrol in an unpleasant series of switchback dives and climbs.

With all Brandon's persistent efforts, the crew of the L33
had apparently hardly noticed his presence, being far too
preoccupied with the results of the previous shell damage.
The ship was now sinking low from loss of gas, and about

quarter to one, when she was north of Chelmsford, Böcker began giving orders to jettison various movable articles to lighten her. Over Broomfield he dropped some spare parts, two aluminum cartridge boxes and a leather machine-gun case; at Boreham, a mile or two farther on, he followed these with a machine gun. At five to one the L33 was somewhere between Witham and Maldon, laboring along, her speed and height decreasing steadily all the time. A second machine gun was thrown overboard, landing in the grounds of "Monctons" at Wickham Bishop. A third machine gun fell at the Gate House Farm, Tiptree. The Zeppelin was near Tolleshunt Major, and very near the ground.

Böcker now made one brief effort to get clear of the coast. At quarter past one the L33 went out to sea near West Mersea. But with his ship almost down Böcker decided that he preferred a hard landing and a chance of life to a soft bed at the bottom of the sea, and turned back over the land. Five minutes later the L33 hit the ground in a field between Little Wigborough and Peldon, about three miles inland and northeast of Mersea, about a third of a mile northeast of Copthall Farm and the adjoining Little Wigborough church, right across a sunken road leading to Peldon Road, her starboard side amidships about twenty yards from New Hall Cottages, her bows about twenty-five yards from New Hall Farm.

The airship landed heavily. There was a slight explosion and she caught fire, but Böcker had jettisoned the remainder of his bombs over the water and there was so little gas left in the ship that only the outer casing would burn. There was severe damage to the front gondola, and the framework partially collapsed amidship when the fire started, but Böcker and the crew were uninjured and got clear of the ship.

Böcker went immediately across to the nearby New Hall Cottages and knocked on door after door to warn the occupants that he was going to set fire to the great wreck which lay literally darkening their thresholds. He got no reply. The family in one cottage had taken shelter in a cupboard, and the tenant of the other, an elderly lady, was simply too frightened to answer. Böcker then returned to the ship and attempted to complete the job of destruction, but there was hardly any gas left and the airship would not burn.

Böcker called off the crew, fell them in, and marched them up the sunken road, little better than a lane, past New Hall Farm, to the Peldon Road. The party turned right toward Peldon, after Böcker had read his whereabouts from the signpost on the corner.

At a bend in the road, about half a mile from the junction, the marching band encountered Special Constable Edgar Nicholas, coming from the direction of Peldon on his bicycle.

Böcker halted his men and asked, "Can you tell me how far we are from Colchester?"

Constable Nicholas said, "Never mind about Colchester. You come along with me."

Meekly Böcker and his men followed the weaving bicycle along the Peldon Road. Shortly afterward they were joined by Sergeant Edwards of the Metropolitan Police, who was on leave in the district. On reaching Peldon Post Office, Constable (afterward promoted sergeant) Smith of the county police formally arrested the Germans.

When Smith had finished cautioning them and writing down the details in his notebook, Böcker said to him, "May I please telephone my wife's sister?"

The policemen exchanged startled looks, and Sergeant Edwards said: "I'm afraid we can't run to that. It's rather a long way to Germany."

Böcker said, "Oh no, not to Germany. Only to London. She is married to an Englishman."

Constable Smith said, "It's not allowed." He made a note

to investigate the matter, then asked Mrs. Smallwood, the postmistress, to get in touch with the military establishment at West Mersea. While she was trying to reach West Mersea by telephone, the German commander and his men were taken into the adjoining Church Hall. Mrs. Smallwood found she could not get through to the Army, so Mr. Wright of Grave Farm set off for Mersea on his motorcycle. On the way he was involved in a collision, and subsequently died from the injuries he received.

Shortly after he had left, Mrs. Smallwood managed to make contact with West Mersea, and was told that an armed escort would set out at once on the main Colchester road, and that the prisoners should be marched to meet them at once. Once again the German party moved off, escorted by the three policemen, and were handed over to the military on the Strood causeway at about three o'clock. On arrival at West Mersea an hour later, the Germans were put in the Church Hall under guard, and given breakfast. A large and excited crowd gathered outside and remained there to gape as the men were taken to Colchester by motor truck at midday. Another Zeppelin crew were "in the box." It was to be a night of disaster for the naval airship service.

Peterson had followed unwillingly in Mathy's wake toward London. After skirting Peasmarsh he went off toward Hythe and at quarter to twelve was seen over Lydd. He then flew near Appledore and Cranbrook to Tunbridge Wells, which he reached at ten past twelve. From here he went north, and at half past twelve dropped a sighting incendiary. At ten to one the L32 was over Crockenhill and Swanley Junction, and when a searchlight opened upon him Peterson aimed seven high explosives at it, which missed. Carrying on north, the L32 went over Dartford, crossed the Thames east of Purfleet, and was immediately caught and held in the searchlights north of the river, where the mist which shrouded the ground on the southern side had not penetrated.

Almost at once she was under a heavy fire from the guns between Beacon Hill and Tunnel Farm, and the latter gun later claimed two hits on her, which were not substantiated. At three minutes past one the rattled Peterson answered this fire by dropping nine high explosives, including two 220-pound bombs, and six incendiaries, which fell at Aveley.

It was at this moment that Brandon, whose engine had at last begun to function properly again, saw the Zeppelin in the lights and made for it. Sowrey, patrolling at the bitterly cold and unprecedented height of 14,000 feet from Sutton's Farm across the river to Joyce Green, had seen it too, a tiny slender shape at the end of a beam of light which illuminated her obliquely through the clouds. He tried to see which way she was heading, and thought, This ship's going out. The Zepp was some miles east of him, approximately over Tilbury, going northeast at about the same height as he himself. He turned and flew toward it. Presently he was near enough to make an attack. He maneuvered his machine into a position directly underneath the hull and a little aft of the center, throttled down to the speed of the airship, which was about sixty miles an hour, and went in as close as he possibly could. When he was so close that he could see the propellers revolving above him he opened fire and flew down the airship's length, pouring in a steady fire.

Brandon, about 2,000 feet below, and still some way off saw the sparklet glowing in the darkness and, as he said in his report, the Zeppelin "being hosed with a stream of fire."

Sowrey could see his tracers hitting but there was no apparent effect. After his first burst a continuous machine-gun fire had opened up on him from the airship's gondolas. He finished his first drum with no more result than to make the airship turn and twist to avoid him. He threw the empty drum overboard and fixed a fresh one on the gun. By the time he had done this he had strayed away from the Zeppelin and had to turn and get in position again under its belly. Once again he sprayed the hull with bullets but the second drum had no more effect than the first. For the third drum he changed his method of attack. Instead of spraying the envelope from end to end he concentrated all his fire upon one spot near the middle of the ship.

This time his bullets hit one of the cylindrical fuel tanks stowed along the airship's central gangway. After about thirty rounds he saw a light inside the hull at the spot where his bullets were going in. In a matter of seconds fire had raced round the inside of the airship's great hull. Then huge flames burst out of it and the whole ship was ablaze.

As soon as he saw the fire start, Sowrey put his nose down and turned to get out of the way of the burning mass. He was just in time. It roared and crackled past him and he watched it all the way down, burning red and yellow until it struck, when the lake of flame turned green. By this time Sowrey had not the slightest idea of his whereabouts, and the visibility had become much worse. He flew due west and eventually picked up some flares which he recognized as those of Sutton's Farm. He landed very cold about quarter to two. Robinson and Bowers met him with congratulations. After a mug of hot cocoa he telephoned the information to Major Morton and asked for permission to go at once and inspect the wreckage.

"Yes," said Morton, "you can go there and see it—after you've written your report."

The report did not take him very long. Then he, Bowers and some others piled into Robinson's Prince Henry Vauxhall and tore off at top speed to find the scene of the crash.

All Hornchurch, first awakened by the bombs which Böcker had thrown at Sutton's Farm, saw the Zeppelin burst into flames in the night. She crashed at Snail's Hall Farm, Great Burstead, south of Billericay, Essex, and everyone on board died with her. The wreckage afterward burned for an hour, and one of the few things found reasonably intact afterward was Peterson's favorite long gray coat, which was thrown clear. It was not possible to identify the commander himself.

When the Vauxhall reached the scene, the Sutton's Farm party had heated words with a pompous general who only let Sowrey go through the cordon of soldiers to see the wreckage, and that reluctantly, when he was told that this was the man who had shot down the airship. Sowrey was further amused to overhear an airman informing an inquiring civilian, "I'm 'appy to tell you, sir, it was Mr. Leefe Robinson's pal that done it!"

Both wrecks were put under guard. The remains of the L33, of very great value in their almost completely preserved state, were particularly well supervised as the experts swarmed over them, though the public were allowed to view the site, when all important parts had been removed, from a distance of about 200 yards. A fee of two pence a head was charged for admission to the area, the proceeds being devoted to the Red Cross and other charities. About $400 was collected in this way. Among those refused admission to the immediate vicinity of the wreck was Captain Leefe Robinson. A daughter was born to Mr. and Mrs. Clark of Little Wigborough at about the time of the crash. She had the misfortune to be christened "Zeppelina," as a result of the coincidence.

The effects of the night's achievements were decisive. Brandon's and particularly Sowrey's efforts had both finally established the power of the airplane in the air defense and all but knocked the heart out of the German Zeppelin offensive. After this, with three of their airships destroyed and one in British hands, with the fear of a fate like that of those in the Schütte-Lanz and the wretched Peterson in the L32 lying uneasily in the minds of every airship aviator, there was only one more serious attempt at a Zeppelin raid on London. On October 1st, a week after Peterson's death and Böcker's slightly farcical capture, eleven naval Zeppelins left Germany for England. Of these, however, it was only Mathy, the greatest of all the captains and the sole survivor of the core of veterans, who made a dash for London, out of revenge for his comrades and with his cold-willed courage untouched by the terrible fate of his messmates burned alive in the sight of the cheering people of the city they had come to destroy.

He came on a Sunday, in the finest weather any Zeppelin raider had ever had. An extensive anti-cyclone of smiling weather, with its center over Holland, covered the whole North Sea area, and the fair conditions were as yet little affected by a depression off the southwest coast of Ireland. The wind over the whole area was very light, with a velocity nowhere greater than eighteen miles an hour at 1,500 feet, and over the central and southern parts of the North Sea there was practically a calm. There was a great deal of cloud, but very little mist or fog.

At seven o'clock Second Lieutenant Tempest was ordered to stand by to take the first patrol from Sutton's Farm. Tempest was a slight young man, and like both Robinson and Sowrey, had been wounded in France. He looked neither particularly strong nor well, and was in fact never in the same robust health as the tall, fair athletic Robinson or the swarthily handsome Sowrey.

Three quarters of an hour after this Mathy in his by now well tried L31 passed over the masthead of the Cross Sand Lightship and five minutes later the St. Nicholas Lightship. Then he crossed the coast at Corton and flew over Lowestoft, Wrentham, Blythburgh, Framlingham and Needham Market. Maintaining the same general direction, he passed Hadleigh at nine o'clock, and went on to Sudbury and Halstead. He stopped his engines for a few minutes to check his position, then altered course more to the south to pass between Braintree and Terling and on to Chelmsford and Blackmore. Mathy knew the quality of the Kelvedon Hatch gunners, and when the searchlight there picked him up he turned off in a northeasterly direction.

When the L31 was near Ongar, Tempest was ordered to take off and patrol at 8,000 feet. Like the other machines at Sutton's Farm, his B.E. was stripped down to its Lewis gun. They had had many awkward moments on official inspections as a result of their unorthodox action, but stuck to a method which enabled their machines to fly three or four thousand feet higher than a B.E.2c could usually go. Tempest reached the normal operational height of 10,000 feet and went on climbing into the icy darkness.

Meanwhile, Heinrich Mathy was passing over Harlow. At quarter past ten he was over Much Hadham and stopped engines again to check his position. When he was near Buntingford he turned the L31 on to a southwesterly course to attack London from the north. He flew south of Stevenage to west Welwyn, passed Hatfield, heading southeast, and went over Hertford. Here he shut off his engines and drifted slowly with the slight north-nor'west wind in the direction of Ware. He started them up again, headed south at very high speed and soon came under a heavy fire from guns at Newmans and Temple House.

This gunfire was so accurate and intense that it forced Mathy to abandon London, and he dropped most of his bomb load, thirty high explosives and twenty-six incendiaries, at Cheshunt. Here he demolished four houses, damaged three hundred others, and destroyed some six and a half acres of glass houses, though only one woman was injured.

At quarter to twelve Tempest was patrolling over southwest London at 14,500 feet. There was a heavy ground fog and it was bitterly cold, but the night was beautiful and lit with stars at that altitude. Looking toward northeast London, where the fog was not quite so heavy, he saw that all the lights in that quarter were concentrated in an enormous pyramid. At the apex he saw, as he says, "a small cigar-shaped object" about fifteen miles away heading straight for London. He had chased clouds before that had looked like Zepps, but this was the real thing.

He turned and passed through the bursting shells, and Wulstan Tempest and Heinrich Mathy flew toward one another across London. All at once the Zeppelin sighted the British airplane, dropped a large batch of bombs in one volley, swung around, tilted up her nose and raced away northward, climbing rapidly as she went, having been at about 11,500 feet when she dropped her bombs. Tempest pursued her from 15,000 feet, gradually overhauling her, but buffeted by countless shell bursts as he went. All the time the Zeppelin was turning and twisting, rising and falling in an effort to dodge the shells and the pursuing aircraft.

When Tempest was about five miles behind the airship his fuel pressure pump broke down. This meant that he had to operate the hand pump constantly to keep up the pressure in his fuel tank. This enforced exercise at such great altitude was very exhausting besides giving him one hand less to operate with when he came up with the Zeppelin and had to begin firing.

Presently he began to draw up with the airship, and found to his relief that he was free of the anti-aircraft shells, the nearest of which were now bursting a good three miles away. The Zeppelin was now at almost 15,000 feet and climbing fast. He put the nose down and dived on her, for, although he had a slight advantage in speed, she was leaving him behind. Giving one tremendous pump at his fuel tank with all his energy, he dived straight at the airship, firing bursts into her as he came. He gave her another burst as he passed beneath the hull, then banked the machine over, positioning himself under her tail, and flew along beneath her, putting all his bullets into the great shape. He could see tracers flying from her in all directions, but was too close for them to do him any harm.

He was still firing when he noticed her begin to go red inside, "like an enormous Chinese lantern." Then a flame shot out of the front part of her and he realized that he had got her. She shot up about 200 feet, hung there, then came roaring down upon the B.E. before Tempest had time to get out of the way. He nose-dived for all he was worth, with the Zeppelin tearing after him, expecting every minute to be engulfed in flames. He put the machine into a spin and just managed to corkscrew out of the way as she fell past him, roaring like a furnace. He righted his aircraft and watched the airship hit the ground with a shower of sparks. Heinrich Mathy was dead.

Tempest fired off dozens of green Very signals in his exuberance. Glancing at his watch he saw that it was about ten minutes to twelve. He suddenly began to feel very sick and giddy and exhausted, and had great difficulty in finding his way to the ground through the fog. In landing he crashed and cut his head on his machine gun.

The D.S.O. which he was awarded for this night's work was doubly well earned, for he had not only put out an effort of will and courage deserving of the higher decoration; he had rung the death knell of the German airship service.

Never again, after this night, did Zeppelins raid London. From the middle of February 1917 to May 1918, the Germans switched from airships to airplanes for the task, long-range bombers of five hours' endurance which could easily make London and back. They came at first in daylight, then at night. More telling in effect than the Zeppelins, they were a more serious threat while they lasted, and were beaten only by the most strenuous efforts of a combined defense built up to enormous size upon the embryo organization which defeated the Zeppelins. The Gothas and Giants did more damage, killed and injured more people, than the Zeppelins. But they did so on the broken back of the airship, and somehow they were never so frighteningly sinister as the monsters from Friedrichshaven, and history will not find as big a place for them. In any case, theirs is another story.

What followed the defeat of the L30's in the way of Zeppelin attacks was a number of more or less isolated sorties, disasters, acts of skill and courage, a sprawling process of mopping up.

Eight weeks after the end of the L31 ten Naval Zeppelins left Germany to raid northern England. The treatment they received rubbed salt in the smarting wounds inflicted by Robinson, Sowrey and Tempest. The new L34, on her maiden raid, was attacked by Second Lieutenant Pyott of No. 36 Squadron, and fell burning into the sea off West Hartlepool. Soon all that was left of her was a scum of burning oil. Three of the other airships turned about and fled as soon as their commanders saw the L34 on fire. As dawn broke, the L21, nine miles off Lowestoft, was overtaken by Flight Lieutenant Cadbury, Flight Sublieutenant Fane, and Flight Sublieutenant Pulling, of the R.N.A.S. All three got in attacks, and it was Pulling who eventually fired the Zeppelin, which fell stern first into the sea and was swallowed up beneath her own burning trail.

Attacks were made in 1917, but without any of the Zeppelins' previous success, though isolated acts of spectacular success by British airmen remain to be chronicled.

On June 17th four German naval airships made for England. Two turned back without crossing the coast, one bombed Ramsgate, did considerable damage, killed three persons, injured another sixteen, and got clean away. The other, the L48, did not. Two pilots made successful attacks on her and shared in her destruction.

This Zeppelin, commanded by *Kapitan-Leutnant* Eichler, with *Korvetten Kapitan* Victor Schuetze, Commodore of the North Sea Airship Division, on board, came in at Orfordness, passed close to Wickham Market, then steered south past Woodbridge and dropped bombs near Martlesham, without causing any damage. At the Experimental Station at Orfordness, two pilots in the flight commanded by Captain Robert Saundby, M.C., had been specially trained in night flying to go up against Zeppelins. As soon as he received the raid warning Saundby sent them off in the B.E.2c and F.E.2b aircraft provided for the job. He did not think very much of their chances, as neither machine could climb beyond 12,000 feet, and the Zeppelins by then were flying at 15,000 feet and more.

It was about one o'clock in the morning when Saundby himself saw the Zeppelin from the ground, shining in the searchlights about fifteen miles away to the south over Harwich, apparently moving westward. Instinctively he longed to go up and attack her himself. He had never flown at night, and all he had available to fly in was a single-seater pusher D.H.2 fighter, which he had recently acquired to carry out some special diving trials. He had recently done some hundreds of hours on this type on the Western Front in France—the D.H.2 was the machine which overcame the Fokker monoplane threat—but single-seater fighters had never been flown at night before, and the machine had no dashboard or navigation lights, no flying instruments other than bubble, altimeter and airspeed indicator. But it was a clear night, and he had enough fuel to stay up until after dawn. The thought of making a dash against the Zeppelin had occurred to him when the warning came through, and he had ordered the machine to be made ready in case one came over. When he sighted the airship in the searchlights he decided to take off.

He ran to the machine and scrambled into the cockpit

right up in the nose of the machine, with its unrestricted field of fire forward. With its air-cooled rotary engine little warming-up was needed, and he was in the air in a minute or two. He kept his eye on the Zeppelin, which seemed to be at a great height with naval anti-aircraft shells bursting many thousands of feet below it. As he climbed toward it he was impressed by its tremendous size and apparently slow movement. When he reached 14,000 feet he judged that he was less than 1,000 feet beneath it. Raising his gun to an angle of forty-five degrees, he let fly at about three hundred yards' range with a double drum of incendiary bullets, aiming at the nose of the ship with the hope of actually hitting somewhere farther aft and all in one spot. When he began firing the airship crew saw his tracer bullets and shot back with a heavy, slow-firing machine gun, but he had time to get off the double drum before it was necessary to jink out of the way.

Second Lieutenant L. P. Watkins, a Canadian, of No. 37 Squadron at Goldhanger, had taken off about two o'clock in a B.E. 12, a machine especially designed and equipped for Zeppelin fighting. He climbed to 8,000 feet over the airdrome, then struck off in the direction of Harwich, still climbing. When he was at 11,000 feet over Harwich he saw the anti-aircraft guns firing and several searchlights playing on the same spot. A minute later he saw the Zeppelin about 2,000 feet above him.

As he climbed toward the Zeppelin he saw the other machine, Saundby's, come up from the north and fire a short burst at the airship from the side. After climbing about 500 feet he himself fired off a drum of amunition into the tail of the Zeppelin, but there was no result. He climbed to 12,000 feet and fired another drum into the tail, but he could still see no effect. He decided to wait until he could get to close range before firing another drum. He climbed steadily and saw the other airplane going from north to south across the airship's bows. Watkins fired three short bursts of about seven rounds, then the remainder of the drum. The Zeppelin burst into flames at the tail, the fire ran rapidly along both flanks, and the whole ship took fire and fell burning.

At somewhere about the same time Saundby's bullets had also taken effect. He had let off seven whole drums of ammunition with no result. Then he put on his eighth and last drum and pressed the trigger. As the gun stopped firing he saw a dull red glow, oblong in shape, appear not far from the bow of the ship. While he was wondering what this could be, a ring of red oblong shapes encircled the airship, and he realized that she was on fire. Within seconds there was a violent spurt of flame, and soon she was blazing from bow to stern.

The airship broke into a huge V and fell slowly past Saundby, the flames roaring so loudly that he could hear them above the sound of his engine. He followed her down as she sank earthward, which took a long time. She struck the ground at the bottom point of the V. The shock forced out the remaining gas in a huge tower of flame, then the Zeppelin crumpled and lay still, a pathetic skeleton of metal girders. She fell in a field belonging to Holly Tree Farm near Theberton, Suffolk.

Saundby returned to Orfordness in the dawn light to find to his alarm that a low white mist covered the landing ground. He nosed cautiously down into the mist, and was relieved to feel and hear his wheels gently rumbling on the grassy surface. He found everyone on the station waiting for him, wild with excitement, as they had been able to see the whole spectacle and follow the exchange of tracer fire. Two men in the airship had a miraculous escape. The forward gondola remained just clear of the ground after the impact, and its occupants survived. One of them, an engineer named Mieth, never returned to Germany, but went

subsequently to Kenya, where he lived until his death after
the Second World War.

On October 19, 1917, eleven naval Zeppelins took off to
attack the industrial Midlands. By this time the German
airships had been forced to operate at such great heights that
the ships themselves were constantly at the mercy of the
harsh atmospheric conditions, and the crew suffered the
paralyzing effects of intense, icy cold and height sickness.
All these miseries afflicted this sortie.

The ships flew at 20,000 feet. At that height neither the
British guns nor airplanes could reach the Zeppelins. If
they had tried they would only have helped the airship
bomb aimers. So the raiders were left alone to do what damage they could from the ice house of their lofty prison, and
the affair became known as "The Silent Raid." Only the
L45, *Kapitan-Leutnant* Kölle, did any serious harm. Having
dropped her main load of bombs over Northampton, with
very little result, she followed the London and North-West-
ern Railway line south to London. Here she dropped
bombs on Hendon and Cricklewood and one in Piccadilly,
which made a big hole in the road next to Swan and Edgar's,
killed seven persons and injured eighteen more. The L45
then dropped two big 660-pound bombs at Camberwell
and Hither Green, which killed twenty-four persons and
wounded thirty. Trying to make her way home, however,
the airship was the victim of engine failure, airplane attacks
and the furious buffeting of a gale and finally crashed in
France, where Kölle set fire to her. The L50 also crashed in
France. The control car was torn free at the first impact
and sixteen men managed to jump off the ship. Free of the
weight, the hull rose and became the sport of the winds. Attacked in vain by airplanes, she eventually disappeared completely, drifting over the Mediterranean. The L44, hit by
anti-aircraft fire over France, caught fire and fell at Chene-
vières, killing all her crew. The L55 succeeded in reaching

Germany but was totally wrecked when trying to land. Many of the others had serious trouble regaining their bases.

The last German airship raid on Britain was made on August 5, 1918, and it was in almost every sense the final effort of the Zeppelin arm.

On the evening of the 5th near the R.N.A.S. air station at Great Yarmouth, Flight Lieutenant Edgar Cadbury's wife, Mary, was singing at a concert in aid of charity. Her husband and Nita, a cousin of hers, were enjoying the music when an orderly caught Cadbury's eye and told him that he was wanted at headquarters. As Cadbury ran along the front he saw to his intense surprise the stark silhouette of an airship sharply etched against the extremely bright, clear, northerly evening light. At Headquarters he was told that three Zeppelins were hovering together at a point about fifty miles northeast of Yarmouth, well to seaward.

Knowing that there was only one aircraft available, a D.H.4, with the necessary speed and climb, he rushed off to the station as fast as his ever-ready Ford would take him. There he grabbed a scarf, goggles and helmet, tore off his streamline coat and with an old jacket thrust under his arm sprinted all-out and took practically a running jump into the front cockpit of the D.H.4, while his observer, Leckie, clambered into the rear nacelle.

Cadbury saw the Zeppelins as he left the ground and gave immediate chase. The machine was not climbing as well as she should have done, even when Cadbury jettisoned his bombs to rid himself of the weight. But both airmen were experienced in attacking Zeppelins, Leckie having actually shot one down over the North Sea when in a flying boat. Slowly they began to close on the Zeppelins. The three airships, flying in a V, saw them and altered course north. Twenty-five minutes later Cadbury had drawn abeam of one of them, about 2,000 feet below her. He climbed to

within 600 feet of her and attacked head-on, slightly to port
to clear any obstructions such as observation cars which
might be suspended from the airship.

Leckie trained his gun on the bow of the airship, and
concentrated his fire on a spot underneath the Zeppelin
three-quarters of the way aft. The bullets blew a great hole
in the fabric and a fire started which quickly ran along the
entire length of the Zeppelin. She raised her bows once as if
to escape, then plunged seaward, a blazing wreck. In about
three-quarters of a minute she had been completely consumed by the flames. They saw a big fuel tank detach itself
from the framework and fall blazing into a heavy layer of
clouds at about 7,000 feet below. The two other airships
broke away and altered course to escape.

At this moment Cadbury's engine cut out completely,
with a block in the fuel system. It was a bad moment. They
were thirty or forty miles from land, and the weather had
become very violent and thick. But after a few splutters and
bangs Cadbury got it going again, and immediately gave
chase to the next nearest Zeppelin. Again he attacked bow
on and Leckie opened fire when they were about 500 feet
away. Fire immediately broke out in the midships gondola
of the airship. Then Leckie's gun jammed from a double
feed. He struggled with the fault but in the darkness it
could not be cleared. By now the fire on the Zeppelin had
been put out. Cadbury was unable to use his front gun as
they had reached their ceiling, but they held on to the airship for five minutes until it was obvious that Leckie was
not going to be able to clear the stoppage on his Lewis.
By then they were lost in the cloudy darkness over the sea.
For the next half an hour they flew through murky blackness and layer after layer of thick cloud in a machine which
they had been told could not be landed safely at night, even
if they ever made land again. At last they sighted the flares

of the night landing ground at Sedgeford, landed without mishap, and reported their victory to base.

So ended the L70. It was no ordinary loss, for on board her had been the *Fuehrer der Luftschiffe* himself, Peter Strasser, who thus died with the final failure of his life's ambition. It was an end which he would probably have sought.

It is too much to say that the Zeppelins failed, though they were forced to leave their main goal unattained—the destruction of London as the heart of the enemy war effort. This they might have accomplished had they not, so surprising to the world, fallen into the error, supposed to be such a characteristic of their enemy, of bringing "too little, too late" to the job. Had they attacked on the very declaration of war, or before, as the Japanese were to do at Pearl Harbor, with all their available airships, when London and all England were fearful and unprotected, they must have done very great damage which, reacting mutually with the drive into France and a similar all-out U-boat campaign, might well have won them the war. But the Germans were not as thorough as they or the rest of the world imagined. Their swollen dream of power, gas-blown and thin-skinned, soared beyond safe altitudes and exploded for want of the ballast which the realism of a more pragmatic people provides.

Short of the greater victory, the Zeppelin service's greatest achievement was that, by tying down a great organization of men and equipment in Britain, it made the most brutalizing war in modern history a few weeks, perhaps months longer.

By the end of 1916, 17,340 officers and men were in the British home anti-aircraft service, and twelve R.F.C. squadrons comprising two hundred officers, 2,000 other ranks and 110 airplanes remained on Home Defense duties, despite the desperate need for them in the Somme battles. Vital war work was held up and communications halted all over the country.

It was in 1917, when he must have been able to see that the second great ambition of his long and fiercely striving life had failed, that the aged Count Zeppelin died, still breathing fire and destruction, with his plan for a special fleet of his own giant bombing aircraft well under way. The real end of the terror called "Zepp" had come on that September night of fiery horror for a few wretches and hysterical joy for a watching multitude, when William Leefe Robinson had won his authentic hero's place upon the rarefied plateau of glory only reached by those beings of superior courage who also happen to be the men of the hour.

On his achievement his country was able to build something positive and real—a shield which defended her not only in that war to end all wars which did not fulfill its promise, but in the greater test of strength and heart which followed twenty years after. As for Zeppelin . . . even in peace his creation was to fail tragically and disastrously for want of strength against the elements of fire and air, time after time until it could be trusted no more, and was abandoned finally in favor of the other aircraft which had first proved its master in the anxious night duels over London. In his book *Western Germany,* Dr. Monk Gibbon writes: "Farther on we come to Friedrichshaven, which was the scene of the labors of Count Zeppelin. No one need shudder at the name today. Actually the Count was exploring an aeronautical cul-de-sac."

Appendix A

THE DÜSSELDORF RAID

On the morning of August 27th, 1914—the morning after the Zeppelin Hansa's raid on Antwerp—Commander Samson's Eastchurch squadron, the best unit of the Royal Naval Air Service, which for a short time had been operating from Skegness on patrol, flew across to Ostend to carry out reconnaissance work in support of a Marine brigade which had been landed there to hold the port. The squadron took with it ten pilots and a collection of airplanes comprising three B.E.2 biplanes, two Sopwith Tabloid biplanes, two Blériot monoplanes, one Henri Farman biplane and one Short seaplane which had been converted from floats to wheels.

On August 30th, their work done, both the Marines and Samson's squadron were ordered to return to England. The squadron's machines flew to Dunkirk on the first leg in their return flight, but there Flight Lieutenant Lord Edward Grosvenor so damaged his Blériot on landing that the whole unit was kept waiting for three days while the machine was repaired. On September 1st, while they were still there, Samson was ordered by telegram to remain in Dunkirk and operate against German Zeppelins from there, specifically "to deny the use of territory within a hundred miles of Dunkirk to German Zeppelins and to attack by aeroplanes all airships replenishing there." This plan by the First Lord of the Admiralty, Winston Churchill, was an expression of his strategy of countering the Zeppelins by attacking them at their continental bases before they could reach England.

Samson's unit should have comprised three squadrons of twelve machines each, and he was considerably under strength. Efforts were made to reinforce him, and on September 3rd Squadron Commander E. L. Gerrard brought three new machines to Dunkirk for the particular object of carrying out a bombing raid upon the Zeppelin sheds at Düsseldorf and at Cologne. On the 12th Gerrard was in Antwerp looking for a suitable airdrome there from which to mount the raids when a very heavy gale struck the machines at Dunkirk, which, owing

231

to lack of proper hangar facilities, had been pegged down in the open, and wrecked several of them. However, within a few days the machines had been replaced and a base set up near Antwerp.

On September 22nd two machines took off to attack Düsseldorf, and two to bomb Cologne. They had to face thick mist when they took off, and unfortunately only one pilot, Flight Lieutenant Collett, reached his target. He dived to 400 feet and dropped his bombs on the airship sheds. There were no Zeppelins inside at the time, but he did some damage.

A second attempt was more successful. On October 9th Commander Spenser Grey and Flight Lieutenant R.L.G. Marix were ordered to bomb the Zeppelin sheds at Cologne and Düsseldorf respectively. The Germans were now pressing close to Antwerp, and at half past eleven on the morning of the 8th the first heavy bombardment of the city began. The airplanes were quickly wheeled out of their hangars and pushed into the middle of the airdrome to avoid damage by splinters in case the field were hit. Shells were whistling overhead all the time as the airdrome was directly between the enemy and the city.

The weather was misty throughout the forenoon of the 9th, but the time was spent in tuning up the two machines in case the weather improved. With the Germans advancing rapidly on Antwerp, the last chances of making a raid at all were speeding by. Then at one o'clock the mist cleared. Marix, in a Sopwith Tabloid single-seater, took off for Düsseldorf at half-past one, flew low over the trees to the west, circled the city and headed east for his target. He made the hundred miles without mishap, a considerable feat in itself with a temperamental 1914 aircraft.

Locating the Zeppelin hangar he executed what was in fact the first dive-bombing run in history, pulling out and letting his bombs go at 600 feet. He could not see whether one or both of the little twenty-pound bombs had hit the shed, but within thirty seconds he had the satisfaction of seeing the whole roof of the shed cave in. Then a huge column of flame shot up from it to a height of 500 feet, and Marix knew that there must have been a Zeppelin inside, fully loaded with hydrogen. The Germans had had time since Collett's visit on September 22nd to move in more anti-aircraft batteries and site machine-guns on the hangar roofs, and Marix came under heavy fire from these and from rifles, and his machine was badly hit. But he managed to keep it under control until he had returned to within twenty miles of Antwerp, when he ran out of gas. He made a good forced landing in a field, and borrowed a bicycle from a Belgian peasant who had stopped to goggle at him, on which he pedaled wearily into Antwerp.

The attack had been a brilliant success. British Intelligence reported that a brand new Zeppelin, Captain Horn's Z9, had been totally destroyed together with a machine shop alongside the airship shed. Marix's well-placed bomb had killed a mechanic standing on the roof of the Z9's hangar, crashed through and set fire to the ship. Captain Lehmann, whose *Sachsen* had partnered the Z9 in several reconnaissance flights to Antwerp and Ostend, when Horn had been getting his hand in with the new airship, came over from Cologne to see the damage for himself and found the hangar almost intact, but the Zeppelin herself a twisted mass of wreckage, with only the motors worth salvaging. The Z9 had actually been loaded with bombs at the time of the attack, but they were not fused, and when the blazing hydrogen from the ruptured tanks melted the bomb racks they had dropped harmlessly to the ground.

Other reports from Berlin described shock and surprise there at the daring raid. English clerks working at the American Embassy were seized by the Germans and accused of passing information which had made it possible. Spenser Grey did not, unfortunately, have the same success at Cologne. Fog obscured the airship sheds there, although he did manage to bomb the main railway station as second best.

Appendix B

THE FRIEDRICHSHAVEN RAID

On November 10, 1914, Lieutenant N. Pemberton Billing, R.N.V.R., well known in prewar years as a flying enthusiast and seaplane designer, joined the transport *Manchester Importer* at Southampton in accordance with secret orders. Already aboard were four new Avro 504 airplanes, transferred within the hour from the special train which had brought them straight from the Avro works at Manchester, and two pilots, Squadron Commander Briggs and Flight Commander Babington, both late of Samson's crack Eastchurch squadron, and eleven air mechanics of the Royal Naval Air Service. After a brief conference with Briggs and Babington, Pemberton Billing left again to join the Havre packet, which was due to leave before the *Manchester Importer*, so that he would arrive at Le Havre ahead of the R.N.A.S. contingent in plenty of time to complete the arrangements there for unloading and their dispatch by rail to the final destination.

When he reached Le Havre the sublieutenant in charge there reported all the arrangements previously ordered for a special train complete. Pemberton Billing had the train shunted on to the quayside. When the *Manchester Importer* came alongside, the machines were hoisted under cover of darkness straight out of her holds and on to the railway trucks. In the middle of this hurried activity the Le Havre electrical power plant broke down, and all the heavy crates had to be manhandled aboard the train. They got away at half past eleven that night and sped through the night across France. At half past nine on the following morning they arrived at Belfort, the French fortified stronghold on the Alsace border. They were briefed to mount from there an attack upon the great Zeppelin plant at Friedrichshaven on Lake Constance.

The train was shunted into a disused factory siding until nightfall. Then, with the assistance of Roger Seyrig, French captain of staff at Belfort, the men and machines were transferred by army

234

truck to their aerodrome. This move was completed by half past eleven on the following morning. The whole R.N.A.S. contingent then worked nonstop, and in four hours the entire job of unpacking and erecting the four aircraft was completed, bombs shipped and their release gear tested, fuel and oil tanks filled. The main bodies of the airplanes, Avro 504's Nos. 179, 873, 874 and 875, were new, but the 80-h.p. Gnome engines were not. These were tried and tested motors and would need no further trials before the raid. No such thing as a standard bomb rack existed at this time, and the Avro Company had designed and made the racks for the machines. "They were a Heath Robinson job," A. V. Roe said, "but they worked." Stowage was provided for four 20-pound high-explosive bombs and four incendiaries, though for the raid each aircraft carried only four high explosives.

The machines were ready and the weather was favorable. There remained only the arrival of the two other pilots selected for the raid, Squadron Commander Shepherd and Flight Lieutenant Sippe. Pemberton Billing telegraphed to the Admiralty, "Ready to start. No news Shepherd or Sippe." The reply was not encouraging. "Sippe Shepherd may be Dijon. Get in touch as soon as possible."

He telephoned Dijon, Jenvissy and Le Havre, with no results. His two pilots were adrift "somewhere in France." He asked the authorities at Dijon to have a car ready at a moment's notice to bring Shepherd and Sippe straight to the aerodrome if they showed up there. Later the same evening Dijon Staff telephoned to say that the two missing officers had arrived by car and were being sent off to Belfort at once. The frequent challenges of sentries posted on the major roads of wartime France at night made travel a slow business, and Shepherd and Sippe did not arrive until half past ten the following morning, Sunday, November 15th. Shepherd was tired out and complained of illness, so the raid was cancelled for that day.

On the Monday morning the spell of fine weather which had held for some days broke down and grounded the airplanes. The glass fell, the wind went into the east blowing a stiff breeze, and the temerature fell as low as 7°C. Frail aeroplanes could not operate in such low temperatures. There were nearly 300 miles to go to the target and back across the Vosges Mountains, a severe test for the little Avros, an uncharted voyage.

The weather remained bad until the morning of Saturday, November 21st, with the exception of Tuesday morning, the 17th. They could have gone that day, but Shepherd decided to test his machine, and on landing shattered the propeller, sprang the fuselage, buckled the left wheel, and broke a wing tip skid. The raid was postponed again. Next day Pemberton Billing telegraphed, "Weather bound. Otherwise all correct."

Throughout the dismal weather the machines were kept in readiness for an immediate start, except that the castor oil, which was especially susceptible to the cold, was kept out of the engines and specially heated in the shed. Oil tanks were kept wrapped in red and white flannel. Every two hours meteorological balloons were released to gauge the velocity of the wind at a variety of different altitudes, and Pemberton Billing kept in touch by telephone with the two weather stations of Ballon d'Alsace and Vol Sellons, each of them 2,000 feet high, to get a daily picture of atmospheric conditions. During these anxious days, Shepherd's health grew worse, and he could neither eat nor sleep. Pemberton Billing and Briggs talked it over with him and it was decided that the spare pilot, Flight Lieutenant Cannon, should take his place.

At last, on the morning of Saturday, November 21st, conditions looked favorable. The sky was clear, the glass steady, the temperature reasonable. The meteorological ballonets found an easterly wind at 2,000 feet blowing twenty-five to thirty-five miles an hour, and above that height blowing due west at twenty to twenty-five miles an hour.

The pilots were already very well briefed. A month previously Pemberton Billing had visited Belfort and worked out the best route to Friedrichshaven and a detailed plan of the Zeppelin works. But the hazards were great. They would have to fly a hundred and twenty-five miles each way, which was very near the limit of their gas endurance. The route would have been shorter and easier if Pemberton Billing had not had to plot a crooked course round the northern border of Switzerland to avoid infringing Swiss neutrality, before laying off a straight course south between the two arms of Lake Constance for the target. They would have to negotiate the Black Forest Mountains, which rose to 3,500 feet, and be on the lookout for the seasonal mist which often lay upon the Rhine valley, 3,000 feet thick. The prospect was difficult and dangerous. They had the very best machines, but all the aircraft of the day were temperamental, and the little Avros had engines of only 80 h.p.

At half past nine in the morning the four machines were pushed out of their hangars. After a final careful inspection they were lined up in position on the western side of the airdrome, and after a three-minute engine and bomb release test each plane was sent off in turn until the first three were in the air. Briggs in Avro No. 873 took off at quarter to ten and climbed immediately to 1,000 feet. Babington in No. 875 took off five minutes later and followed Briggs, who was circling the field. At five minutes to ten Sippe's No. 874 joined the circle.

Three minutes later Cannon's machine was released by the mechanics and he opened the throttle. But the aircraft could not work up enough airspeed to get off the ground. Cannon tried again but the same thing happened, and this time the Avro slewed round and broke its tail skid. Pemberton Billing decided immediately to cancel Cannon's flight. His engine was running a hundred revolutions short, the machine was damaged, and the other three aircraft had decided not to wait any longer for the slow starter and were now almost out of sight at a height of about 3,500 feet.

The weather stayed fair all the time the machines were away. The morning was spent dismantling and repacking Cannon's machine, with many anxious glances at the hazy sky to the west.

At half past one in the afternoon an aircraft was sighted coming in from the northwest. It flew closer and was plainly an Avro. As it approached the field they made out the number 874. It was Sippe's machine. As it touched down its starboard wheel crumpled and it careered across the ground, full of bullet and shrapnel holes. An hour later Pemberton Billing was wiring to the Admiralty:

"Raid successful. Sippe returned 1.45 reports considerable damage to workshops. Missed Briggs and Babington during attack under shell and rifle fire no news of them probably landed in Switzerland. Have communicated with British Minister Berne. Wiring again later."

While they waited for news of Briggs and Babington, Sippe gave Pemberton Billing the details of his part in the attack. Early in the flight Briggs had drawn ahead of Babington and Sippe, and they had seen no more of him. By twenty past ten they were over the gleaming Rhine at Basle. They shaped course down the river valley, flying at a height of about 4,000 feet, and by half past eleven they had become separated in cloud between Schaffhausen and Constance, with Sippe about three miles ahead of Babington and over the extreme edge of the Lake.

Sippe immediately went down low on the surface of the Lake to avoid detection as long as possible, and headed for Friedrichshaven, passing Constance at a height of about ten feet above the water. Crossing the Lake, he hugged the north shore until he was about five miles from the target. Then he started to climb to 1,200 feet, noticing shrapnel bursts to the north of Friedrichshaven which he presumed were being aimed at Briggs. The mass of the Zeppelin sheds gleamed silver ahead but he could not make out the other Avro anywhere.

When he was half a mile from the sheds he put the machine into a dive and came down to 700 feet. He dropped one bomb into an enclosure to put the gunners off their aim, then two into the works and hangars. The fourth bomb stuck in the rack and he could not dislodge it. Rifles and anti-aircraft guns were firing at him all the time, and the little Avro tossed violently in the turbulent air from their bursts. He dived, flew north until he was out of range of the guns, then turned back and made an attempt to get rid of his fourth bomb over the big waterside shed. But the bomb remained fast in the rack and he came under a heavy fire from machine guns. He dived again and escaped along the shimmering surface of the Lake to make the long flight home, arriving back at Belfort almost four hours after he had left.

At twenty past two anxiety over the safety of the other two pilots was partly relieved when Babington rang up to report that he had made a successful attack and force-landed near Belfort. Pemberton Billing at once telegraphed to the Admiralty: "Babington just telephoned forced landing near Vesaul thirty miles away. Reports further damage from his attack. Still no news Briggs."

Babington had followed Sippe in to the target. At seven minutes to twelve he was abreast of the waterside shed—which he had time to notice was empty—and steering down the shore of the lake. He saw Sippe escaping low down across the water, shrapnel bursting behind him. A few seconds later shrapnel was threatening his own machine, bursting about a thousand feet below him to starboard. He continued on course until the sun was in line with his gun sights. Shrapnel was now bursting close behind him.

He went into a steep curving dive over the sheds and let go two bombs at 950 feet. The shrapnel was bursting well above and behind him now. At 450 feet, with the machine nearly vertical, he released his other two bombs. Seconds later his aircraft rocked as the blast wave from his first two bombs struck him. As he pulled up and away he saw smoke, unmistakably from bomb explosions, drifting over the sheds to leeward of the points of impact. Workmen were running madly to and fro, and panic appeared to reign. He made a detour inland and turned back over the Lake again, flying very low through a screen of machine-gun bullets from the waterside shed, which he left on his starboard beam. Then he shaped course over the Lake towards the sun. At half-past twelve he was flying down the Rhine valley, and at ten minutes past one he was over Basle and shaping course by the sun for Belfort. A mist obscured the base and he had come down at Largewells. He made a safe landing and hurried to telephone Belfort to report his attack.

On the afternoon of the next day, November 22nd, all the troops in Belfort were paraded to see Babington and Sippe receive the Légion d'Honneur, and Pemberton Billing was able to tell Mr. Churchill that Briggs, wounded and a prisoner in a German hospital, would live to collect the same award. On the 23rd Mr. Churchill made this statement in the House of Commons:

"On Saturday a flight of aeroplanes under the command of Squadron Commander E. F. Briggs of the Royal Naval Air Service, with Flight Commander J. T. Babington and Flight Lieutenant S. V. Sippe as pilots, flew from French territory to the Zeppelin Airship Factory at Friedrichshaven.

"All three pilots in succession flew down to close range under a heavy fire from guns, machine guns and rifles, and launched their bombs according to instructions. Commander Briggs is reported to have been shot down, wounded, and taken to hospital as a prisoner. Both the other officers have returned safely to French territory, though their machines were damaged by gunfire. They report positively that all bombs reached their objectives, and that serious damage was done to the Zeppelin factory.

"This flight of 250 miles, which penetrated 150 miles into Germany, across mountainous country, in difficult weather conditions, constitutes with the attack a fine feat of arms."

The impact of this announcement upon the House in November, 1914, must have been about equal to the very similar one which the same Minister, in the same capacity, made in the same place in November 1940, when he had the great pleasure of telling the whole world of the victory of the Fleet Air Arm over the Italian Battle Fleet at Taranto. Both were naval air occasions of major significance. The flight of Briggs, Babington and Sippe in their fragile little machines was, for its time, a little epic which foreshadowed in some of its details the very much heavier Dam Busters raid of 1942.

The Friedrichshaven Raid was an especially shrewd conception on the part of the Admiralty, as it struck right at the almost sacred heart of the whole great Zeppelin venture. It was at Friedrichshaven and over the smiling face of Lake Constance that Graf von Zeppelin had worked his mechanical miracle. Here he and Eckener had brought the airship from a state of doubtful, ramshackle airworthiness to one of enormous potentialities for the German people. The place had been untouchable, almost a scientific shrine. After the raid nothing seemed safe from British Naval bombs.

While the dust and ash were settling over the gutted plant at Friedrichshaven, accounts came pouring in confirming the heavy damage done and filling in some of the details. *Le Matin* for November 27th reported: "Basle, 26th November. In spite of information received from German sources, the news is confirmed that a Zeppelin was completely destroyed during the bombardment of the sheds at Friedrichshaven by English aviators. Besides this, the factory suffered severe damage." A Swiss engineer who had been working temporarily on the installation of new plant at the Zeppelin Factory had the wry satisfaction of watching its destruction from the window of a hotel uncomfortably close to the works. Methodically he counted nine bomb explosions, and was able to tell reporters later in Basle that he had seen the British commander's machine hit by a shell and crash in flames. He denied a rumor, which was never substantiated, that the wounded Briggs had been slashed across the face by a German officer. Briggs had actually been struck a blow across the head by the butt of an excited soldier's rifle.

The attack caused a wave of frantic reorganization at the Zeppelin works. Defenses were hurriedly trebled in strength, a curfew was introduced in the town, and strict security measures put into force to guard against spies. Three days after the raid an old Zeppelin was sent cruising down the Lake in an attempt to "double" for the new airship which should have come out on trials, but the veteran ship fooled no one. On December 20th the Berne correspondent of *Le Matin* reported that all trials by Zeppelins over Lake Constance had ceased since the raid.

Appendix C

THE CUXHAVEN RAID

By the end of December, 1914, the young Lieutenant Horst von Buttlar Brandenfels, stationed at bleak Nordholz, the new Zeppelin base on the coast a few miles from Cuxhaven, was feeling frustrated and stale from continual inaction. On Christmas Eve his impatience got the better of him and he telephoned the Director of the Naval Airship Service, Peter Strasser, demanding to be sent out on patrol. Wisely, Strasser allowed him to blow off steam and sent him on a patrol the next day, the first Christmas Day of the war. Two Zeppelins, Hirsch's L5 and von Buttlar's L6, took off in the darkness of early morning and steered north on a reconnaissance of the North Sea.

Dawn came up cold and clear over a smooth, pearly sea as the L6 passed over Heligoland, still heading north. Buttlar was looking out over the side of the open control car at the distant island of Amrum when his executive officer shouted, "Sir! Looks like enemy ships ahead!"

Looking down, Buttlar saw three steamers moving slowly through the water. They were auxiliary warships of some kind, and as the L6 drew close he judged them to be minelayers. At once he gave orders to code up a message for the reconnaissance flagship lying in Jade Bay, the battle cruiser *Seydlitz*, anxious to cut off the British ships. The signal was quickly coded, but as the operator began sending, the set went dead. Hurried efforts to repair the set failed, and Buttlar's spirits sank as he saw a splendid opportunity slipping from his hands. Then a seaplane was sighted on their port side coming from Heligoland. Buttlar immediately ordered the signalman to flash her. Anxiously he waited, then the seaplane fired a green star to indicate that she understood. Quickly they flashed the coded signal for the Senior Officer, Reconnaissance Ships, and asked the seaplane to turn back and repeat the signal via the coastal wireless station on Heligoland. Twenty minutes later they could hear over their own receiver, which was working normally, Heligoland passing the message to the *Seydlitz.*

Had Buttlar been on the scene a little earlier it might have been received with far greater consternation then it in fact was. The ships were not minelayers, but the seaplane carriers *Empress, Engadine* and *Riviera,* and half an hour before the Zeppelins came in sight—about seven o'clock—seven seaplanes, lowered overboard from their hangars, had taken off from the ideally smooth water to attack the Zeppelin hangars at Nordholz and to reconnoitre the Wilhelmshaven Basin, the Schillig Roads and the mouth of the Elbe. Two seaplanes which had developed engine trouble at the moment of take-off had been hoisted inboard again and stowed out of sight in their hangars before Buttlar came upon the ships and mistook them for minelayers.

The L6 came down low to observe the ships more closely, and Buttlar saw that one of the three was lagging behind the others, apparently with engine trouble, so he decided to bomb the straggler. As he was heading in for the attack he sighted in the west two British cruisers and eight torpedo-boat destroyers steaming for the scene of impending action at full speed. These were the escorting warships of the British attack force, commanded by Commodores Tyrrwhitt and Roger Keyes.

The L6 carried three 100-pound bombs, not a very dangerous load, and just had time to drop one of them over the lame duck before the cruisers started firing at her. The three bombs were tied to the catwalk beneath the Zeppelin's hull by lengths of seaming twine. Schiller, the L6's bombing officer, climbed up out of the for'ard control car on to the covered catwalk, took rough aim by eye, and sawed through the twine with his dirk. The bomb plopped into the sea a hundred yards short. The ship below began to zigzag, and the Zeppelin had to climb abruptly to avoid the shrapnel which had begun to burst below her.

She sheltered in cloud for a short time, then came in to attack from a different quarter. At 2,000 feet Schiller slashed the twine holding the second bomb. This one also missed, though by twenty yards less. Smoke from the shrapnel bursts actually made the Zeppelin crew cough and blink as it drifted aft over the control car, and once again the L6 climbed away in a hurry. Hidden by cloud she went up to 3,600 feet and steered south. Presently the cloud began to thin and a clear patch revealed the lame ship still struggling along below. The Zeppelin came lower this time. Her third and last bomb fell just twenty yards short of the carrier's bow. As she rose into the clouds again, crewmen aboard her laughed to see men on the ship below potting at the huge Zeppelin with rifles.

Buttlar was determined to hold on to his contact. He brought the airship down once more, but the cloud had thickened considerably and the L6 sank dangerously low without being able to shake it off.

When she finally broke clear it was to find herself 400 feet from the sea and immediately above her target. Buttlar himself rushed to the machine gun in the control car, leaving Schiller to grab the wheel. In the engine car aft the chief artificer engineer swung another machine gun toward the ship below. A few bursts and her decks were clear of riflemen. As the British cruisers opened fire again the L6 climbed clear. She ascended slowly, then the elevator helmsman shouted, "There's something wrong with the ship, sir! I can't get her to move. She's as heavy as lead."

Buttlar thought quickly. Perhaps some of the shrapnel had hit them. "Rigger!"

"Sir?"

"Get aft on the double and check the gas-bags for leaks."

"Aye aye, sir."

After an anxious wait the man returned. "All the gas-bags are hanging true, sir. No leaks."

The Zeppelin continued to lose height. All Buttlar could do was to drop more and more water ballast. Their wireless transmitter was still out of action, and Buttlar was determined to make Jade Harbor and drop a thorough report, with detailed sketches, actually on the deck of the flagship. But the airship was sinking lower and lower all the time. The engineers searched but could find nothing wrong with her. As they approached Jade Harbor the L6 was so dangerously low that Buttlar had to jettison her first gravity tank, containing six hundredweight of fuel. He had a moment of uneasiness when it looked as if the plunging tank might hit the Jade Harbor patrol lightship, but he finally hit what he was aiming for when the heavy waterproof wallet containing his dispatch, trailing black, white and red streamers, fell on the quarterdeck of the *Seydlitz*.

He steered hopefully for Nordholz and reached there after throwing overboard everything detachable aboard the airship. When they got down the rigger made a closer inspection of the gas-bags, and reported that their brush with disaster had been caused by over six hundred tiny holes made in the bags by rifle bullets.

When the Zeppelin had finally left them, the ships of the British force steamed slowly up and down, waiting for the return of their aircraft, with the cruisers and destroyers strung out in a wide search of the horizon for the German surface attack they were sure would develop.

Then, about ten o'clock, three hours after the attacking airplanes had taken off, aircraft were sighted. In a few minutes three of the British seaplanes were taxiing alongside their parent ships. They were followed closely by enemy seaplanes from Heligoland. Soon geysers of spray were erupting all round the seaplane carriers, though no hits were scored. A second Zeppelin, probably Hirsch's L5, attacked them, but the British captains found her clumsy movements childishly easy to anticipate, and she did no damage. When the Germans had left them alone the British ships searched the Frisian coast for four hours, looking for the missing four seaplanes. The Germans did not attack them again, and when the limit of endurance of the missing aircrafts' tanks had been reached the squadron turned and steamed home. Three of the missing crews had been saved in the teeth of an attacking Zeppelin by the submarine E11 off Norderney Gat. The fourth pilot had force-landed with engine failure near a Dutch trawler, and was later interned in Holland.

The raid had met with mixed success. The attack on the Zeppelin sheds had been a failure, the seaplanes being unable to locate them. The other part of the mission had come off well. Seaplane No. 136 had been particularly successful. Piloted by Flight Commander Kilner, this machine had as its observer Lieutenant Erskine Childers, R.N.V.R. who, as a writer and expert yachtsman, had shrewdly anticipated German war preparations in these very waters in his famous novel, *The Riddle of the Sands*. Childers flew over Schillig Roads and saw a display of massed naval might—seven battleships, three battle-cruisers, three cruisers, ten destroyers and four other naval vessels. He also noted a heavy concentration of shipping in the northern part of the fairway of the Weser, and spotted a force of destroyers east of Wangeroog. The immediate effect of his flight was a hurried shifting of a large part of the German Fleet from Cuxhaven further up the Kiel Canal out of the range of the R.N.A.S.

The raid made an important impression upon German airship policy. Advocates of the bombing of England by Zeppelins now argued that if the airships did not make the attempt soon the R.N.A.S. would destroy them in their hangars before they could start. The next raid might not be so abortive. This point of view was not shared by von Falkenhayn, the Minister of War, and others, who considered that airship strength, in spite of substantial additions, was still too low to make really effective attacks upon England. Events were to prove them right, but the Christmas Day raid helped to drown the voice of caution, and it was decided to put pressure upon the Kaiser to withdraw his ban upon bombing England.

Appendix D

WARNEFORD'S REPORT

No. 1 Naval Aeroplane Squadron,
7th June, 1915.

Wing Commander Longmore.

Sir,

I have the honour to report as follows:

I left Furnes at 1:0 a.m. on June the 7th on Morane No. 3253 under orders to proceed to look for Zeppelins and attack the Berchem St. Agathe Airship Shed with six 20 lb. bombs.

On arriving at Dixmude at 1:5 a.m. I observed a Zeppelin apparently over Ostend and proceeded in chase of the same.

I arrived at close quarters a few miles past Bruges at 1:50 a.m. and the Airship opened heavy maxim fire, so I retreated to gain height and the Airship turned and followed me.

At 2:15 a.m. he seemed to stop firing and at 2:25 a.m. I came behind, but well above the Zeppelin; height then 11,000 feet, and switched off my engine to descend on top of him.

When close above him, at 7,000 feet I dropped my bombs, and, whilst releasing the last, there was an explosion which lifted my machine and turned it over. The aeroplane was out of control for a short period, but went into a nose dive, and the control was regained.

I then saw that the Zeppelin was on the ground in flames and also that there were pieces of something burning in the air all the way down.

The joint on my petrol pipe and pump from the back tank was broken, and at about 2:40 a.m. I was forced to land and repair my pump.

I landed at the back of a forest close to a farmhouse; the district is unknown on account of the fog and the continuous changing of course.

I made preparations to set the machine on fire but apparently was not observed, so was enabled to effect a repair, and continued at

3:15 a.m. in a southwesterly direction after considerable difficulty in starting my engine single-handed.

I tried several times to find my whereabouts by descending through the clouds, but was unable to do so. So eventually I landed and found out that it was at Cape Gris Nez, and took in some petrol. When the weather cleared I was able to proceed and arrived at the aerodrome about 10:30 a.m.

As far as could be seen the colour of the airship was green on top and yellow below and there was no machine or gun platform on top.

I have the honour to be, Sir,
Your obedient servant,
(Sgd.) R. A. J. Warneford,
Flt. Sub-Lieutenant.

Meier & Frank Co.

DATE DUE